The Enlightened College Applicant

The Enlightened College Applicant

A New Approach to the Search and Admissions Process

Andrew Belasco and Dave Bergman

ROWMAN & LITTLEFIELD
Lanham • Boulder • New York • London

Published by Rowman & Littlefield
A wholly owned subsidiary of The Rowman & Littlefield Publishing Group, Inc.
4501 Forbes Boulevard, Suite 200, Lanham, Maryland 20706
www.rowman.com

Unit A, Whitacre Mews, 26–34 Stannary Street, London SE11 4AB

British Library Cataloguing in Publication Information Available

Library of Congress Cataloging-in-Publication Data Available

ISBN 978-1-4758-2690-6 (cloth : alk. paper)
ISBN 978-1-4758-2691-3 (pbk. : alk. paper)
ISBN 978-1-4758-2692-0 (electronic)

Printed in the United States of America

To mom.

—A.B.

For Leslie and Clara, my two loves.

—D.B.

Contents

List of Figures

Acknowledgments

We gratefully acknowledge the support and suggestions of our partner, Michael Trivette. Michael, this book couldn't have been possible without your help.

We also wish to sincerely thank our editor at Rowman & Littlefield, Sarah Jubar, whose exceptional dedication to every aspect of *The Enlightened College Applicant* throughout the publishing process truly went above and beyond.

Our literary agent, Anne Devlin, has our sincere gratitude for all of her hard work connecting us with Rowman & Littlefield. We also wish to express thanks to all of our colleagues at College Transitions for their input and continued commitment to helping our clients. Last, Andrew, in particular, wishes to thank his wife, Eva, and his daughters, Anna and Abigel, for being a constant source of support and inspiration.

The Enlightened College Applicant

An Introduction

Early in Lois Lowry's classic young adult novel *The Giver,* a group of adolescents nervously await their fate at The Ceremony of Twelve, where town elders will single-handedly and irrevocably determine their vocational futures. For the book's protagonist, Jonas, and his peers, everything is riding on this one moment. How they will spend every day of their lives going forward rests fully in the hands of these powerful decision-makers.

At the ceremony, some are selected to high-prestige posts like doctors, scientists, or engineers and others to more modest posts like street cleaners, landscapers, or general laborers. In this fictional society, The Ceremony of Twelve is the watershed moment in young people's lives, and also one in which they have absolutely no agency.

Sadly, more than a decade and a half into the new millennium, the way in which the college admissions process is approached by many Americans might as well be termed the *Ceremony of Eighteen.* Each April, swarms of teens await word from their prospective universities with bated breath, their hopes and dreams unhealthily tied to gaining acceptance at a very select subset of name-brand schools.

Prospective college students, we do not envy you. You live in the age of information overload, where advice about college admissions is abundant to a fault. Chatter and hearsay on the topic is ubiquitous. In affluent neighborhoods, this phenomenon runs on overdrive: "If he doesn't get into Columbia, I just don't know what he'll do," says the woman in line at the deli as she waits for her chicken salad order to be filled.

The news media throws petrol on the inferno, regularly highlighting shrinking admission rates at elite colleges. Attempts to navigate through the cacophony of voices often result in students and families left adrift in the proverbial mile-wide, inch-deep ocean of cyberspace. Going down the Internet rabbit hole, they land on College Confidential or some other online forum, taking as gospel the words of some of the most negative, misinformed fear mongers on the planet (Insert FoxNews/MSNBC joke, depending on your political affiliation).

An internal monologue begins to develop in the heads of even the most reasonable, logical young people. "If I don't get into this school, my chances at success are doomed." Level-headed parents, even, ironically, those who attended nonelite colleges themselves and went on to outstanding career accomplishments and financial success, suddenly believe that if their child is rejected from Duke, they will be relegated to a life of menial labor.

It's natural to get fixated on a particular *name school*, the type of recognizable and respected university whose bumper sticker would evoke jealousy in anyone breathing your exhaust fumes, whose presence adjacent to your child's name in their high school graduation program will stun that one teacher who never seemed to totally believe in him and cause other parents in the stands to ooh and ahh and say, perhaps with a wisp of jealousy, "Now that young person is going places." And that highfalutin lady in the deli? Well, she'll be crying in her chicken salad when she finds out that your kid got into Elite U and her son is stuck at State.

We get it. Encouraging people to adopt a more holistic and consumer-minded approach to college selection is about as easy as reprogramming the Manchurian Candidate. After all, messages about the overwhelming importance of your child attending a prestigious school have been gradually scaffolded in your brain, embedded deep within your subconscious, and, after 17–18 years of reinforcement from family, friends, media, and popular culture, likely entangled with your own sense of self-worth.

The Giver slowly revealed the dark underbelly of an at-first seemingly utopian society. From an outsider's perspective, it's easy to accept the college admissions process, like Lowry's fictional world, at face value. In a kind and innocent, *Richard Scarry*-like world, admissions officers would operate with pure intentions and egalitarian zeal, only wishing to further the noble cause of educating the next generation of responsible citizens. Of course, they would also probably be aardvarks.

Unfortunately, real life admissions officers have other, more institution-driven motives. Faced with financial pressures and a persistent need to climb the rankings of *U.S. News* and other publications, many devote considerable effort to drum up applicants for the purpose of rejecting more students and therefore enhancing their selectivity and status. Institutions have fed the aforementioned admissions insanity by implicitly perpetuating a myth that where one attends college is going to be the greatest determinant of future success. Lois Lowry, a two-time Newbury Award winner and author of over thirty books that have sold tens of millions of copies worldwide, might be one of the countless leaders in their respective fields who would firmly disagree; she graduated from the University of Southern Maine.[1]

THE BETTER ANGELS OF OUR NATURE

We are encouraged by the paradigm shift that has begun to take place in the college admissions discourse in recent years. Strong national voices like Frank Bruni and Lynn O'Shaughnessy, among others, have begun to peel away the fear-based and pretentious layers of the college admissions onion, urging families to consider fit before prestige, while highlighting the many postsecondary pathways to success.

The better angels of our nature finally seem to be emerging, as these saner voices have begun to take the college admissions dialogue in a healthier direction. Yet, there is a need to balance idealism with reality and to provide a more data-driven examination of college admissions in America—one that is capable of distinguishing fact from fantasy. *The Enlightened College Applicant* will disabuse you of the notion that college admissions is all about *getting in* to an elite school; however, it will also honestly confront the ways in which college selectivity and reputation still matter. Of equal importance, this book will provide you and your child with the knowledge needed to make savvy college-related choices and win admission into institutions that account for the *bigger picture* of a student's academic, professional, and personal life and that ultimately provide optimal returns on your educational investment.

We have spent the last decade working with thousands of high school and college students in a host of capacities: certified college counselors, teachers, college professors, and administrators. In addition to this experience *on the ground*, we both are higher education researchers with a bird's-eye perspective of the college admissions landscape. Drawing on our practical and academic understanding of the admissions game, our goal is to give you and your child a comprehensive, evidence-based understanding of college admissions and planning and then teach you how to apply such understanding to your unique situation. It is our strong belief that after reading this book you will emerge a better-informed and more thoughtful college consumer.

WHAT OUR BOOK IS NOT

As you've probably noticed, there is no dearth of college guidebooks on the market. We had no interest in publishing information that is readily available elsewhere. As a result *The Enlightened College Applicant* is not a comprehensive resource guide stuffed with SAT/GPA statistics of admitted applicants, prestige rankings, application deadlines, popular majors, admission rates, and the like. While valuable, you can easily track down hard admissions data in any of the phone book–sized volumes that tower over this modestly proportioned text.

Anecdotes and generalizations about life on campus/the student body are likewise absent from this book. Some guidebooks will tell you if *hard liquor is popular on campus* or if *no one cheats*. Such generalities may capture something about the milieu on a given campus, but they should not guide your child's college selection. There are students at every college and university who are more focused on illicitly purchasing bottles of Smirnoff than attending class, and someone at even the allegedly most honest campus is plagiarizing their thesis on eighteenth-century Scottish currency as we speak.

This is not a step-by-step how-to guide covering the basics like how to fill out the FAFSA or how your child should submit supplemental materials as part of their application. Many excellent procedural texts already exist. Ideally, your child's counselor will be able to assist them in these areas as well.

OUR GOALS FOR YOU: CHAPTER BY CHAPTER

The layout of *The Enlightened College Applicant* is designed and sequenced so that readers can achieve specific learning goals in each chapter that, in the end, allow you to help your child identify the right colleges (for them) and get the most out of their higher education experience. The outline of the chapter-by-chapter learning goals below is provided to give you a coherent sense of where we are headed.

Chapter 1: You will emerge with a firm grasp of the financial realities of a college education in today's world and the unexpected ways in which college-related choices, made at the age of 18 or younger, can impact your child's life well into adulthood. With this in mind, you'll learn how to account for the *bigger picture* and help your child decide on a college and course of study that improves their prospects for long-term success in work and life.

Chapter 2: You will come to understand the true, in-depth answer to the question of *Does it matter where my child goes to college?* Oversimplified answers to this question abound. We'll show you what the premier research has to say regarding the relationship between college prestige and professional success. We'll also highlight the often-overlooked institutions and institutional features that provide for a productive and profitable undergraduate experience.

Chapters 3–5: Now that you have a better understanding of what characteristics to look for when helping your child identify their target destinations, it's time to get into the *meat* of our text. These chapters are loaded with invaluable advice on everything you need to know about the admissions process, including what number of Advanced Placement (AP) classes your child should take, whether they should apply early, how they can write a winning essay, and much more. We begin in chapter 3 by dispelling the most popular college admission myths. Chapter 4 covers what students can do, even before the application process begins, to maximize their admissions prospects. Finally, in chapter 5, we'll discuss strategies for crafting an effective college application.

Chapter 6: You'll understand that adopting a smart consumer mindset is critical. Accepting that higher education is actually a buyer's market will open your eyes to financial aid and merit-based scholarship opportunities, as well as cost-saving strategies, and will help you and your child avoid commonly made fiscal mistakes.

Chapter 7: Our "So You Want to Be a . . ." chapter will provide your child with a detailed roadmap to entering some of the most popular careers: doctor, lawyer, engineer, software developer/programmer, teacher, financial analyst, psychologist, journalist, and professor. In addition, this chapter will include a series of Top Feeders lists revealing which colleges send the highest percentage of students to top jobs and graduate schools, as well as a data-driven discussion of whether attending a prestigious college actually gives students a leg up in each of the aforementioned fields. This is a great place to just explore professions of interest, or for those high schoolers who have already settled on a vocation, specific guidance on how to approach their undergraduate education.

NOTES

1. Lois Lowry began her academic career at Brown University, left to marry a naval officer, and then resumed her education at Southern Maine later in life, graduating at age 35. She is an excellent example of someone who obviously had the ability to gain acceptance at an Ivy League school not needing the name on the diploma to achieve wild success in her chosen field.

Chapter 1

The Big Picture

Let's begin by posing and answering the most basic question about college in the mid-2010s: Is a college education still worth the investment?

We'll save the drama—even in an era of bloated tuition costs, ballooning student loan debt, and a weakened American job market, the answer to the general question of whether a college degree is still worth the investment remains a resounding *yes*.

Yet, this affirmative answer is strapped with a Barry Bonds–sized asterisk; not every degree from every school for every individual *is* actually worth the investment. A more extensive and more personalized analysis is necessary to be of any useful guidance. We lead off with the examination of a basic question: Is today's average college graduate still better off than an average high school graduate?

COLLEGE VERSUS HIGH SCHOOL GRADS

Survey any high school guidance counselor's assortment of wall hangings, and you will likely spot some sort of infographic clipped from a newspaper, showing the difference in projected lifetime earnings for the average college grad versus the average high school grad—the estimate is about 1 million dollars or more for the degree earner. It's no secret that more years of education equate to higher earning potential. In fact, a recent study showed that a degree increases one's hourly earnings by 98%.[1]

The advantage doesn't end with salary; benefits such as health insurance and retirement packages are also slanted in favor of college grads. Over 75%

of college graduates have access to employer-provided health insurance compared to just 50% of high school grads.[2] A similar gap exists when looking at access to retirement plans. College grads also report being more satisfied with their jobs, tend to live longer and healthier lives, and are far less likely to wind up unemployed or in a state of poverty than their nondegree-holding counterparts.

Forgoing higher education is clearly a perilous road, but so is thinking that you've got it made just because you are college bound. Over the last decade, earnings for college graduates have actually decreased, when accounting for inflation.[3] This income stagnation runs concurrent with college tuition prices continuing to skyrocket and 7 in 10 college graduates emerging from their undergraduate years with educational debt.

Educational debt, in and of itself, is not bad, especially if it leads to better job prospects and improved earning potential. However, a frightening number of graduates take on too much debt, attending unnecessarily expensive schools and programs that fail to provide sufficient returns, despite the fact that equally beneficial yet more affordable options exist.

THE LIFE-ALTERING IMPACT OF STUDENT LOAN DEBT

The myopic nonchalance with which students willingly take on needless debt to attend one university over another is a startling aspect of college selection in the twenty-first century. We'll explore why, in spite of well-publicized information about the horrors of student loan debt, the great mass of applicants choose to plunge right into IOU financing when better options rest within their reach. Hopefully, we'll convince you that the debt-free (or debt-reduced) road, while less traveled, is worth exploring.

Negatively charged adjectives—*crippling*, *burdensome*, and *overwhelming*, just to name a few—frequently accompany sound bites and headlines on the topic of student loan debt. Student loan debt is a *crisis*, people are drowning in it, and it is seen as a threat to the economy at large. It is hard not to come away with an appropriate level of concern regarding student loan debt, yet, in admissions cycle after admissions cycle, swarms of college applicants continue to make decisions that set themselves up to be just as financially crippled, burdened, and overwhelmed in adulthood as the headlines forewarned. The first question is—why?

Some blame lies in the pervasive belief that a student should strive to attend the most prestigious school to which they are accepted. Such a narrow mindset takes *value* and how one's undergraduate experience fits into *the larger picture* completely out of the equation, leading many to believe that paying exorbitant tuition costs, while something to grumble about, is ultimately a fait accompli—an unpleasant but unavoidable reality.

Another key factor is that teenagers, even exceptionally bright examples of the lot, are notorious for concluding that known dangers will never personally affect them (i.e., "I am aware that drunk driving can be deadly, but I know that *I'll* be fine."). Not surprisingly this same faulty bravado seems to enter into decisions around financing higher education.

In the last thirty years, tuition prices are up 538%,[4] aggregate student loan debt is now in the trillions, and the average debt load is around $30,000.[5] But we acknowledge that numbers, even numbers this staggering, can seem distant and abstract. Thus, we aim to present the very real and tangible ways in which student loan debt can impact a young person's life, in an attempt to impart that decisions made at 18 can have significant consequences at 25, 30, and beyond.

Impact on Career Options

A recent survey found that only 13% of workers worldwide actually enjoy their jobs—talk about a depressing statistic.[6] No one's goal is to join the 87% for whom work leaves something to be desired, but being boxed in by cumbersome student loans makes someone far more likely to be part of this unsatisfied cohort. While there are plenty of people satisfied and fulfilled by their careers in lucrative professions, there are also many who despise their jobs but are stuck in a type of indentured servitude, working long, stressful hours just to meet their massive monthly student loan payments.

Those carrying student loan debt are less likely to choose careers in the nonprofit or public interest sectors. To a teenager, this might elicit a response along these lines: "Big deal, I'll just have to take a job where I have to make more money." However, as this same individual progresses through college, they may realize that their true passion lies in a field like social work, teaching, or public service. Unfortunately, because of loans already accrued, a switch into a lesser-paying field may prove untenable. In a world where workers switch jobs an average of every 4.6 years, this desire or need to shift careers on a dime can likewise be hampered by the burden of debt.[7] Student loan debt is simply the number-one enemy of career flexibility.

Individuals with high levels of student loan debt are also statistically unlikely to start their own businesses. Acquiring a small business loan typically requires being relatively debt-free. Even if indebted graduates could get financing to start their business, those needing to make monthly payments cannot afford to endure the growing pains inevitable with any independent venture. Eliminating this option from consideration is a shame, as a recent survey indicated that 55% of small business owners are happy with their jobs—a pretty big jump over 13%.[8]

Effect on Lifestyle

The only debt burden larger than student loans that most people will encounter in their lives is that of a mortgage. In recent years, thirty-year-olds with student loan debts have become less likely to take on mortgages than their debt-free counterparts—some by choice, others solely because they cannot get one. Those with high levels of debt are also more likely to be refused more simple lines of credit such as credit cards or car loans.

Debt can have other powerful effects on available choices in adulthood, which would have seemed eons away at 18. Holders of student loan debt are far more likely to delay marriage for financial reasons than those without. One survey found that 43% of graduates choose to put off having kids until their student loans are paid off.[9]

Future Education

It's important to realize that a college degree, while necessary, is no longer sufficient for entry into many of the most sought-after professions. If a student plans on getting a graduate degree to enter the profession of their dreams, they should be sure to explore that cost before committing to taking on massive undergraduate loans.

The average cost of attending a top MBA program is over $111,000,[10] and that doesn't even account for living expenses and the opportunity cost of forgoing two years' worth of paychecks. The average law degree will also run a total in the six figures. The cheapest medical school will still cost over $200,000.[11]

Many graduate degrees that allow entry into lower-paying jobs also cost a good deal of money. Obtaining a master of fine arts degree will more than likely cost two to three times your future annual salary. If your passion lies in the arts, let no one dissuade you from the plan, but you need to have exactly that—*a plan*. Racking up massive undergraduate debt and then taking on additional graduate debt for the purposes of entering a low-paying job is a setup for disaster, or at the very least, living with one's parents until the age of 45 (which, even if you love your parents, likely still qualifies as a disaster).

The Overeducated Barista

Tales of debt-saddled college grads lining up for jobs at Starbucks abound in popular media. In this case, popular perception is backed by statistical proof. In the United States today, over 46% of recent college grads report to jobs that do not require a four-year degree—nearly 20 million Americans overall fall into this category.[12]

Over 300,000 of this group are working as waiters and waitresses, almost half a million as customer service reps, 115,000 as janitors, 107,000 as laborers, 83,000 are tending bar at an establishment near you, and the list goes on and on (mail carriers, flight attendants, landscapers, and construction workers all have large contingents of college-educated workers as well).

Of course, there is nothing wrong with making an honest living through any of these means. The real question is whether this was the working life these folks envisioned when they started their higher education journey. Did the server at your local IHOP anticipate delivering Rooty Tooty Fresh 'N Fruity pancakes to tables of teenagers when he decided to incur 40 grand in educational debt to pursue an art degree? Are the majority of the nation's educated custodians actually math geniuses trying to pull a Matt Damon from *Good Will Hunting*? Life can always take us down unexpected roads, but it seems unlikely that anyone would willingly desire to chart such a challenging course.

So, how does one avoid this pitfall? Is it sheer luck? Perhaps Branch Rickey, the baseball executive who famously brought Jackie Robinson to the Brooklyn Dodgers, said it best, "Luck is the residue of design."

Whether someone is building a 1940s baseball team or their own educational and career goals, thoughtful design can be the difference between success and failure.

Keep Focused on the Bigger Picture

Author Stephen Covey, in his *The Seven Habits of Highly Effective People,* suggests that it is wise to *begin with the end in mind* when approaching any big, multistep decision. Applying this concept to college planning, if as a high school senior, a student's dream is to one day pursue a PhD in Marine Biology, they would plan accordingly, working backward to ensure that their ducks are in a row (a pun if we're talking about sea ducks). This student might consider the following questions:

- Where do most marine biologists live?
- Where are they employed?
- How much do they make?
- What are the best PhD programs in the field?
- What do those programs look for in terms of undergraduate candidates?
- Which institutions did these candidates attend and what did they study?
- Which of these colleges can I afford?
- Is prestige a big factor in this field?
- How much would I owe in student loans if I attend my first choice and how might that influence the other future steps I've outlined above?

Of course, not every high school senior can map out their entire young adulthood from soup to nuts. Reality is, most cannot, and that's absolutely okay. Even if your son or daughter will be entering college with an *undecided* label, there are still financial realities that can be projected into the future and considered. They may want to become a banker; they may want to open a bakery. Either way, it would certainly be nice to have the choice.

Designing Your Education

In today's globalized and competitive economy, skills and/or relevant experience matter as much or more than a diploma, primarily because a diploma doesn't mean what it used to. While degree attainment was pretty close to a surefire meal ticket a generation ago, simply possessing a credential from an institution of higher education is still necessary but not adequate for most *college-level* jobs.

Although demand for college-level work has grown, many new degree holders have failed to acquire practical skills valued in the job market, resulting in widespread unemployment and underemployment among recent graduates. In light of these trends, it is essential that today's college applicants explore academic programs that lead to genuine learning and distinction, not just a vanilla degree.

CHOOSING A COLLEGE MAJOR: WHAT YOU NEED TO KNOW

Buridan's ass is a well-known (and unfortunately named) philosophical paradox where a famished donkey sits equidistant between two similarly delicious bales of hay and, unable to find a rational reason to select one over the other, ultimately starves to death. Strangely enough, this rather absurd and morbid fourteenth-century tale is relevant to the dilemma faced by many college students today.

Never before in human history have young people had such an endless array of desirable career paths as they do in twenty-first-century America. The US Department of Education presently recognizes over 1,500 academic programs offered by the nation's colleges and universities.[13] These include everything from your run-of-the-mill liberal arts, social science, and STEM majors to your more unique upstart disciplines such as blacksmithing (Southern Illinois University), puppet arts (University of Connecticut), and race track management (University of Arizona). Given this cornucopia of potential career paths, it is little surprise that settling on a major is a difficult enterprise.

The Age of Exploration

The concept of a 4-year undergraduate degree is becoming an urban legend on the scale of Bigfoot and the chupacabra. At non-flagship public institutions nationwide, only 19% of students graduate on time. At flagship institutions, the number climbs to just 36%. Shockingly the *6-year* graduation rate across all public and private colleges and universities in the United States is only 56%.[14] There are a multitude of factors behind these abysmal numbers, but the process of settling on a major is right at the forefront.

Research tells us that the best-laid plans of high school students frequently falter early into their postsecondary experience. It is estimated that 75% of college students will change their major at least once—the average student will switch a stunning three times before graduating.[15] Even at Princeton University, a campus filled with some of the most driven and focused young people in the world, an internal study revealed that 70% of this elite student body elect to pull the old major switcheroo.[16]

Let's pause to point out that switching a major is not inherently a *bad* thing and is in some cases an unavoidable outcome. Not every high school senior can be expected to map out their entire academic and career path in permanent ink. It is perfectly normal for one's interests to shift and develop as new experiences unfold, and nothing is worse than sticking with an academic path one knows is the wrong choice. As the saying goes, "It's better to be at the bottom of a ladder you want to climb than halfway up one that you don't."

While changing majors is inevitable for some, others end up abandoning their initial pathway because of poor planning, lack of information, or following misguided outside influences. Math and science departments tend to see the largest exodus as freshmen receive first- and second-semester grades far lower than anticipated. These students typically did not seek out the most rigorous options at their high school to ensure that they could handle college-level STEM coursework. Any student pursuing a STEM field should avail themselves of advanced math and science classes in high school. Your first college-level course should not feel exponentially more challenging than those experienced in 12th grade.

Passion Matters

Another popular category of major switchers are those who selected their initial area of study for the wrong reasons. The majority of high school students, almost two-thirds, select areas of study that do not match their interests—an extremely odd phenomenon and one that is ultimately counterproductive. Studies have repeatedly shown that students who pick a major in an area of high interest earn better grades[17] and are more likely to finish their degree in 4 years.[18]

Yet, despite these findings, many adolescents still feel tremendous pressure from their parents and others to pursue what are considered the most economically viable and/or prestigious fields. Interest, passion, and enjoyment often take a backseat to projected future salary. However, outside of a few fields, salary data based on your undergraduate major can be highly unpredictable.

Starting Salary Data

Articles ranking the highest-paying college majors are easy to find but are typically of little help in selecting a career. A quick glance at any such list will make you notice that just about all of the degrees producing the handsomest return on your tuition dollars end with the word *engineering*. This is great news for anyone interested in becoming a petroleum, computer, chemical, civil, electronics, nuclear, mechanical, or electrical engineer and wholly irrelevant news for the other 95% of prospective college students.

The fact that the average petroleum engineering major makes $93,500 right out of college does not mean that all the future humanities majors out there should abandon all of their respective passions and immediately register for Introduction to Fossil Fuels.[19] Planning the extraction of crude oil from subsurface reservoirs may be lucrative, but it isn't for everyone.

It goes without saying that the decision on what to do with the next 40 plus years of life after college graduation should not be driven entirely by average starting salary figures. In addition to the obvious reason that people don't want to be stuck in a job that makes them completely miserable solely to earn a few extra bucks, recent studies have actually shown that salaries by major tend to level out in the long run. For example, liberal arts majors may lag behind before the age of 30, but after 50 (their peak earning years), they surprisingly outearn individuals who pursued a preprofessional or professional track in college.

Still, one should be cognizant of their short-term, postgraduate earning potential when selecting what type of school to attend. Ignorance of this factor can be a setup for financial distress later in life—stress that with proper planning could have easily been avoided. College grads in the bottom quartile of earners actually make less than the average high school graduate. Some of the lowest-paying majors include early childhood education, drama/theater, social work, library science, and psychology. Students considering these majors are wise to avoid incurring unnecessary debt in pursuit of their undergraduate degrees. The same goes for graduates in STEM fields that do not typically lead to high-income positions right out of college.

While engineering and computer science grads enjoy solid starting salaries, meteorology, biology, and zoology majors begin their careers paid below the median college grad. Other majors that many assume would have poor starting, and mid-career salaries are actually shockingly strong. For example, philosophy majors outpace their peers who studied marketing, pre-law, and even chemistry in mid-career income.[20] You read correctly—philosophy majors!

As stand-alone credentials, many undergraduate diplomas, even from elite schools, do not alone qualify someone for a high-paying professional job. It is in these situations that salary data broken down by college major becomes particularly hard to interpret.

Majors Dependent upon Grad School

Many bachelor's degrees have limited value on their own but can be parlayed into relatively lucrative careers through continuing one's education. Psychology is perhaps the ultimate example of this phenomenon. Those with bachelor's degrees in clinical or counseling psychology enter the field making less than $35,000 on average. Most will find entry-level employment in the behavioral/mental health field, working in positions such as a drug and alcohol counselor, probation officer, group home coordinator, or social worker.

While engineering majors can call themselves *engineers* upon graduation, psychology majors need to pursue advanced degrees to claim such a credential. Master's level psychologists will more than double up their bachelor's-only peers, and those who eventually earn a PsyD or PhD will see average earnings above $87,000.[21]

If a student plans on entering a grad school-dependent field, make sure they don't break the bank on their undergraduate education. Students with ambitions to enter fields such as law or medicine should account for undergraduate affordability and performance in addition to prestige, given the costs of a professional degree. Aspiring doctors and lawyers, along with would-be professors and scientists, should also realize that graduate school credentials, not undergraduate name, will be most important to their job prospects.

Don't End up a Starving Donkey

As with any element of postsecondary planning, decisions about college majors should be made within the context of the bigger picture of a student's career and life goals. It's important to be aware of financial outcomes for graduates in a chosen area, but future salary considerations are often highly dependent on future educational attainment. A young person's own internal compass should guide the major selection process more than any outside voice.

When it comes to postsecondary choices, young people today possess a level of choice that would make Buridan's donkey's head explode. If a student makes their choice strategically and follows their instincts, they'll be able to successfully pick out the *bale of hay* that best fits into their life plan.

LOOKING BEYOND MAJORS: SKILLS THAT EVERY COLLEGE STUDENT SHOULD ACQUIRE

The selection of an undergraduate major is important but is far from the be-all and end-all of a college experience. It is an overly simplistic view of higher education that people emerge from four years of college with a specific skill related to their primary area of study: education majors learn how to teach, accounting majors learn how to crunch numbers, allied health majors learn skills particular to the health care profession, and so on.

Yet, no matter the primary field of study, there are certain generalized skills that will serve students well in the modern economy where the average worker will change jobs an astonishing 11 times.[22] Abilities in the areas of written expression, public speaking, foreign language, and quantitative analysis can and should be honed while pursuing a degree in any field. If a student emerges from any degree-granting program capable in those four areas, their investment will be rewarded many times over.

Writing

Elect to major in English and only one thing is for certain—you're going to endure at least four years of barbs and jabs from your know-it-all, curmudgeonly Uncle Jerry. At family gatherings, he'll interrupt your attempt to relate your love of Chaucer to a group of elderly female relatives whose names you have never been 100% sure of (Agnes? Gertrude? Doris?) with something along the lines of:

> *Q:* "What's the difference between an English major and a park bench?"
>
> *A:* "The park bench can support a family of four . . . hardy har har."

Light laughter and stares of pity from the rest of the room follow.

What Uncle Jerry and his peanut gallery don't realize is that becoming a highly literate person actually makes you a very marketable person in the modern economy. Reports, emails, memos, newsletters, press releases, and presentations are just a handful of the ways in which written communication is required on a daily basis in most places of business. Good writing sets a tone for a company, as of course does inferior writing. Poor grammar, misspellings, and subpar sentence structure in workplace communication can be the equivalent of showing up for a client meeting sporting a mustard-splotched tie (something Uncle Jerry would totally do).

Whether or not a student majors in English, it behooves them to sharpen their writing skills throughout college—chances are they'll use them in their future profession. Survey executives from literally any industry and they all say the same thing—quality writing is a necessary skill for most jobs. In fact, within American companies, over two-thirds of salaried employees have some level of writing responsibility.[23] As a result, the vast majority of companies take writing ability into consideration when making hiring and promotion decisions.

Many employers bemoan the level of writing ability demonstrated by recent college grads, even those from elite schools. At risk of sounding like the aforementioned Uncle Jerry, in a world filled with daily texts, tweets, and Facebook posts, the average college grad's grammar, punctuation, and sentence structure are simply no longer up to the standards of many hiring officials. This, however, is good news for all of those strong young writers out there, as their skills have never been in greater demand.

Public Speaking

Warren Buffett once opined that for those entering the business world, becoming an effective public communicator can boost one's future earnings by an estimated 50%.[24] Unfortunately, this bump in income would be viewed by most people as full-blown hazard pay—public speaking is simply that terrifying an endeavor.

Fear of public speaking runs so deep that, in survey after survey, Americans report fearing the act of oratory more than any more traditionally nightmarish situation you can conjure up: heights, plane crashes, sharks, getting stuck in an elevator, getting stuck in an elevator filled with sharks, and most famously—death itself.

In trying to avoid public speaking, one might first cross off the obvious list of professions requiring the practice: minister, motivational speaker, broadcaster, and actor. Unfortunately, the list doesn't end there: purchasing agents, marketers, nonprofit fundraisers, sales reps, public relations specialists, teachers, professors, realtors, and corporate trainers all are required to speak to groups, large and small, on a regular basis. In any profession, even ones almost completely devoid of social interaction, most employees will still likely have to go through a harrowing interview process, participate in staff meetings, and discuss one's worth at some type of annual performance review. Public speaking, in one form or another, is pretty darn close to unavoidable.

To fully comprehend the value of quality public speaking, reflect on the practitioners of the art that you have witnessed every day for the last 12 or so years—your K-12 teachers. Sadly, a great many of this cohort were probably such poor presenters that they made your brain melt on a daily basis (coincidentally, brain melting is #174 on the list of Americans' fears). On the other end, the best teachers you had were able to transcend the monotony of the school day, engaging, enlightening, and inspiring you, while even on occasion evoking laughter and tears. Imagine what possessing such a skill set would do in any chosen profession.

Some colleges and universities require that all graduates take a course in public speaking; most do not. Either way, we recommend that students seek out opportunities to practice this intimidating but extremely worthwhile craft. Taking a public speaking course is a good start, but it shouldn't stop there—students should ask around and find out which elective courses require presentations and consider joining a club or activity that requires public speaking. College presents a unique time to work on becoming comfortable presenting yourself and your ideas to others—a skill that will pay off mightily in a future career.

Foreign Language

The Soviet launching of Sputnik in 1957 is widely recognized as the impetus for President Eisenhower's initiative to improve science education in America's public schools. The strong push for STEM education persists in the modern era, this time with the revised aim of preparing US youth to compete in the global economy.

Lost to history, though, is the fact that Eisenhower also spoke of the equally pressing need to help American pupils become proficient in foreign languages. By the 1960s, over two-thirds of higher education institutions required students to learn a foreign language as part of their bachelor's degree; today that number has fallen to just 50%.[25]

The Cold War may have crumbled with the Berlin Wall, but we now reside in a globalized marketplace where knowledge, trade, and investments know no borders. For anyone entering fields such as business, finance, information technology, software development, government, law enforcement, or health care (just to name a few), fluency in a foreign language has never been more advantageous.

The ability to converse with international clients in their native tongue is of great value. Bilingual college grads entering the private sector right now can expect a pay increase right off the bat; those conversant in Mandarin Chinese, German, Japanese, and Arabic may demand even higher compensation.[26] As a secondary bonus, research shows that the process of language acquisition is the mental equivalent of a P90X workout. Bilinguals develop increased gray matter in their brains, which leads to heightened creativity, focus, and decision-making ability.

While studying language may no longer be required at many colleges and universities, we recommend that students consider completing multiple levels of a foreign language and take advantage of now-commonplace study abroad programs. Learning a language during one's college years will be easier than one-day listening to Rosetta Stone recordings in the car as you drive your screaming kids to day care.

Data Analysis

News flash: Analyzing data is no longer done exclusively by middle-aged men in pocketed, short-sleeved white dress shirts, robotically inputting punched cards into giant mainframe computers. In a world with *Moneyball*, Nate Silver, *Freakonomics*, and widespread fantasy sports participation, stats have officially entered the mainstream.

It goes without saying that individuals majoring in areas such as math, engineering, actuarial science, pre-med, or architecture will be required to become fluent in the likes of calculus, geometry, and trigonometry. On the other end of the spectrum, many liberal arts majors manage to take just one basic math course in college or even eschew mathematics entirely. Math-phobic individuals tend to cast the quantitative out of their lives forever as soon as they are able to—a move that may not prove altogether wise.

Some level of data analysis is now a requirement in a surprising number of non-STEM fields including but by no means limited to business, politics, nonprofit work, health care, and education. Becoming a human calculator is less important in today's workplace than being able to accurately interpret data. Traces of an increasingly data-driven society are everywhere. Analytics are increasingly being utilized by human resource departments for recruiting, measuring productivity, and workplace planning. Companies like Walmart and Amazon have famously used logistical models to revolutionize retail. Even the formerly quaint world of public education becomes more and more data-reliant each year in this age of accountability.

In an effort to cultivate data literacy, we recommend students take at least one statistics course and one economics course (preferably in microeconomics) during their undergraduate years. Possessing some level of ability to analyze data will enhance their employability in just about any field.

FINAL THOUGHTS

In this chapter, you've learned many of the basic tenets of what is genuinely important when planning for postsecondary education—what students study and what skills they acquire matter as much or more than where they go, college planning should be done with long-term life goals in mind, and taking on too much unnecessary debt can have a sweeping, negative impact on a student's future. In spite of these acknowledgments, however, it's understandable if you're still not ready to take the leap and reframe your approach to college admissions.

Don't worry, you're right where you should be. Just lend us your ears, approach chapter 2 with an open mind, and discover what research and data actually say about the relationship between college selectivity and student outcomes.

NOTES

1. Pew Research Center, "Is College Worth It?" May 15, 2011, accessed December 6, 2015, http://www.pewsocialtrends.org/2011/05/15/is-college-worth-it/.

2. Elise Gould, "A Decade of Declines in Employer-Sponsored Health Insurance Coverage," Economic Policy Institute, February 23, 2012, accessed December 6, 2015, http://www.epi.org/publication/bp337-employer-sponsored-health-insurance/.

3. Elise Gould, "2014 Continues a 35-Year Trend of Broad-Based Wage Stagnation," Economic Policy Institute, February 19, 2015, accessed December 6, 2015, http://www.epi.org/publication/stagnant-wages-in-2014/.

4. Mamie Lynch, Jennifer Engle, and Jose L. Cruz, "Lifting the Fog on Inequitable Financial Aid Policies," The Education Trust, November 2011, accessed December 6, 2015, http://edtrust.org/wp-content/uploads/2013/10/Lifting-the-Fog-FINAL.pdf.

5. The Institute for College Access & Success, "Project on Student Debt: State by State Data," accessed December 6, 2015, http://ticas.org/posd/map-state-data-2015.

6. Steve Crabtree, "Worldwide, 13% of Employees Are Engaged at Work," Gallup, October 8, 2013, accessed December 6, 2015, http://www.gallup.com/poll/165269/worldwide-employees-engaged-work.aspx.

7. U.S. Department of Labor, Bureau of Labor Statistics, "Employee Tenure in 2014," September 18, 2014, accessed December 6, 2015, http://www.bls.gov/news.release/archives/tenure_09182014.htm.

8. Yodle, "Survey: SMB Owners are 'Happy' Despite Concerns about Healthcare, Retirement & Customer Acquisition," August 22, 2013, accessed December 6, 2015, http://www.yodle.com/company/press-releases/yodle-smb-sentiment-survey.

9. American Student Assistance, "Life Delayed: The Impact of Student Debt on the Daily Lives of Young Americans," 2013, accessed December 6, 2015, http://www.asa.org/site/assets/files/3793/life_delayed.pdf.

10. Patrick Clark, "Debt Is Piling Up Faster for Most Graduate Students—but Not MBAs," *Bloomberg Businessweek*, March 25, 2014, accessed December 6, 2015, http://www.bloomberg.com/bw/articles/2014-03-25/student-loan-debt-piles-up-for-graduate-students-but-not-mbas.

11. Janet Lorin, "Medical School at $278,000 Means Even Bernanke Son Has Debt," *Bloomberg Businessweek*, April 11, 2013, accessed December 6, 2015, http://www.bloomberg.com/news/articles/2013-04-11/medical-school-at-278-000-means-even-bernanke-son-carries-debt.

12. Richard Vedder, "Why Did 17 Million Students Go to College?" *The Chronicle of Higher Education*, October 20, 2010, accessed December 6, 2015, http://chronicle.com/blogs/innovations/why-did-17-million-students-go-to-college/27634.

13. Cecilia Capuzzi Simon, "Major Decisions," *New York Times,* November 2, 2012, accessed December 6, 2015, http://www.nytimes.com/2012/11/04/education/edlife/choosing-one-college-major-out-of-hundreds.html?_r=0.

14. Doug Shapiro et al, (2013, December), "Completing College: A National View of Student Attainment Rates-Fall 2007 Cohort (Signature Report No. 6)," Herndon, VA: National Student Clearinghouse Research Center, accessed December 6, 2015, http://nscresearchcenter.org/signaturereport6/.

15. Virginia Gordon, (2007), *The Undecided College Student: An Academic and Career Advising Challenge* (3rd ed.), Springfield, IL: Charles C. Thomas.

16. Corinne Lowe, "70 Percent of Students Change Major After Enrollment, Study Finds," *The Daily Princetonian,* September 18, 2014, accessed December 6, 2015, http://dailyprincetonian.com/news/2014/09/70-percent-of-students-change-major-after-enrollment-study-finds/.

17. Lawrence K. Jones and Juliet Wehr Jones, (2012). "Personality-College Major Match and Student Success: A Guide for Professionals Helping Youth and Adults Who Are in College or Are College-Bound," accessed February 29, 2016, http://www.careerkey.org/pdf/Personality-College_Major_Match_Guide_Professionals.pdf.

18. Jeff Allen and Steve Robbins, (2010), "Effects of Interest-Major Congruence, Motivation, and Academic Performance on Timely Degree Attainment," *Journal of Counseling Psychology,* 57, 23–35.

19. National Association of Colleges and Employers, "Starting Salaries," accessed December 6, 2015, https://www.naceweb.org/salary-resources/starting-salaries.aspx.

20. "Salary Increase by Major," *Wall Street Journal,* accessed February 29, 2016, http://online.wsj.com/public/resources/documents/info-Degrees_that_Pay_you_Back-sort.html.

21. D. W. Rajecki and Victor M. H. Borden, (2011), "Psychology Degrees: Employment, Wage, and Career Trajectory Consequences," *Perspectives in Psychological Science,* 6, 321–335.

22. U.S. Department of Labor, Bureau of Labor Statistics, "News Release: Number of Jobs Held, Labor Market Activity, and Earnings Growth among the Youngest Baby Boomers: Results from a Longitudinal Survey," March 31, 2015, accessed June 17, 2015, http://www.bls.gov/news.release/pdf/nlsoy.pdf.

23. College Board, The National Commission on Writing for America's Families, Schools, and Colleges, "Writing: A Ticket to Work . . . Or a Ticket Out: A Survey of Business Leaders," September 2004, accessed December 6, 2015, http://www.collegeboard.com/prod_downloads/writingcom/writing-ticket-to-work.pdf.

24. Carmine Gallo, "The Soft Skill That Could Mean $1 Million Hard Cash for One Manager," *Forbes,* November 7, 2013, accessed December 2, 2015, http://www.forbes.com/sites/carminegallo/2013/11/07/the-soft-skill-that-could-mean-1-million-hard-cash-for-one-manager/.

25. Natalia Lusin, "The MLA Survey of Postsecondary Entrance and Degree Requirements for Languages Other Than English, 2009–10," Modern Language

Association of America, March 2012, accessed December 6, 2015, http://www.mla.org/pdf/requirements_survey_200910.pdf.

26. Albert Saiz and Elena Zoido, 2002, "The Returns to Speaking a Second Language," Working Papers 02-16, Federal Reserve Bank of Philadelphia.

Chapter 2

The Enlightened College Applicant
What Really Matters in a College

We begin with an analogy. Three racehorses—Cream of the Crop, Above Average, and Run of the Mill—are selected by three trainers of varying quality to prepare for the Kentucky Derby. Trainer A is world renowned, highly sought after, and thus has his pick of the litter. Without hesitation, he scoops up Cream of the Crop, who has the most natural ability of the three equine athletes. Trainer B won't work with just anyone—he generally gets strong horses who don't quite catch the eye of Trainer A. Not surprisingly, he chooses to work with Above Average, whose name aptly sums up his natural talent. Trainer C spends more time sipping mint juleps and ogling women in oversized derby hats than actually working with the horses. He takes Run of the Mill because, well, that's who is left.

If Cream of the Crop wins the Kentucky Derby, Trainer A will bask in his horse's glory and claim all the credit. The question is, what does taking in elite thoroughbreds and churning out winners actually prove about Trainer A? If Cream of the Crop had worked with Trainer B, would he not have still won the Derby? What if Cream of the Crop had elected to work with that ol' lascivious lush, Trainer C? Could he still have emerged victorious given his immense natural talent?

Now let's step out of the analogy. Substitute students for horses, colleges for trainers, and future earnings for winning the Kentucky Derby, and you should be left with similar questions. In order to begin to find answers to these types of questions related to college choice and future earnings, we have to explore a concept known as *returns to selectivity*.

FINANCIAL RETURNS TO SELECTIVITY

In recent years, the rather revolutionary notion that where you go to college will do little to determine your future life and career has exploded in popularity, endorsed by columnists and policy analysts alike. For this we are quite glad. The frenzied *rat race* of elite college admissions causes undue stress and anxiety on students and families. We are firm believers that talented, driven students will thrive at a number of institutions outside of the Ivy League.

That being said, we hesitate at making a sweeping, unequivocal statement saying that it "doesn't matter where you go to college." To do so would be to ignore decades' worth of research on outcomes related to selectivity—research that has uncovered some nuances and important distinctions on the subject of how much a school does or does not impact its students' future success.

The term *returns to selectivity* refers to the financial benefit of attending schools across the selectivity spectrum—from Harvard with its infinitesimal 6% acceptance rate[1] to Northern Arizona University with its generous 91% acceptance rate.[2] The body of research from this field of study will enlighten and surprise you.

Confirming Assumptions: 1999–2008

To briefly return to our horse-training scenario, the first true question is an obvious one: Do Trainer A's, B's, and C's horses actually enjoy different rates of success?

In an effort to scientifically explore the relationship between selectivity and economic returns, researchers in the late 1990s were able to verify that students attending colleges on the high end of the selectivity spectrum do in fact earn higher wages, on average, than students attending less-selective institutions.[3] For example, Yale graduates, as you would have expected, enjoy superior average earnings to graduates of Southern Connecticut State University, New Haven's public and less-prestigious four-year institution.

Nearly a decade later, a study by another researcher reached a similar conclusion about the monetary benefit of attending an elite school over a less-selective school. This research affirmed presumptions about how income is linked to college selectivity but did so only by comparing apples to oranges, students with the credentials to attend ultra-selective schools versus students only able to attend nonselective ones.[4] To uncover more illuminating data, it was time to toss aside the Valencias and line up a pair of nearly identical Granny Smiths.

Apples to Apples: 2009

In an attempt to look at the effects of attending a selective institution on comparable applicants, scholars looked at two groups with almost everything in common, except for one thing—where they went to college.

Students barely admitted into an unnamed flagship university were evaluated against similarly qualified students who were denied admission at the same institution and ultimately, in most cases, enrolled in far less-selective schools. Interestingly, the group of students who attended the flagship eventually earned 20% more, on average, than their rejected counterparts, a sizable discrepancy.[5]

While this outcome tells us something about selectivity's impact on monetary returns, the takeaways are limited because the study was limited to one state, significant findings were limited to white men, and schools attended by the two groups were either moderately selective or barely selective at all; the upper echelon of schools was nowhere to be found.

In essence, what remained unanswered was the essential question: Do students actually benefit from enrolling at the most selective college available to them? In 2011, two researchers would begin to shed light on an answer.

A Complex Picture Emerges: 2011

Prior research confirmed that Yale graduates earn more, on average, than students at Southern Connecticut State University. However, the million-dollar question remained: Do Yale graduates earn more because of the name on their diploma or because of the qualities that allowed them to earn admission at Yale in the first place?

In an effort to better crack this conundrum, Stacy Dale and Alan Krueger[6] set out to distinguish the benefits of college selectivity from personal characteristics that tend to result in professional success, regardless of one's undergraduate institution. The cohorts of students studied by the researchers possessed similar backgrounds, boasted strong identical high school GPAs and SAT scores, and held similarly ambitious attitudes toward their educational and career goals. Here, the authors did find that graduates of more selective colleges realized earnings 7% greater, on average, than graduates of less-selective institutions, but their most intriguing finding was yet to come.

When the authors incorporated an additional control (i.e., adjustment) for *where* students applied, they uncovered something quite interesting: students who applied to a more selective college but who chose instead to attend a less-exclusive school still earned the same wages as similarly credentialed graduates of these choosier institutions. In other words, selectivity of the college one attended didn't really matter; what counted was the selectivity of institutions to where one applied.

This finding suggests that, all things being equal, attitude, rather than undergraduate name drives earnings. In other words, if a student possesses the mindset to strive toward elite college attendance, he or she likely has the disposition and intellectual prowess to achieve high earnings, regardless of whether he or she ultimately attends an elite institution.

Now that we have a clearer answer as to the relationship between college prestige and income, it's time to muddy the waters yet again.

Cases Where Selectivity *Does* Matter

While Dale and Krueger found that the general population experiences little-to-no earnings boost by attending a supremely selective school, there are a couple of caveats. First, Dale and Krueger's study included only elite and moderately selective institutions, so they were unable to test whether similar students attending a minimally or nonselective school would be similarly unaffected. Comparisons were drawn between Penn State and Princeton or Tufts and Tulane, rather than between Elite U and the local community college. Thus, a slight revision to Dale and Krueger's finding is warranted and suggests that you do not need to attend an elite college to maximize your financial returns, *so long as you at least attend a college that is selective.*

Second, the study revealed that African Americans, Latino Americans, and first-generation college students *did* in fact see substantial benefits from attending the most selective institutions. Members of these racial/socioeconomic groups who went on to attend elite colleges earned significantly more than similarly qualified students of the same background who attended less-exclusive schools. The *why* isn't borne out by research, but a likely explanation exists.

Members of the dominant class (white, wealthy, and educated) often run in social circles with other connected, powerful (even in a relative sense) people who possess a high degree of social capital. It stands to reason that while an upper-middle-class student who attends a semi-selective state school is likely to benefit from a network of family and family friends who can help that young person land their first job, a student from a lower-income household may lack these advantages and must therefore forge their own connections, accruing their own social capital only by navigating their way through an elite university.

As such, these groups may uniquely benefit, and thus be more inclined, to choose the most selective college they can attend. In a world of nepotism and networking, an *elite* brand-name college can in fact open doors to students from less-privileged backgrounds.

Back to the Races . . .

Let's head back to our Kentucky Derby analogy to clarify the research-supported effects of selectivity on future income.

The full body of *returns to selectivity* research tells us that, in most cases, similarly equipped individuals will likely achieve similar earnings whether they choose to attend an Ivy like Columbia University or SUNY Stony Brook, a very reputable yet less-selective institution 50 miles to the east. In horse-racing terms, an elite horse like Cream of the Crop is going to get his shot at the Triple Crown whether schooled by Trainer A or Trainer B.

Trainer C's story, on the other hand, is quite different. If our same highly qualified student passed up an opportunity to attend Columbia or Stony Brook in favor of the much less-selective Long Island University, for example, they might not fare as well out in the working world. Schools like Long Island University, due to lack of resources, networks, and similarly abled peer groups, simply cannot provide a comparable undergraduate experience.

This isn't to say that an *individual* from Long Island University cannot be a president of the United States (Ronald Reagan attended Eureka College and Andrew Jackson was rumored to be illiterate) or a Fortune 500 CEO (too many examples to list). It is only to say that graduates of minimally selective schools are not on equal footing with grads of highly selective or moderately selective institutions in their quest to ascend the income ladder.

Conclusions: Selectivity Does Matter but Not Entirely

In light of findings uncovered by the complete body of literature on returns to college prestige, it appears that selectivity does matter, but not in the way that many think. Among elite and moderately selective colleges, there's significantly more variability *within* institutions *than between* institutions. As such, if you have admissions offers from multiple selective schools, don't make your choice on the basis of a *U.S. News* rank; instead, choose a college that provides you the best fit, knowing that your future professional success will likely have more to do with your own ability and effort than the name of the college on your diploma. While it isn't as simple a statement as "it doesn't matter where you go to college," it is one that is actually backed by rigorous research.

COLLEGES THAT ARE PROBABLY BETTER THAN HARVARD

Now that you understand what research has to say about the contextual and often-limited benefits of attending a highly selective school, you may have opened your mind to a few less-competitive yet still wonderful institutions. However, we've worked with enough cream of the crop high school superstars to know that for many, the lure of prestige is just too strong. Ultimately, students and parents alike still want a *name* school.

We get it. The *Harvard* name is the *Harvard* name, and that is an undeniable fact. When an alumni list includes 7 signers of the Declaration of Independence, Teddy and Franklin Roosevelt, John F. Kennedy, and 25 of the current Fortune 500 CEOs in the world, it would be just plain silly to assert that life's doors are not swung wide open for Harvard's graduates (apologies to forgotten nineteenth President of the United States Rutherford B. Hayes and the actor who played Herman Munster for narrowly missing inclusion on this list).

That being said, there are other elite, name-brand colleges and universities that may provide a better undergraduate experience than Harvard. Let us begin by revealing the truth about an undergraduate education at Harvard.

What Does a Harvard Classroom Look Like?

A Gallup Poll survey of 30,000 college graduates found that where one went to school was in no way predictive of happiness in one's future life or career.[7] There was, however, a strong correlation between close mentorship by one or more faculty members in college and future satisfaction. Graduates who felt emotionally supported by faculty and were encouraged to learn on a deep and experiential level by their professors found themselves far more engaged in their work years down the line than those who did not. The average college consumer's method of discerning how much of this highly important personal connection and intimate interaction takes place is to look at a school's student-faculty ratio. Yet, this figure can be highly misleading.

Harvard touts a remarkably low student-faculty ratio; some years, it is the very best in the nation. Unfortunately, their stated 7:1 ratio does not necessarily mean that classes are small and that classes are taught primarily by their eminent, full-time faculty. The average class size at Harvard is below forty and a handful of introductory classes are filled by hundreds of students.[8] According to the *New York Times*, many Harvard graduates lament making it through four years and not even getting to know a single professor well enough to ask for a letter of recommendation.[9] While this factoid is a bit anecdotal for our research-based tastes, a significant amount of hard data is suggestive of its veracity.

While there exists no shortage of Nobel Laureates, Pulitzer Prize winners, and leaders in government and business on the Harvard faculty, the undergraduate teaching duties for these individuals range from limited to nonexistent. With over 1,200 instructional graduate assistants at their disposal, a surprisingly large number of Harvard's undergraduate courses are taught by either graduate students or *undergraduate teaching fellows*. Yes, you heard it correctly—some courses at one of the world's most prestigious colleges are taught by fellow undergrads. In the fall of 2013, Harvard hired 32 graduate students and 32 undergraduates to help teach statistics courses. That same year, sections of a popular computer science course were led by 16 undergraduate teaching fellows overseen by one graduate assistant.[10]

A 2005 survey conducted across 31 elite campuses found Harvard undergrads ranking 27th in overall student satisfaction.[11] The main reasons given were the faculty's emphasis on research over teaching, lack of faculty availability, quality of instruction, quality of advising, and student life factors such as sense of community and social life on campus. While the school has since put together committees geared toward addressing these issues, student ratings of professor engagement and availability continue to lag well behind many other premier academic institutions.

Elite Schools with a Superior Commitment to Teaching

Swarthmore College in suburban Pennsylvania has a slightly higher student-faculty ratio than Harvard (8:1) but boasts an average class size of only 15 students and an average laboratory class of fewer than 10 students.[12] Take a moment to visualize the difference between sitting in a class of 40 and a class of 15. The educational implications are obvious: higher engagement, more discussion, more face time with your professors—heck, they might even take the time to learn your name.

Harvard and Swarthmore both have some of the toughest admissions standards in the country. The competition for a spot at either institution is a case of valedictorian-on-valedictorian crime, and perfect SATs are by no means a guarantor of acceptance. Clearly, if you are sitting in a classroom at either school you're surrounded by peers who are also incredibly bright and driven individuals, the intellectual 1%. The difference is that at Swarthmore, a liberal arts college without any graduate programs, the instructor in your class is guaranteed not to be a grad student and certainly won't be a fellow undergraduate. Further, Swarthmore students, as a whole, rate their faculty as being ultra-accessible.[13]

Over on the west coast, in Claremont, California, sits Pomona College, a school that is remarkably similar to Swarthmore in terms of student body size, class size, professor accessibility, and a generally happy and satisfied student body. Student accounts of their professors almost universally laud them as accessible, friendly, and caring. Only 15% of Pomona's professors are not full-time instructors, and there are no courses taught by graduate students.[14] Opportunities for undergraduate research abound through grants, research assistantships, and summer studies. Undergrads present with professors at conferences and even coauthor academic papers on a regular basis.

Perhaps the stark difference between the commitment to undergraduate teaching at Pomona and Harvard is best illustrated in the two schools' own words. In a recent job posting for an instructor in physics and astronomy, Pomona declared that "candidates must have a strong commitment to high-quality undergraduate teaching in a liberal arts environment, and those with significant teaching experience are especially encouraged to apply."[15] Compare this to a recent Harvard posting for an instructor in life sciences, which emphasized skills around "supervising and training a staff of approximately 30 teaching fellows, as well as a team of undergraduates who run weekly help sessions."[16]

Swarthmore and Pomona are hardly the only ultra-elite schools known for their commitment to the classroom experience of their undergraduate students. Located a mere 15-minute drive from Swarthmore, Haverford and Bryn Mawr both offer comparably wonderful educational experiences. These three schools also work on the same academic calendar and allow their students to take courses or even major on each other's campuses. Within a stone's throw of Pomona stand the other four members of the Claremont Consortium, and all have a similar arrangement. Scripps, Claremont McKenna, Harvey Mudd, and Pitzer are all prestigious schools with low student-teacher ratios and a high level of student engagement and personal connection with faculty.

Outside of these two geographic hotbeds of liberal arts glory, there are many schools fitting this profile right in Harvard's own region of New England. Amherst, Middlebury, Bates, Bowdoin, Williams, and Wesleyan all offer a chance for the best and brightest students to learn from faculty strongly invested in teaching and student success. Other phenomenal options are scattered between the coasts such as Carleton and Macalester in Minnesota, Oberlin in Ohio, and Grinnell in Iowa.

Pomona, Haverford, Macalester, and company may not inspire the same awe among the general public as an Ivy name. However, you can rest assured that the people who need to know—graduate schools and employers—are familiar with the quality and prestige of these institutions. In other words, these colleges still very much qualify as the type of *name* schools that many students crave.

Not All Ivies Are Created Equal

When seeking a school with a deep commitment to undergraduate instruction, you don't necessarily have to look beyond the Ivy League. Yale, Princeton, and Dartmouth, for example, have long been known for their balanced commitment to research and teaching.

Yale's storied residential college system is emblematic of the school's commitment to an intimate undergraduate experience. All Yalies are divided into one of twelve residential colleges prior to their freshman year and remain part of a cohort throughout their four years together. Each residential college is overseen by a dean and a master, distinguished faculty members who live on site and regularly eat meals with students, allowing these anointed shepherds to better advise and mentor members of their flock.

The senior thesis requirement at Princeton ensures that no student will ever exit the university without having had close contact with at least one faculty member. Working in a one-on-one capacity with a professor, students begin crafting an original piece of scholarship in their field during their junior year. Seniors typically take a reduced course load so they can focus on completing this culminating project, which usually hovers in the 80–100 page range.[17] Many alums say that the chance to generate a legitimate academic work was part of what made the Princeton experience so special, unless of course you speak with those who ended up running for high office or were nominated for the Supreme Court, in which case the words they penned at age 21 were dug out of the stacks, publicized, and scrutinized to the nth degree (see Michelle Obama, Elena Kagan, & others).

Dartmouth College prides itself on providing undergraduate students with structured research opportunities. Their First-Year Research in Engineering Program allows freshmen to work with research faculty up to 10 hours a week for an entire year. The Women in Science Project matches female students with researchers in fields where women are underrepresented, such as computer science, mathematics, and physics. These samples only scratch the surface of the abundance of opportunities at Dartmouth—in total, 600 undergrads participate in student-faculty research each year.[18]

Relax, Harvard Folks . . .

Harvard University was founded in 1636 and has a historical and deep-rooted place in American life. The pride of being accepted to and graduating from such an institution is understandable; it's one hell of an achievement. Obviously you will be surrounded by an unsurpassed (but not unparalleled) peer group as well.

If you are one of the 37,000 brilliant, talented, and hyper-motivated individuals who will be applying to Harvard next year, we want you to do so with your eyes fully open. Should you emerge as one of the 2,000 odds-defying souls who gain admission, do your homework to make sure that Harvard is truly the best fit for you. If you end up joining the 35,000 who ultimately get rejected, revel in the fact that you have now been granted a new beginning, released from the mesmeric allure of Harvard's iconic status. As T.S. Eliot once said, "What we call the beginning is often the end. And to make an end is to make a beginning. The end is where we start from."[19]

Of course that's easy for him to say—Eliot was a Harvard alumnus.

LOOK TO THE LIBERAL ARTS

It's not hard to see why Swarthmore, Pomona, and other schools of this ilk are desirable. Not only do they possess an impressive name but also, more importantly, set the standard for high-quality day-to-day education of undergraduate students. Of course not everyone enters the college selection process sitting in the catbird seat with near-perfect grades and SATs, getting to choose between an Ivy and a top-ranked liberal arts school. However, this doesn't mean that your only choices will be schools with a football stadium large enough to house the citizens of several countries combined (Ohio State's stadium could seat everyone from Liechtenstein, Monaco, and Vatican City with about 30,000 seats to spare).

There are many liberal arts colleges for less-than-perfect students that offer many of the same laudable qualities possessed by the aforementioned schools, including accessible faculty, small class sizes, and an emphasis on undergraduate (vs. graduate) education. In addition, and as hinted to previously, students at liberal arts colleges have access to certain extracurricular activities that would otherwise be unavailable to them at large universities, such as joining a varsity sport or assisting their favorite professor in a research project. At a liberal arts college, you do not have to compete with a PhD student or NFL prospect to represent your college and reap the personal and social benefits that come from deep involvement in an extracurricular activity.

So, yes, liberal arts colleges do offer a variety of benefits to students during their undergraduate years. But maybe you're not as concerned about what liberal arts schools do for students during college as you are with what these institutions do for students *after* they have graduated. What about job prospects and prospects for admission into graduate school? Well, the following are just a few facts confirming that liberal arts schools do indeed prepare their students for life after college: Liberal arts colleges constitute seven of the ten postsecondary institutions that graduate the highest percentage of eventual PhDs.[20] As of 2014, almost one-third of Fortune 1000 CEOs held liberal arts degrees.[21] By mid-career, liberal arts majors earn more, on average, than graduates of preprofessional programs.[22]

As evident from these findings, bigger isn't always better when it comes to choosing a college so, if your child is the kind of student who desires a close-knit, intimate learning environment and a chance to participate in all aspects of campus life, consider sacrificing the big name car window decal for the opportunity to enjoy a substantive and very meaningful four years.

Private Colleges Can Offer Great Deals

Many families on some kind of postsecondary budget assume they will not be able to afford this type of experience, and, admittedly, the list prices of these institutions are often high. This is where it pays to be a knowledgeable college consumer.

Many of the nation's top liberal arts schools are able to offer a world-class education at a cost well below the book-price tuition figure. In fact, students at premier schools such as Pomona and Haverford College typically pay between one-third and one-half of the stated price tag. The only problem is that these schools are among the most selective in the entire world, meaning that the vast majority of applicants are left out in the cold.

Fortunately, many other quality liberal arts schools also offer generous aid, a fact that strong but not quite elite applicants cannot afford to ignore. Here are a few examples:

Skidmore College

An excellent liberal arts school located in beautiful Saratoga Springs, New York, Skidmore has an intimidating annual cost of 45K, which might make middle-class families instantly rule it out as a possibility. Yet, if you dig deeper into their numbers, you'll find that the average net price actually paid by the 2,500 Thoroughbreds (their mascot) on campus comes in at just over $22,500.[23]

St. John's College

With campuses in Annapolis, Maryland, and Santa Fe, New Mexico, St. John's offers students an opportunity to participate in their Great Books curriculum in an unparalleled intimate environment of under 500 total students on either campus. You might expect such a uniquely small educational institution to collect every penny of stated $46,000 annual tuition, but that simply isn't the case. Students from middle-class families can study at either campus for somewhere in the neighborhood of 18–25K.

Hendrix College

Located about half an hour outside Little Rock, Arkansas, Hendrix is a small liberal arts school with an enrollment under 1,500 students. Hendrix is known for providing unique opportunities for hands-on learning, particularly through its nationally recognized study abroad and internship programs, offerings that sound expensive, and yet are enjoyed by the average student for $22,000 per year—$15,000 less than the official tuition cost.

FINDING VALUE: PUBLIC LIBERAL ARTS COLLEGES

We understand that even with the steep discounts at schools like Skidmore, St. John's, and Hendrix, attending a liberal arts college is still too expensive a proposition for some.

Fortunately, hidden gems can be found in the form of public liberal arts colleges. Outside the awareness of the average college consumer, 27 public liberal arts schools are spread across the United States, offering some of the best values in higher education. A quick profile of a few of these schools will give you a taste as to why.

Truman State

Located in Northern Missouri, Truman State is a selective institution (1205 mean SAT) offering a fantastic education for a bargain price. Truman students pay an average annual net tuition price of just $13,000. For residents of the *Show-Me State*, that cost drops to just over 7K, meaning that you can have a bachelor's degree from Truman State for the same price as a single semester at George Washington University or NYU. The average class size is 24 students, but some courses will be in the single digits, translating to an intimate educational experience.

New College of Florida

Formally a private institution, New College became part of Florida's public education system in 2001 and has since produced a disproportionately high number of Fullbright scholars and winners of other internationally recognized academic awards. Located right against scenic Sarasota Bay, New College educates a student body of just 800 and boasts a miniscule 10:1 student-to-faculty ratio. It is even more selective than Truman State, with the average admitted student sporting a 1270 SAT and a 4.0 GPA. With a list price of 27K but at a net price of just 12K, New College provides strong students a prestigious college education for a shockingly reasonable sum.

St. Mary's College of Maryland

A bit pricier at $14,800 in-state, St. Mary's still represents a relative bargain for the 1,800 students who grace its 361-acre campus. While it sounds like a religiously affiliated school, St. Mary's has surprisingly been a secular institution since its founding in 1840. Designated as a public honors college, St. Mary's has a 12:1 student-to-faculty ratio and boasts a 70% 4-year graduation rate. Like Truman State and New College, St. Mary's is selective but accessible to B students with solid SATs—their admit rate is 69%.

Other highly reputable (and often affordable) public liberal arts colleges include the following:

- College of Charleston
- Georgia College

- SUNY Geneseo
- The College of New Jersey
- The Evergreen State College
- University of Minnesota—Morris
- University of North Carolina at Asheville

Simply being aware of public liberal arts colleges makes you more knowledgeable than the average parent or prospective college student. Even though 23 states in the United States do not have a public liberal arts college, meaning that in-state tuition is off the table, many of these institutions offer such reasonable out-of-state tuition rates that they are still worth your careful consideration.

HONORS PROGRAMS

While there is much to love about liberal arts colleges, we also acknowledge that many students are understandably drawn to the bright lights of a large campus, the big-time sports, and the chance to be part of a large and passionate student community. For some, those qualities are simply synonymous with the quintessential *college experience*.

Not to sound like Ron Popeil on an infomercial hocking food dehydrators but—now it's finally possible to enjoy the best of both worlds—the honors college! While honors programs have existed in one form or another since the GI Bill first brought an influx of talented but cost-conscious students to public universities in the postwar era, the full-blown honors college is a more recent phenomenon. The majority of honors colleges were born in the 1990s, designed with the aim of drawing Ivy League caliber students to public institutions. Today, it is hard to find a large, public university that does not advertise some type of honors distinction. Yet, determining the quality and value among these ubiquitous honors programs can prove challenging. Below are some key considerations.

Class Size and Number of Honors Courses

Ideally, an honors college will offer a wide variety of honors-only courses with low class sizes, in the 15–20 range. In reality, these two factors vary widely across schools. The University of Mississippi, for example, boasts over 70 honors courses and class sizes of fewer than 15 students. Arizona

State, Indiana, Penn State, and the University of Georgia offer a similarly vast array of honors courses as well as class sizes under 20 students.

However, you need to be discerning when checking out average class sizes on university websites. Some programs may truly offer honors courses with 15–20 students, but provide so few specialized courses that honors students may often find themselves in 300-seat lecture halls, along with the rest of the general student population. As such, make sure to ask your prospective college for a complete list of honors courses.

Does the "Honors" Experience Extend Outside the Classroom?

Fairly serious students may benefit by being surrounded by other academic-minded students outside of the lecture hall. Find out if a prospective school offers special honors living arrangements. At the University of South Carolina and Boston University students are required to live in a designated honors dorm as a freshman. At Drexel University, all honors students live in a dorm that features special guest lecturers and faculty dinners on a regular basis. Other schools such as Michigan State leave it up to the student—they can elect to reside on specified floors of certain dorms if they so choose. Pitt also makes honors housing optional and, interestingly, also allows serious-minded but non-honors students to elect to live in the honors residence hall.

Cost Considerations

It's no secret that state schools (sans financial aid) have a significantly lower sticker price than most private colleges. However, given that many *honors* students also qualify for substantial merit aid from the larger university at which they enroll, honors programs can be an absolute bargain. For example, students admitted into Penn State's Schreyer Honors College automatically qualify for an Academic Excellence Scholarship valued at $4,500 per year, while students at Arizona State's Barrett Honors College have exclusive access to scholarships ranging from $1,000 to as much as $20,000 per year.

Ultimately, honors colleges can be a cost-effective and highly rewarding undergraduate experience for top-notch students. In the best-case scenario, students can enjoy all the benefits of a large university (research opportunities, athletics, and a diverse student body) while still profiting from an intimate, rigorous, and individualized experience usually reserved for elite liberal arts colleges.

In compiling this list, we looked to several indicators of program quality, including honors graduation requirements, honors class size, the range and type of honors course offerings, access to honors housing, and the high school credentials of admitted honors students.

Arizona State University (Barrett)

Indiana University (Hutton)

Michigan State University

Penn State University (Schreyer)

University of Georgia

University of Kansas

University of Maryland

University of Michigan (LSA)

University of Minnesota

University of Mississippi (Sally McDonnell Barksdale)

University of North Carolina at Chapel Hill

University of Oregon (Clark)

University of Pittsburgh

University of South Carolina

University of Texas at Austin

University of Virginia (Echols)

University of Washington

Figure 2.1   Top Honors Colleges

THREE IMPORTANT FACTORS MOST PEOPLE
OVERLOOK WHEN CHOOSING A SCHOOL

Whether a student is seeking a liberal arts school or a large university experience, there are three key qualities to look for in any institution, which often fly under the radar: the presence of a strong alumni network than can help to land a job down the line, the importance of a college's location when trying to enter certain fields or score a position with a specific company, and the strength of a college's career services office that can help students take full advantage of the previous two factors. A prestigious name can have value, but as we'll see momentarily, if a teen wants to work for Microsoft, they may end up being better served by Washington State University than an elite college on the East Coast.

#1) Alumni Networks

For many freshly minted college graduates, the satisfaction of completing an undergraduate degree morphs into job search-related anxiety before the Gothic font on their diploma even has a chance to dry. Many proceed to blindly send out an entire Redwood's worth of resumes, obsessively update their LinkedIn profile, and in true moments of desperation, actually start considering whether those craigslist *opportunities* to make $5,000 a week working from home are legit.

Landing a dream job or even just *a* job is often determined, in part, by the old cliché of *who you know*. Outside of those lucky enough to have helpful family connections, most unemployed 22-year-olds only know other unemployed 22-year-olds, which makes networking within their current social circle a rather incestuous and futile exercise. This leaves students with two choices: hope that their American Girl doll collection will fetch enough on eBay to pay the rent or begin tapping into their college's alumni network.

How Alumni Networks Can (and Cannot) Help

Rid yourself of any *Skull and Bones* fantasies—the notion that attending a certain college will automatically open doors to a life of luxury and privilege is not realistic. While sharing an alma mater with a potential employer or networking contact can be helpful in the job search/career development process, simply showing up to an interview with a fellow Michigan alumnus, sporting a Wolverine lapel pin is not going to cause the boss to say, "A fellow Wolverine!!?? Scrap this interview. Here's a cigar. Let me show you to your corner office." Similarly, a desperate cold call to a random member of a student's school's alumni database is not likely to land them a job (or even a polite reply).

To effectively take advantage of alumni networks, students should work on cultivating meaningful relationships with alumni in their potential field throughout their college experience. Your teen should attend alumni events and call or email alums in their field, and ask if they could speak with them about their career path. Most people will be happy to speak with them and offer advice. The Bureau of Labor Statistics estimates that 70% of jobs are found through some form of networking.[24]

While there are no statistics revealing the exact percentage of college grads who find employment specifically through alumni connections, it is safe to assume that the number is sizable. It is also a logical bet that schools with stronger alumni organizations will offer better networking opportunities than schools with less-established and less-enthusiastic alumni communities.

Identifying a "Strong" Alumni Network

Two primary indicators of institutions with strong alumni networks are sheer size and alumni generosity. Penn State has the largest dues-paying alumni network in the country with 177,000 members.[25] Other large universities such as the University of Illinois, Indiana, University of Michigan, Ohio State, and UCLA also boast an insane number of graduates, but judging how connected they are to their alma maters (and therefore to you, a potential networker) requires additional data.

Identifying institutions with impressive percentages of alumni choosing to donate to their school is one way to gauge a sense of connectedness and *strength* of a network. In this arena, smaller liberal arts schools such as Bowdoin, Williams, Middlebury, and Carleton lead the way. This can be a more helpful metric than the overall endowment an institution boasts. For example, University of Hawaii alumnus Jay Shidler, a real estate mogul, has donated over 100 million dollars to his alma mater.[26] While this undoubtedly has a positive impact on the school's endowment, it is not necessarily indicative of a strong alumni network (good luck getting Hawaii's wealthiest resident on the phone to dispense career advice).

It can also be helpful to explore a prospective college's career services webpage for how they assist current students in connecting with alumni. You should see evidence of upcoming events such career and internship fairs, alumni panels, and employer information sessions.

Another question worth asking is whether a given institution's network has regional, national, or international reach? If a student has a goal to work in a particular field or even for a specific company within that field, such considerations can be of critical importance.

#2) The Importance of Location

It would be correct to assume that the colleges at which premier tech companies most heavily recruit include your usual suspects: Stanford, MIT, Berkley, etc. Yet, what many don't know is that Redmond, Washington-based Microsoft plucks an even greater number of employees from nearby institutions such as the University of Washington, Washington State, and Western Washington University. Apple, located in the heart of Silicon Valley, draws a large portion of its workforce from nearby San Jose State and Cal Poly.[27]

The world of Wall Street finance is similarly surprising. Rutgers University and Baruch College rank right up there with the Ivies and a host of more-selective liberal arts schools in terms of career outcomes in the finance industry.[28] With a large alumni base and close proximity to New York City, aspiring financial workers may be better served at these schools than at a more prestigious school in a different region of the country.

In the last decade, more and more large companies have begun forming partnerships with colleges and universities right in their own neighborhoods.[29] This leads to a steady flow of interns from the school to the company and allows businesses the chance to scout top talent firsthand. It also saves them a bundle on both the cost of corporate recruiting and the cash doled out to new hires for relocation expenses. Access to eager interns 365 days a year is a huge advantage for companies and a wonderful opportunity for talented students to audition for a job after graduation. These partnerships are truly a win-win, and it's important to find out which schools have them and with whom.

Understandably, many companies like to partner with larger institutions that have a large and academically well-rounded student body—the larger the talent pool to pluck from, the better. The University of Michigan's massive and extremely bright student body have enticed a gaggle of US and even foreign companies to migrate into their backyard. Google even set up a sales and operations office in Ann Arbor just to tap into this never-ending stream of collegiate talent.

#3) Career Services

Ideally, career centers provide information that enables students to find good-fit jobs and make the most of their undergraduate years. In truth, however, too many colleges possess career centers that are understaffed and underutilized, and which do little to help students' professional prospects. At these institutions, students may earn an excellent education yet graduate without the knowledge and networks to capitalize upon their accomplishments. Given this reality, we encourage students to investigate career service offerings *before* applying. They should reach out to the career centers at each of their prospective schools to inquire about employment rates, graduate school placement, and salary statistics. Although career services staff may not be solely or primarily responsible for collecting postgraduate data, they should be able to tell students where and how to access such information.

Moreover, while outcomes data can prove extremely useful, general statistics may not be sufficient to address questions and/or concerns that are particular to every student. Perhaps one wishes to enroll in an under-subscribed major, work in a specific part of the country/world, or pursue employment in a highly specialized field. In these cases, these students need to dig deeper and ask questions that yield information more relevant to their unique objectives, such as these: Which employers recruit on campus? Which jobs (in their area of interest) have been posted on the college's site? Where have students from their desired major(s) attended graduate school? Does the college partner with other institutions to offer job fairs or networking opportunities that provide students with access to professionals in their desired field?

Finally, your child should inquire about how career center staff prepare them for the world of work. How and when do staff engage students? Do staff provide services related to career assessment, resume development, and/or interview prep? What internship and co-op opportunities are available? What percentage of students utilize career services?

As students begin to develop their list of prospective schools, it's important to remember that college should offer them more than a degree. It should provide skills and experiences that contribute to their professional development—long after anyone remembers or cares to ask about the school name on their diploma. With this in mind, look beyond admission statistics and evaluate those who are responsible for connecting students to the opportunities that college is supposed to—but is not guaranteed to—provide.

We've spent the bulk of this chapter laying out what a college should offer: accessible professors, a focus on undergraduate teaching, a strong alumni network, ability to connect students directly with employers, and a school with a solid (but not necessarily spectacular) reputation for the purpose of keeping open all future graduate school and career-related opportunities. Now it's time to cover the other end of the spectrum—the schools that you should avoid like a rabid raccoon.

COLLEGES TO AVOID

A quick glance at the *around-the-web* links housed underneath legitimate news articles on an unfortunate number of sites tells us two things: (1) people like lists and (2) people like lists slamming someone or something—20 Celebrities Who Got Fat, 15 Grossest Cruciferous Vegetables, 17 Child Actors Busted for DUIs. Whether it's morbid curiosity or pure schadenfreude, human nature seems to draw us to such lists.

While a like-minded bash list of Colleges to Avoid would titillate, it would also be disingenuous and ultimately unhelpful to prospective college students. This is due to the fact that the colleges that should be avoided are context-dependent and will vary by individual circumstance. Components such as geographic location, the strength of the applicant, and family income level are all determining factors. If you're on any kind of postsecondary budget, there are a litany of schools that should be avoided; in fact, there may be hundreds or even in excess of 1,000 schools that should be avoided.

What Type of College Should I Avoid?

For any money-conscious college student, paying exorbitant tuition amounts and taking on large quantities of debt for the sake of attending a low-to-moderately prestigious school can be a monumental mistake. Unless they are dropping in excess of 40K on a school that can provide them with a high return on their investment—a proposition that may be more dependent on their desired field than the name brand of the university—it is worth pursuing better values in the higher education marketplace.

As you will see, many of the schools that students should avoid are not *bad* schools by any means. In fact, quite often they are excellent institutions, but not at all worth the sticker price when weighed against other choices that educational consumers, stunningly, rarely even pause to consider.

Net Price by Income

Highly prestigious schools typically have eye-popping list prices but, thanks to endowments that resemble Scrooge McDuck's vault, those with any degree of financial need often receive a steep discount.

Duke University, for example, has an intimidating price tag of $67,000, yet the average price actually paid by attendees is $19,000 per year. Families making a net income under $75,000 per year pay an average of just over 14K per year, a 79% savings. The average student debt incurred during undergraduate study at Duke is $20,000, across all income levels. On top of the reasonable price of attendance, a degree from Duke, thanks to its reputation and powerful alumni network, can lead to a high return on investment.

Compare these numbers to a school like Baylor University in Texas, a school with a solid reputation, but one that wouldn't be categorized as elite. Baylor's official price tag is $59,000, which is less than Duke's; yet, unlike, Duke, most students, even those coming from families making under $75,000 per year, pay the majority of the sticker price. Those from lower-income brackets still pay nearly 27K while the average student qualifying for need-based aid still forks over close to 30K per year. As a result, the average Baylor freshman student (with financial need) can expect to take on nearly $12,000 worth of debt during the first year, which spread out over the next four years, is over $28,000 more, on average, than your standard Duke grad.

No one would put Baylor on a generic list of *schools to avoid*. It's a reputable school that easily cracks many *top-college* guidebooks. However, for students lacking unlimited education funds, crossing Baylor off of their list may be an extremely wise decision.

Low Prestige + High Debt = Avoid

While our previous example pits a topflight school against a lesser, but still very competitive school, there are countless examples of schools that charge high tuition, offer minimal aid, and do not provide students with promising job prospects needed to pay down the debt they accrue.

Take, for instance, the University of Tampa, a private school costing a little over 40 grand. The net price, what students actually end up paying, is roughly 27K and family income plays a minimal role in the distribution of aid, meaning that those in the lowest bracket pay the still pay close to 25K per year. As a result, the mean debt load a student graduates with is around $45,000, a number which easily eclipses the average salary a University of Tampa grad will find early in their career. Therefore, a cost-conscious teen should avoid the University of Tampa.

We're not picking on the University of Tampa. There are countless other schools with similarly disheartening numbers. Other universities where the average student is saddled with a five-figure debt total every year include Drexel, Quinnipiac, and most likely, a handful of moderate-to-less-selective private institutions not far from your home.

In the absence of a comprehensive list, how will you be able to spot a school along these lines? Simple. Look for colleges with high acceptance rates, high net price tuition (remember, not sticker price), and excessive graduate loan debt (as a barometer, the national average for four years is $30,000) and avoid, avoid, avoid.

Out-of-State Publics

Another category of school that wise consumers will do well to steer clear of are out-of-state public schools. Flagship universities such as Penn State, UCLA, Michigan, the University of Wisconsin–Madison, UVA, and UNC are all, understandably, a big draw to students from all over the country. They are premier research institutions with a smorgasbord of areas of study, a wealth of resources, big-time sports programs, top-caliber professors, and attractive campuses brimming with student amenities. So why would such fine institutions be on anyone's list of colleges to avoid? It's all about the Clevelands ($1,000 bill) or even Salmon P. Chases ($10,000 bill).

Flagship universities rarely offer significant packages to out-of-staters leaving families stuck with the nonresident sticker price. Annual, out-of-state costs at the University of Michigan run nearly 60 grand, more than double what Michigan residents pay. UCLA charges nearly $25,000 more to those who hail from outside the Golden State. The University of Connecticut, a bargain for Connecticut residents at 30K per year (including room, board, and other expenses), climbs to 52K for outsiders, and after accounting for need-based and merit-based financial aid, proves more expensive than Wesleyan, Connecticut College, or Trinity—three elite colleges in the same state. Amazingly, thanks to the generosity of those three schools, each carries an average net price of 20K per year or less for students demonstrating financial need.

If you do your homework, the colleges and universities that grace your personal *avoid* list may surprise you and, on the contrary, schools that you may never have considered as being financially within reach may end up as viable options. If this piece left you craving actual lists—please Google *32 Unforgettable Justin Bieber Mishaps* or *21 Diva Diet Secrets* and brace your-self for a time-killing trip down the Internet rabbit hole.

FINAL THOUGHTS

We hope that we have succeeded in reframing your understanding of what matters when selecting a college. In citing many examples of excellent schools, we've given you a taste of the outstanding institutions at which students can enjoy a high-caliber educational experience for a price that won't limit their opportunities later in life. To view a comprehensive menu of schools that may be an ideal destination point, refer to our "So You Want to Be a . . ." reference guide in chapter 7, where we'll give you a list of recommended schools for students with various career-related interests and goals.

Of course, no matter where a young person decides to apply, they're still going to be worried about step 1—getting in! The following three chapters cover everything you could possibly want to know about college admissions, straight from the mouths of two experienced private college admissions coun-selors who have helped students gain acceptance at institutions throughout the United States, from Swarthmore to Stanford and nearly every selective institution in between. We will begin by dispelling the most common myths we hear perpetuated among students and families and then dish the insider's scoop on how to approach standardized tests, essays, extracurriculars, Advanced Placement classes, early admission, and other subjects that we are most routinely asked about by our clients.

NOTES

1. *U.S. News & World Report*, "Harvard University," accessed December 6, 2015, http://colleges.usnews.rankingsandreviews.com/best-colleges/harvard-university-2155.

2. *U.S. News & World Report*, "Northern Arizona University," accessed December 6, 2015, http://colleges.usnews.rankingsandreviews.com/best-colleges/northern-arizona-university-1082.

3. Dominic J. Brewer, Eric R. Eide, and Ronald G. Ehrenberg, "Does It Pay to Attend an Elite Private College? Cross Cohort Evidence on the Effects of College Type on Earnings," *Journal of Human Resources* 34, no. 1 (Winter 1999): 104–23.

4. Mark Long, "College Quality and Early Adult Outcomes," *Economics of Education Review* 27, no. 5 (2008): 588–602, doi:10.1016/j.econedurev.2007.04.004.

5. Mark Hoekstra, "The Effect of Attending the Flagship State University on Earnings: A Discontinuity-Based Approach," *The Review of Economics and Statistics* 91, no. 4 (2009): 717–24, doi:10.1162/rest.91.4.717.

6. Stacy Dale and Alan Krueger, "Estimating the Return to College Selectivity over the Career Using Administrative Earnings Data" (NBER Working Paper 17159, June 2011).

7. Julie Ray and Stephanie Kafka, "Life in College Matters for Life after College," Gallup, May 6, 2014, accessed December 6, 2015, http://www.gallup.com/poll/168848/life-college-matters-life-college.aspx.

8. Harvard University, "Harvard at a Glance: About the Faculty," accessed July 8, 2015, http://www.harvard.edu/about-harvard/harvard-glance/about-faculty.

9. Sara Rimer, "Harvard Task Force Calls for New Focus on Teaching and Not Just Research," *New York Times*, May 10, 2007, accessed December 6, 2015, http://www.nytimes.com/2007/05/10/education/10harvard.html?pagewanted=1&sq=harvard%20task%20force%20calls%20for%20new%20focus%20on%20teaching%20and%20not%20just%20research&st=nyt&scp=1.

10. Brian C. Zhang, "CS Leads Concentration Growth in SEAS," *The Harvard Crimson*, February 13, 2013, accessed December 6, 2015, http://www.thecrimson.com/article/2013/2/13/cs-seas-more-concentrators.

11. Margaret W. Ho and Joshua P. Rogers, "Harvard Students Less Satisfied Than Peers with Undergraduate Experience, Survey Finds," *The Harvard Crimson*, March 31, 2005, accessed December 6, 2015, http://www.thecrimson.com/article/2005/3/31/harvard-students-less-satisfied-than-peers/.

12. Swarthmore College, "Swarthmore College Class Size Summary," accessed December 6, 2015, http://www.swarthmore.edu/Documents/administration/ir/ClassSize.pdf.

13. Lynn O'Shaughnessy, "12 Colleges with Great Professors," CBS MoneyWatch, November 19, 2013, accessed December 26, 2015, http://www.cbsnews.com/news/12-colleges-with-great-college-professors/.

14. Robert Franek and Princeton Review (Firm), *The Best 376 Colleges* (New York: Random House, 2011).

15. PER Jobs, "VAP at Pomona College (CA)," February 22, 2012, accessed December 6, 2015, http://perjobs.blogspot.com/2012_02_01_archive.html.

16. UniJobs, "Preceptor in the Life Sciences," accessed December 6, 2015, http://www.unijobs.us/harvard-university-jobs/G2PF/preceptor-in-the-life-sciences.

17. Princeton University Department of Politics, "Senior Thesis," last modified July 27, 2015, accessed December 6, 2015, https://www.princeton.edu/politics/undergraduate/independent-work/senior-thesis/.

18. Michael Qian, "College Aims to Focus Undergraduate Research," *The Dartmouth*, October 19, 2014, accessed December 6, 2015, http://thedartmouth.com/2014/10/19/college-aims-to-focus-undergraduate-research/.

19. T. S. Eliot et al., *Little Gidding* (London: Faber and Faber, 1942).

20. Lynn O'Shaughnessy, "The Colleges Where PhD's Get Their Start," The College Solution, January 26, 2012, accessed December 6, 2015, http://www.thecollegesolution.com/the-colleges-where-phds-get-their-start/.

21. Kenneth C. Tsang, "From College Graduate to Chief Executive: A Closer Look at Education and the Fortune 1000 CEOs," *NACE Journal* 75, no. 1 (September 2014): 12–18.

22. Debra Humphreys and Patrick Kelly, "How Liberal Arts and Sciences Majors Fare in Employment: A Report on Earnings and Long-Term Career Paths," Washington, DC: Association of American Colleges and Universities, 2014.

23. U.S. Department of Education, Institute of Education Sciences, National Center for Education Statistics.

24. Glassdoor, "How to Stay Positive with Your Job Search," July 15, 2014, accessed December 6, 2015, http://www.foxbusiness.com/personal-finance/2014/07/15/how-to-stay-positive-with-your-job-search/.

25. Penn State Alumni Association, "Alumni Association Overview," accessed December 6, 2015, http://alumni.psu.edu/about_us/overview.

26. University of Hawaii at Manoa Shidler College of Business, "$100 Million: A Visionary Gift," accessed December 6, 2015, http://shidler.hawaii.edu/visionary/gift.

27. Will Oremus, "Where Do Googlers Go to College? A Look at Tech Companies' Top Feeder Schools," *Slate,* May 23, 2014, accessed December 6, 2015, http://www.slate.com/blogs/future_tense/2014/05/23/tech_company_feeder_schools_stanford_to_google_washington_to_microsoft_sjsu.html.

28. Data collected from LinkedIn University Finder https://www.linkedin.com/edu/university-finder?trk=edu-rankings-to-uf, accessed February 1, 2016

29. Teri Evans, "Penn State Tops Recruiter Rankings," *The Wall Street Journal,* September 13, 2010, accessed December 6, 2015, http://www.wsj.com/articles/SB10001424052748704358904575477643369663352.

Chapter 3

Getting In

Admission Mythbusters

Books and articles that profess to offer *the secrets* to the college admissions process are not at all difficult to find. We hate to be the bearers of bad news, but these tips are worth about as much as your creepy neighbor's prized VHS movie library—that is to say, very, very . . . one more . . . *very* little. Like other promises of *secret* and *easy* ways to lose weight or become a millionaire, shortcuts and gimmicks related to college admissions are not based in reality. Just as you are unlikely to actually lose weight by strapping on a vibrating ab belt while inhaling two quarts of mint chocolate chip ice cream, it is equally improbable that you will earn admission through implementation of a top-secret admissions strategy while sporting a GPA and standardized test score that is less than adequate.

Although there may not be secrets to winning admission, there are best-practice strategies that, when implemented together, can significantly improve an applicant's chances of earning acceptance. In order to ensure that this book isn't *just another admissions guide*, we devote the next three chapters almost exclusively to topics that cannot be researched through a quick Google search or found in your average nuts-and-bolts admissions book. We will uncover several strategies students can employ to strengthen their academic and extracurricular profile (see chapter 4) and prepare impressive applications (see chapter 5). We begin, however, by debunking several admission-related myths that are most commonly echoed by the students and parents with whom we meet.

MYTH #1: AN APPLICANT SHOULD TRY TO PRESENT AS "WELL ROUNDED" TO PLEASE ADMISSIONS COMMITTEES

This myth remains pervasive among nervous applicants and their families. Sadly, this misconception usually ends with many applicants entering their admissions interviews dressed in a safari outfit while simultaneously riding a unicycle, playing a didgeridoo, and explaining their design plans for a squirt gun that combats diabetes. Okay, maybe a slight exaggeration, but the bottom line is that well roundedness is a gravely misunderstood concept.

It is true that college admissions committees seek to have well-rounded classes comprised of individuals who have a serious passion for something—but this can be and usually is just *one* thing. As we'll discuss later, delving deeply into two or three related pursuits is always better than superficial participation in a laundry list of things. Plus, playing an oversized Australian wind instrument without proper footing is a major safety hazard.

MYTH #2: RECOMMENDATION LETTERS FROM INFLUENTIAL FIGURES WILL HELP MY ADMISSIONS CHANCES

Local members of congress must employ a secretary whose sole job responsibility is the mass production of generic college letters of recommendation for the children of their influential constituents. Parents with connections often think that such letters from government officials, celebrities, or other notable public figures will give their kids a big edge in the high-stakes battle for admissions at prestigious schools. In a majority of cases, this simply isn't true and the insight added by these recommendations is rarely anything other than superficial.

Think about it. Let's say that a given congresswoman actually met your child once or twice at a fundraiser. What insight could they possibly provide that would not be otherwise evident in an application? "So and so is committed to community service." Great, an admissions officer could glean that same information in a more genuine, thorough way from a teacher or school guidance counselor who watched your child's commitment to service grow over a period of years.

Same goes for letters from other influential folks parents might happen to know. Which is more likely to persuade a committee to accept an applicant interested in a history major: An enthusiastic letter from Doris Kearns

Goodwin saying that your child has great potential as a historian or a letter from the student's Advanced Placement history teacher who has taught them nearly every day for the past year and who can attest to their abilities and work ethic inside the classroom? Common sense tells you the answer.

MYTH #3: I GOT A LETTER FROM THE DEAN! I'M IN!

For a high school student, there is something undeniably exciting about being the recipient of an unsolicited brochure from a prestigious university, or even better, a personalized letter from the dean of admissions practically begging them to apply. Unfortunately, this material usually has about as much value as the L.L. Bean catalog that arrived in the same stack of mail.

It's no great secret that in the age of *U.S. News* rankings, colleges are engaged in a never-ending battle to reject more applicants, thereby improving their (perceived) selectivity. The truth about these mass mailings is that their sole purpose is to drum up additional applicants. If you took the PSAT, chances are you'll be inundated with *junk* mail from various colleges, regardless of your score; so, students should do themselves a favor: view all recruitment efforts through a skeptic's lens and rely on one's own research to develop a list of prospective schools. You'll know that a college truly wants a student when they receive a letter of admission, and even more so, a substantial merit aid award.

MYTH #4: GETTING INTO A GOOD COLLEGE IS HARDER THAN EVER

Parents, educators, and even a few of our fellow admissions consultants are often guilty of spreading this one. They cite dropping admission rates at Harvard, for example, to claim that earning admission into selective institutions of higher education has become practically impossible; however, they fail to account for the bigger picture. The truth is that many colleges have experienced slight declines in the number of applications they have received—a trend that may be attributed to a potential shortage of college-qualified high school graduates.[1]

Moreover, increasing application numbers at other selective institutions do not necessarily indicate that earning admission has actually become harder. As the Common Application continues to proliferate, and as savvy college-recruiting strategies become more commonplace, selective institutions are receiving more applications from unqualified students who have little chance of being accepted and who ultimately do not impact a particular college's incoming student profile. In other words, the same types of students admitted several years ago are likely the same types of students being admitted today.

MYTH #5: THE MORE I SUBMIT, THE BETTER

Applicants often feel that more is inherently better when it comes to their application file and proceed to send along everything from editorials penned for the school newspaper to 5th-grade book reports plastered in gold stars and *seals of approval* (featuring an actual seal. Get it?). Such offerings are highly unlikely to sway the admissions gods.

If a student decides to include ancillary materials, they should do so judiciously. First ask, "Will this item tell the admissions committee something important about me that they will not be able to extract from the rest of my application?" If so, send along an addendum or two. Admissions officers are busy, and if they want a copy of the play a student wrote at summer camp when they were 12 years old about Gandhi coming back to life as a hip-hop artist, they'll ask for it (but really, they won't).

MYTH # 6: COMMUNITY SERVICE AND VOLUNTEERING WILL HELP MY COLLEGE APPLICATION

Many families still believe that evidence of scattered, unfocused altruism is a prerequisite for admission at highly selective universities. It is not. Volunteering is a wonderful thing to do in life, but spending a couple hours at a community hospital or a few days at the local soup kitchen will have little, if any, impact on your admissions prospects.

Instead of worrying about the number of service hours, students should focus on the activities about which they are truly passionate and that will offer evidence of their unique talents, leadership potential, and/or long-term dedication. Students are best served by engaging in extracurriculars because they are part of what makes them *who they are*. Doing so will enable them to present as a more authentic and attractive applicant.

MYTH #7: MY SOCIAL MEDIA POSTS WON'T AFFECT MY COLLEGE APPLICATION

The majority of college admissions officers rarely, if ever, Google applicants' names, rifle through their Facebook accounts, carefully pore over their archived tweets, or analyze their *selfies* on Instagram. For some officers, this is a moral issue; your social media should be your private space. For others, such as those at universities receiving 80,000 plus applicants, stalking long-abandoned Myspace pages for evidence of middle school misdeeds would be a terribly wasteful use of precious time.

While most admissions officers steer clear of online snooping, the practice has trended upward over the last several years. In 2008, Kaplan reported that only 10% of officers bothered looking at applicants' social media pages.[2] Today, that number has increased to 40%, and a similar number of officers report at least googling an applicant simply to see if any relevant information, positive or negative, can be gleaned.[3] Almost one-third of those surveyed reported ultimately finding something that negatively impacted their view of an applicant.

Students should not post anything online (or keep anything active online during the admissions process) that they do not feel represents their best selves. There is nothing wrong with having a Facebook page, but be cognizant of the fact that many admissions officers may frown upon the contents of a student's Spring Break 2015 Facebook album, unless, of course, he spent that time at a robotics competition in Dayton, Ohio, rather than guzzling Keystone Lights with his bros at Daytona Beach. Even if the majority of schools never peer into a student's online life, there is simply no good reason to risk jeopardizing their chances of admission for the sake of maintaining a risqué Instagram account.

MYTH #8: COLLEGE RANKINGS SHOULD GUIDE MY COLLEGE SELECTION

Like most people, we love ratings systems and refer to them when purchasing a variety of things, like computers or household appliances. But let's face it, paying for a higher education is not the equivalent of buying a toaster—the best college for me isn't necessarily the best college for you. Yet, *U.S. News* and other publications unabashedly assign a rank number to hundreds of colleges, whose missions, attributes, and learning environments are as varied as the millions of students who apply to college each year.

College ranking systems appear to suggest that an ordering of institutions was devised through definitive and rigorous means, and that there is a significant reason as to why Princeton is ranked 6 spots higher than MIT or why Amherst is rated 10 spots higher than Vassar. But there is no reason, really — formulas for college ranking systems are largely subjective and consist of measures that the magazine chooses, not what the research community deems as indicative of institutional quality.

For example, *U.S. News* employs a measure indicating undergraduate academic reputation, which currently comprises 22.5% of the magazine's ranking formula and is determined primarily by college presidents and deans of admission, many of whom are too engrossed in the business affairs of their own institutions to possess sufficient knowledge of other colleges. *Forbes* makes a more genuine effort to incorporate objective measures into its ranking system, but the data it collects on retention, graduation rates, and the number of Rhodes Scholars, for example, still says more about incoming students than the quality of an institution.

It's also important to understand that college rankings can be manipulated. There are numerous, well-documented examples of colleges soliciting applications from unqualified applicants (to *improve* selectivity); requesting nominal donations from alumni (to *improve* giving rates); and bumping students from certain classes (to *improve* class size) — all done for the sole purpose of advancing one's ranking.

Other colleges simply cheat, and report false numbers, causing students and families to make college-related choices that are based on inaccurate and misleading information. Some reputable institutions that have been caught lying to *U.S. News* in the past several years include Tulane University, Claremont McKenna College, Bucknell University, Emory University, and George Washington University.[4]

MYTH #9: STANDARDIZED TEST SCORES DON'T MATTER AS MUCH AS THEY USED TO

In the last decade, the idea that colleges no longer care that much about standardized test scores has become prevalent in the admissions discourse. Many schools themselves like to brag about how they view test scores as just one of a multitude of factors in the admissions process. Yet like a 7th-grade boy who spends two hours in front of the mirror every morning trying to perfect his Justin Bieber bangs while simultaneously proclaiming that he "doesn't care what anyone thinks," the facts about test scores quite simply belie the claim.

Despite media talk and institutional reports of the SAT and ACTs diminishing role, the data suggests that standardized test scores have actually become more important in recent years. Rankings are still driven by test scores. The admissions process is still beholden to and driven by the almighty rankings. In fact, *U.S. News* recently upped the importance placed on test scores in their methodology. Not surprisingly, the *top* schools remain the ones whose freshman classes have the highest SAT scores. Today, 56% of colleges state that test scores are of *considerable importance* in their admissions decisions, placing them third behind grades and a rigorous curriculum. Twenty years ago only 43% of schools said the same.

As a general rule, larger schools rely more on test scores than do smaller liberal arts colleges merely as a tool to pare down a massive applicant pool. In a pragmatic sense, it would be difficult for admissions officers at a school like UCLA to wade through 60,000+ applications, sans SAT/ACT data, without feeling like a harried cashier in a Weimer Republic farmer's market ("I'll get you your cabbage as soon as I finish counting your 200,000,000,000 marks!").

Yet, the last decade has indeed seen a rise in *test-optional* schools. Wake Forest, George Mason, Ursinus, American, Bates, Bowdoin, Franklin & Marshall, Union, and Connecticut College are just a sampling of the highly selective schools that have adopted a *test-optional* policy. While this choice may open doors for the test averse, don't mistake the intent of the policy as wholeheartedly charitable or representative of a sweeping philosophical shift. Test-optional schools generally only receive scores from applicants who excelled on the test, which ends up raising the average scores they can report to *U.S. News*. Thus these institutions can accept lower-performing applicants with full impunity.

Ultimately, excellent test scores are still necessary for admission at the vast majority of highly selective schools. At smaller institutions, a student with an excellent overall profile but weaker test scores may receive a closer look, but unless that school is test optional or that applicant can throw a 60-yard tight spiral, the scores still stir the drink.

MYTH #10: EXCELLENT GRADES AND TEST SCORES WILL GUARANTEE MY ADMISSION INTO AN ELITE COLLEGE

Every year, we encounter students who feel their academic accomplishments entitle them to entry at an Ivy League school and that the word *safety* simply does not apply to them. With such students in mind, we launch into our story about Mark, a student whose family came to us in May of his senior year.

Mark was a highly accomplished student with excellent grades and stratospheric test scores. He talked often about his friend, Jim, who possessed a similar class rank and who was admitted into Princeton the previous year. As a result, Mark believed that admission into an Ivy League school was a virtual lock. He decided to apply to all eight Ivy League institutions, and at the suggestion of a family friend, also submitted applications to three prestigious, out-of-state institutions, including the University of North Carolina, the University of Virginia, and the UC Berkeley—Mark considered these three colleges to be his *safety* schools, despite their excellent reputation and competitive admissions process, especially for out-of-state students.

April arrived and Mark was dismayed to learn that he was denied admission at each Ivy League school, and was also waitlisted at UNC, a university with an average SAT score well below his. Although Mark was admitted into UVA and UC Berkeley, he soon discovered that out-of-state rates at both schools were prohibitively expensive. As high school graduation neared, Mark was scrambling to find a list of colleges still accepting applications, and dreamed of donning Carolina blue—a color that didn't seem all that attractive only a few months ago.

There are several important takeaways from Mark's story. First, no matter your background or credentials, never assume admission into an Ivy League institution. These schools receive applications from many more top-notch students than they are able to admit, so unless you're an Olympic athlete with flawless academic credentials or the child of a US president, there are no guarantees. Always expand your list of prospective schools to include colleges outside of the Ivy League.

Second, earning entrance into out-of-state public colleges and universities can be more difficult than you think. Several reputable institutions have admissions policies that overwhelmingly favor in-state residents, and as a result, reject a high number of elite, out-of-state residents every year. It is not uncommon for students to earn admission into colleges like Penn, Cornell, or Washington University, while being denied admission at universities like UVA, UNC, or UC Berkeley, in large part, because of their out-of-state status. Therefore, prior to finalizing an applicant's college list and regardless of their academic background, check to see if the public schools on their *safety* list give admission preference to in-state students.

Third, every college list should include at least two to three *safety* schools, where a student is very likely to be admitted *and which they can afford*. Remember, *safety* schools are not safe if there exist factors that may ultimately prevent a student from enrollment, whether personal, financial, or admissions related.

NOTES

1. Paul Fain, "Nearing the Bottom," *Inside Higher Ed,* May 15, 2014, accessed December 26, 2015, https://www.insidehighered.com/news/2014/05/15/new-data-show-slowing-national-enrollment-decline.

2. Kaplan Test Prep, "Kaplan Test Prep Survey: More College Admissions Officers Checking Applicants' Digital Trails, but Most Students Unconcerned," October 31, 2013, accessed December 26, 2015, http://press.kaptest.com/press-releases/kaplan-test-prep-survey-more-college-admissions-officers-checking-applicants-digital-trails-but-most-students-unconcerned.

3. Kaitlin Mulhere, "Lots More College Admissions Officers Are Checking Your Instagram and Facebook," *Money,* November 9, 2013, accessed January 31, 2016, http://time.com/money/4179392/college-applications-social-media/.

4. Scott Jaschik, "How Much Admission Misreporting?" *Inside Higher Ed,* January 28, 2013, accessed December 26, 2015, https://www.insidehighered.com/news/2013/01/28/bucknells-admission-raises-questions-about-how-many-colleges-are-reporting-false.

Chapter 4

Getting In

Improving Your Odds

In this chapter, we shift gears from mythbusting to answering the questions that we most frequently receive from parents in our consulting practice. Again, these are not *When is the SAT offered* type of questions that can be answered in two seconds by Siri but rather more complicated questions requiring nuanced, research-based expert advice. We begin with a question that we often receive from parents of our youngest clients who are just about to enter high school.

IS THERE A PRIVATE SCHOOL ADVANTAGE IN COLLEGE ADMISSIONS?

Prior to the 1920s, attendance at a topflight prep school was nothing less than a prerequisite for admission into an Ivy League college. Absurdly, a diploma from a blue-blood boarding school actually trumped academic superiority in the elitist admissions landscape of early twentieth-century America. Today, nearly 100 years later, 62% of Harvard students hail from a public high school.[1] For a less Ivy-centric view, consider that fewer than 6% of college students in 2012 had attended private, nonreligious high schools. So this begs the question: Do private schools still offer an admissions advantage at our nation's most selective colleges and universities?

The Argument for Private School

Let's begin by acknowledging that there are some undeniable admissions advantages to private schools. For example, counselors in public high schools report spending only 28% of their time on college-related counseling, while their private school counterparts spend a far healthier 60%.[2] Moreover, three-quarters of private high schools employ a counselor who is solely dedicated to matters of college admissions, something very few public schools are able to offer.

Private school students are also more likely to be completely surrounded by highly motivated, college-bound peers, which research suggests raises expectations and performance. Roughly 86% of private high school grads immediately go on to four-year postsecondary institutions compared with 51% of public school grads.[3]

Academic powerhouses such as Harvard-Westlake, which services Hollywood's elite, or the Trinity School in New York City, which caters to the children of Wall Street, still serve, as prep schools did back in the day, as direct pipelines to Harvard, Princeton, Yale, and MIT. A staggering 6% (yes, in this case 6% qualifies as staggering) of Harvard's Class of 2017 came from just *ten* high schools.[4] Considering that there are over 30,000 public and private high schools in the country, that is a shockingly disproportionate number. While some look at the close relationship between premier magnet high schools and elite colleges and bemoan the sad state of meritocracy, there is still evidence that public schools may offer an equal or even better chance at admission to an Ivy than spending four years at Groton or some other Hogwarts-looking prep school.

The Argument for Public School

Public schools, of course, vary greatly in quality. The dilapidated state of too many urban and rural schools in the United States is a well-chronicled tragedy. Yet, a large number of suburban public high schools offer many of the amenities of a private school, including a full slate of Advanced Placement (AP) and other college-level or honors courses, as well as a lineup of strongly credentialed, dedicated instructors.

Students may also gain an edge by being a big fish in a small pond, or if you prefer a less overused analogy, a gargantuan begonia in a miniature greenhouse. Studies have shown that when you control for scholastic ability, attending a school surrounded by fellow academic superstars actually has a negative effect on your admissions chances at an elite college.[5] This is in part because a highly abled student, who attends a good public high school, is more likely to stand out among her peers (and to an admissions committee) than a similarly abled student attending a top-of-the-line private school.

Ultimately, colleges admit high school students, not high schools. The *who you know* intangibles of the elite private school experience undoubtedly exist but are tough to quantify. If you are a student who can finish at the top of your public school class while securing the support needed to navigate the college admissions process, then you may be better off as a giant gerbil in a pint-sized Habitrail.

WHEN IT COMES TO YOUR COURSES, CHOOSE WISELY

"It's not whether you win or lose, but how you play the game." This age-old maxim applies not just to sports, but to high school and to college admissions as well. Many students would be surprised to discover that their strength of curriculum, or the types of courses in which they enroll during high school, is often times viewed as more important in the admissions process than grade point average or standardized test performance. If a student hopes to win admission into competitive, four-year colleges, they should consider adopting the following four strategies:

1. *Enroll in a fourth year of science and math.* Although most high schools only require that students complete three years of math and science to graduate, competitive colleges like to see a fourth year in these subjects. Opting for math and science during senior year demonstrates to an admissions office that a student is intellectually motivated and willing to negotiate the rigors of a college curriculum. It may also improve their prospects for college success, at least according to a widely cited US Department of Education study:

   The highest level of mathematics reached in high school continues to be a key marker in precollegiate momentum with the tipping point now firmly above Algebra II. The world has gone quantitative: business, geography, criminal justice, history, allied health fields—a full range of disciplines and job tasks tells students why math requirements are not just some abstract school exercise.[6]

2. *Consider adding an AP/IB course, or two.* Taking Advanced Placement or International Baccalaureate courses during high school signals to prospective colleges that one is enrolled in a challenging course of study, and

thus prepared for college-level work. In a nationwide survey, the National Association of College Admissions Counseling (NACAC) discovered that 70% of all colleges considered AP/IB performance as having some level of importance in the admissions process, and that 94 percent of colleges viewed an applicant's strength of curriculum as being somewhere between *somewhat important* and *very important.*[7]

3. *Enroll in challenging and/or relevant electives.* Instead of registering for a cooking or sewing class, enroll in journalism, psychology, French, or some other academic course that will challenge your child and demonstrate to their prospective schools that they are passionate about learning. Although usually not as rigorous as some core academic courses (in math, science, history, etc.), electives play an important role in the admissions process. If chosen carefully, they can help develop a student's talents and allow them to further exhibit their interest in a particular subject area. If a student is an aspiring architect, for example, choosing an elective in engineering or CAD (computer-aided design) will help her to develop a portfolio of related work (now required by most architecture schools) and capture the attention of an admissions officer or faculty member who is seeking applicants committed to this field.

4. *Finally, know your limits, and don't take on too much.* Adding an AP or IB course is fine, but if a student is enrolled in two AP courses his junior year and opts for five such courses his senior year, he's likely to become overwhelmed and earn less than satisfactory grades. Tom Reason, the former director of admissions at the University of Wisconsin–Madison expressed his views on the importance of striking a balance when it comes to course rigor: "We don't expect students to take every AP or IB course available. We do expect students to have made thoughtful choices that exemplify full preparation for college. Rigorous course work without performance in that course work is not what we're after and will not be fruitful."[8]

Reason's views echo the views of most other college admissions officers and reveal the need for all students to reflect upon their own academic limits and to then challenge themselves accordingly. In doing so, students will not only become happier and more productive learners, they will become better college applicants.

HOW MANY AP COURSES SHOULD I TAKE?

Most students are familiar with the basics of AP courses: they offer a chance to experience a college-level curriculum while still in high school, earn college credits, and impress prospective institutions by undertaking a rigorous course load. From there, questions typically abound. We'll do our best to answer the most commonly asked questions we receive about AP classes, starting with the most frequent one.

Let's begin by saying that taking too heavy an AP course load (relative to the caliber of the student) is never a good idea. If your kid is up at 4 am on a Wednesday morning rereading the footnotes in Immanuel Kant's *The False Subtlety of the Four Syllogistic Figures*, downing their sixth Monster Energy, and it's been three days since their last shower . . . they might be taking too many AP courses.

Some schools such as University of North Carolina (UNC)—Chapel Hill have stated publicly that they will not grant favor in the admissions process to students who took more than five AP courses. This came in the wake of a study which found that while there was a correlation between higher freshman GPA and the number of AP courses taken in high school, the effect flatlined after five courses. In other words, there was no predictive indicator of success if you took ten APs versus five.[9]

Does this mean that 5 is the *right* number for everybody? Not necessarily, but most highly selective colleges generally expect that students will have taken the most challenging course available in math, English, history, science, and foreign language. If an ambitious high schooler believes that they can handle more than 5 APs, they should go for it, but they should do it because *they want to*, not because they think colleges require it.

In the case of students not aiming for Ivies, we wholeheartedly recommend taking AP classes only in their expressed areas of interest/strength. They could try an AP class as a sophomore (if available) or as a junior and go from there. If they're successful, they can take another AP class or two as a senior. This schedule will be rigorous enough to satisfy 99% of the nation's colleges and universities and won't drive them to the brink of insanity.

Is a Student Who Takes AP Classes Better Prepared for College Than One Who Does Not?

The jury is still out on this one. Although several reports reveal a positive relationship between AP participation and college performance, most are sponsored by the College Board (AP's creator) and/or rely on woefully inadequate methodologies. Further, more recent and rigorous studies find little advantage for AP students, and warn that AP classes at most high schools are not necessarily adequate substitutes for a college-level course.[10] In other words, take some AP courses to save money and improve your admissions prospects, but don't expect to enter college more prepared than similar *non-AP* students.

How Much College Credit Will I Actually Receive?

Check the AP credit policies of the institutions that your child is considering. This can vary greatly. For example, at NYU, a "5" on the AP Physics B exam will net them ten college credits, a "4" will earn them five credits, while a "3" and a $1.25 will get them a jumbo pack of Nutter Butters from a campus vending machine. Meanwhile, upstate at Ithaca College, that same "3" will earn them six college credits and a "4" will garner them eight credits. The subsequent savings in tuition could put enough extra cash in their pocket to purchase that obscure, out-of-print, ridiculously pricey textbook authored by and assigned by their most egomaniacal professor, or, if they prefer, a year's supply of Nutter Butters.

DON'T OVERLOOK SUBJECT TESTS

Like AP exams, SAT Subject Tests give students the opportunity to demonstrate mastery of a content area; yet they play a far more important role in the admissions process. Often an afterthought in the mind of applicants, SAT Subject Tests can greatly benefit some applicants and are a near-necessity for anyone with an eye on gaining acceptance to Ivy or Ivy-caliber schools. One might say that Subject Tests are like the Jan Brady of the college application family—easy to forget about when surrounded by the Marcia-like SAT and ACT.

We receive many questions on the topic and hope that the following will give you a complete understanding of what these tests entail and whether or not they should be a part of a student's college application process.

What's on the Menu?

There are over 20 Subjects Tests, but that number implies more variety than is reality. A dozen of the tests are actually in the foreign language arena and include your usual suspect tongues such as Spanish, French, Italian, German, Chinese, as well as lesser-studied languages such as Korean, Modern Hebrew, and Japanese. For several of the language exams, students can choose between a purely written exam or one that includes a listening component.

The eight non-foreign language exams cover literature, two levels of general math, chemistry, physics, American history, world history, and biology, of either the molecular or ecological variety.

What Tests Should I Choose?

In terms of sheer volume, the three most commonly administered assessments are the Math Level 2, U.S. History and Literature exams. Of the science exams, chemistry and biology top the popularity charts. If Subject Tests are not required by any school to which your daughter is planning to apply, avoid tests that are redundant in terms of what they say about her. In other words, if she already has a "5" on the AP United States History exam, taking an SAT Subject Test in the same area isn't going to unveil any significant new information about her ability, even if she registers a perfect score. If tests are required by a student's prospective colleges, she will be best served by focusing on areas of strength and, of course, adhering to any program-specific requirements.

When to Take Subject Tests

We advise students to take Subject Tests immediately after finishing course-work for the subject area in which they will be tested, whether during sophomore, junior, or senior year. This will allow them to maximize their exposure to key concepts in the classroom and sit for the exam while everything is still fresh in their mind. In the case of Math Level 2, make sure that they have had prior exposure to trigonometry and precalculus, as well as a basic understanding of statistics and probability. In the case of language, we advise that they wait to take these exams until late in their junior year, after they have progressed through intermediate and, ideally, advanced coursework. If they are unhappy with their scores, there is always the option to retake an exam or two during senior year.

Required, Recommended, or Considered?

Roughly 160 colleges and universities, mostly of the elite variety, require or highly recommend the submission of Subject Tests as part of an applicant's portfolio. Several top-tier colleges such as Cornell, Carnegie Mellon, and MIT require students to take two Subject Tests of their choosing. Emory, Georgetown, and Duke are among the institutions that recommend or in some cases strongly recommend that Subject Tests be a part of any application

Many other schools do not recommend Subject Tests but will give them serious consideration in the application process. Institutions such as the University of Chicago, Vanderbilt, and Boston College fall into this category.

Finally, several of the most prestigious universities consider, but do not require, students to submit Subject Tests if they have taken the ACT (with writing). These schools include Brown, Tufts, and Wellesley College.

Special Situations

It is worth noting that some schools will accept Subject Tests in lieu of the SAT I. The University of Rochester will accept two SAT II tests in place of the SAT/ACT. Colorado College and Colby College offer the same deal but require three test scores instead of two.

Other schools require more case-by-case research as they only require or recommend SAT II scores from applicants to certain academic or honors programs. For engineering applicants, UCLA and UC Berkeley strongly advise the submission of math and science Subject Test scores. The University of Delaware, George Washington University, and the University of Miami all strongly recommend Subject Tests be included as part any application to their honors programs.

If a student referred to their high school teacher as *Mom* or *Dad*, then they may be compelled to take Subject Tests. Northeastern, Virginia Tech, and American University all request Subject Test results from home schooled or other nontraditionally educated applicants.

A Strong Cohort

While students of varying caliber typically take the SAT I, Subject Tests are mostly the domain of high-achievers. Over 60% of exam-takers are in the top 20% of their respective high school classes.[12] The average Subject Test participant scored over a 600 on both the reading and math section of the SAT I, over 100 points higher per section than the average student.[13] Keep this in mind when interpreting the percentile results of any Subject Test; students are pitted against stiffer competition.

Prepare for the Test

If you're going to shell out the College Board fee (including $26 for registration and $20 per Subject Test) plus the cost of a few number-two pencils (approximately 17 cents) and have your child spend a portion of their Saturday bubbling their demographic information into a Scantron for the millionth time this year, they might as well prep sufficiently so that they can excel on the SAT Subject Tests.

It sounds obvious enough, but some students will take an SAT Subject Test with very little preparation on the assumption that since they aced the class at their high school, they'll nail the Subject Test just the same. Though we advise taking a Subject Test after taking a related course, we warn you that material covered and taught in high school classes will not necessarily be identical to the material featured on the exam.

Unfortunately, it is very possible for a student to ace an honors biology class, sign up for the Molecular Biology SAT II Subject Test, and feel like they have just been thrown a nasty curveball. Remember, unlike in an AP class, a teacher, even in a very rigorous course, is not aligning his or her curriculum to an SAT Subject Test. Thus, it's on the student to learn exactly what is on these exams and then fill in any gaps with supplemental learning.

Students should give Subject Tests the love and attention they deserve, or on test day, they might hear their neglected test booklet uttering the lonely whispered cries of "Marcia, Marcia, Marcia!"

WHAT EXTRACURRICULAR ACTIVITIES LOOK BEST ON A COLLEGE APPLICATION?

We hear this question a lot—often from parents who have come to view the college application process as an exercise in spin, rather than an opportunity to exhibit passion. While the temptation to *amass* activities is strong, especially given the overwhelmingly competitive nature of college admissions, it's important to realize that superficiality will not get students far in life, and it certainly won't help them get into the college of their choice. College admissions officers are interested in meaningful engagement, not perfunctory participation, and are smart enough and experienced enough to distinguish between the two. That being said, here are a few rules to abide by as you plan your extracurricular involvement:

1. *Keep it real.* Every admissions season, colleges strive to admit a diverse community of students with a wide range of talents and interests. If your child isn't interested in sports, student council, or some other typical extracurricular activity, don't worry about it. Colleges are just as intrigued by the student filmmaker or poetry club founder as they are by the starting power forward or student body president. Provided that they demonstrate a deep and consistent commitment, admissions officers will take notice, whatever the activity.

2. *Focus on depth, not breadth.* Students who assume leadership roles and participate extensively (10–20 hours per week) in one or two pursuits will always outshine comparable applicants who merely dabble in several activities. If they want activities to have a meaningful impact, have students find their niche, and improve their college admissions prospects in the process. Suggest that they forget the laundry list and commit to the wholehearted following of their true extracurricular interests.

3. *Take advantage of the summer.* Students want to show colleges that they are serious about their extracurricular pursuits. They should use their summer to secure an internship, take a class, or enroll in a camp that will allow them to further explore their interests outside the classroom. Though there are admission-related advantages to spending their summer months productively, doing so does not require that they spend thousands of dollars on some high-end program, as we explain in our next section.

4. *Get a job.* A job is one of the most underrated activities on a college application. Regardless of where they work, a job demonstrates to an admissions committee that a student is mature, practical, and ready to take on the responsibilities associated with adulthood. If they can get a job in their area of interest, great; if they can't, they should get one anyway. Most of us, at one time or another, have had to find alternative, less attractive ways to fund the pursuit of our passions. This will show colleges that they're not afraid to get their hands dirty.

All in all, extracurricular life is not about building a resume (students will have plenty of time to do that later); it's about finding themselves and their true calling. Students should follow their heart, strive for authenticity, and the admissions process will take care of itself.

SUMMER PROGRAMS: DO THEY MAKE A DIFFERENCE?

In the 1990s, while the rest of society was busy squirting each other with Super Soakers, listening to the Gin Blossoms, and carving Nike swooshes into their hair, colleges finally realized for the first time that their campuses were deserted during the summer. Suddenly, an administrator at a prestigious university had a revolutionary notion, "What if we filled up our dorms with high school students who are caught up in the admissions hysteria and charged triple our normal tuition rate for the privilege?" Hence, the college summer program for high school sophomores and juniors was born.

Cynical pseudo-historical accounts aside, the merit of summer programs varies greatly from campus to campus, and it is important to do your homework before reaching for that Visa card. The following Q&A seeks to address the most frequent queries we receive from parents on the topic.

How Much Do They Cost?

Elite schools such as Harvard, Stanford, Columbia, and Duke charge between $1,500 and $3,000 per week for the privilege of sleeping in their dorms and having a few idle faculty members impart wisdom about the transition to college life. Programs abroad can be even pricier. On the other hand, some programs are actually free of charge and can be far more valuable in both the experiential and admissions sense (more on this in a moment).

Will They Help My Child's Chance at Admission?

In most cases, *no*. A summer spent strutting around Harvard Yard in a borrowed tweed jacket will be viewed by an admissions committee as equal in merit to spending your break restocking packets of Horsey Sauce at an Arby's in a mall food court. Admissions officers know that very few students have the resources to drop ten grand on a three-week equivalent to summer camp and will not grant favor to those who attend. Doing so would be as absurd as NASA deciding to send a group of Space Camp attendees into orbit. Never mind that this scenario actually occurs, albeit by accident, in the 1986 Hollywood mega-flop, *Space Camp* . . .

Do They Have Any Admissions-Related Value?

Indirectly, perhaps. As with any experience a young person undertakes, a high-cost summer program could indirectly have a positive impact on a future application. For example, a summer program attendee might work on a project that ignites a passion which becomes ideal fodder for a future application essay. In some cases, a student may impress a faculty member to the point where they are willing to write a glowing, committee-swaying letter of recommendation.

Yet, it is critical to be aware that the programs with the highest value are actually the ones that are cost free or relatively affordable, and highly selective. For example, MIT offers several free programs that allow a select group of high school juniors to intensively study subjects such as the human genome or robotics.

These competitive summer programs not only provide for an enriching experience but also look impressive on a college application.

Program	Location
Asian American Journalists Association – JCamp	Washington, DC
Boston University – RISE	Boston, MA
Canada/USA Mathcamp	Waterville, ME (Colby College)
Carnegie Mellon University – SAMS	Pittsburgh, PA
Endevvr	Multiple Locations
Foundation for Teaching Economics – Economics for Leaders	Multiple Locations
Hampshire College Summer Studies in Mathematics (HCSSiM)	Amherst, MA
Indiana University Young Women's Institute	Bloomington, IN
Jackson Lab Summer Student Program	Multiple Locations (CT or ME)
MIT Launch	Cambridge, MA
MIT MITES	Cambridge, MA
Michigan Math and Science Scholars	Ann Arbor, MI
Michigan State University HSHSP	East Lansing, MI
Monell Center Research Apprenticeship Program	Philadelphia, PA
NIH Summer Internship in Biomedical Research (SIP)	Multiple Locations
Ohio State University – Ross Mathematics Program	Columbus, OH
Program in Mathematics for Young Scientists (PROMYS)	Boston, MA
Research Science Institute (RSI)	Cambridge, MA (MIT)
Stanford University Mathematics Camp (SUMaC)	Stanford, CA
Telluride Association Summer Program	Multiple Locations (NY or MI)
Texas Tech University Clark Scholars	Lubbock, TX
University of Iowa Secondary Student Training Program	Iowa City, IA
University of Notre Dame Leadership Seminars	Notre Dame, IN
University of Pennsylvania – Leadership in the Business World	Philadelphia, PA
Yale Young Global Scholars	New Haven, CT

Figure 4.1   Selective Summer Programs

Bottom Line

If you have unlimited resources and your son or daughter feels they would benefit from the experience, there is absolutely no harm in attending a high-end summer program. However, it is important to be realistic about what you're paying for. Some *elite* programs accept as many as 70% of applicants.[14] Again, we recommend first exploring more selective, cost-free programs that are merit-based and geared toward a discipline of genuine interest. And, if all else fails, don't underestimate the value of a normal teenage summer experience. After all, you have to admit, the Sisyphean task of Horsey Sauce packet replenishment would make a damn original essay topic.

COLLEGE ADMISSION CREDENTIALS THAT YOU CAN DO WITHOUT

So much misinformation about the college admissions process is transmitted through the *you have to do x, y, and z* admonitions of peers, relatives, media outlets, and message boards.

The items on this list tend to cause students and parents undue stress and, in the end, add little-to-no value to the application process. To be clear, we are not advising students *not* to engage in these activities if they hold intrinsic value to them. We are merely saying that none of the following are *essential* components of a successful college application.

1. National Honors Society

Belonging to the local chapter of NHS can be a wonderful thing. Eligibility requirements vary from school to school, but all chapters require an impressive number of service hours, community involvement, academic excellence, and upstanding behavior. So, why does it make our *overrated* list? For one, there are roughly one million NHS members in the United States so it isn't exactly an exclusive credential that is going to set admissions officers' hearts aflutter. Secondly, belonging to this group isn't any more impressive than achieving the prerequisites for admittance independently. In other words, an honor roll student who engages in community service work is just as impressive as someone doing the same under the auspices of NHS.

2. Participation in a Sport

Very few admissions officers are going to sprint into the dean's office after reviewing an application to exclaim, "You'll never believe this . . .

The third-string kicker on a high school football team wants to come to our university! And there's more . . . he also played volleyball for three months as a sophomore!" This, of course, is to take nothing away from less-gifted athletes who choose to dabble in high school athletics for the love of the game. However, some non-sports enthusiasts feel the need to join teams solely because they feel it will enhance their college application. Unless a student's athletic endeavors show evidence of talent or leadership, they will be of little help to their admission prospects.

3. Alumni Recommendations

If the campus library is named after the person who wrote a student's letter of recommendation, they might be in luck. Otherwise, letters of recommendation from alumni are only as valuable as the academic-related insights they contain. A generic letter from a student's father's boss's cousin's uncle who graduated from Colgate University in 1973 is not going to guarantee a place on the prestigious Hamilton, New York campus next fall.

4. Pay-for-Award Programs

The most notorious of this group was the now defunct *Who's Who Among American High School Students,* a book whose only purchasers, presumably, were the selected students' proud grandparents. High school students continue to be deluged with offers from various honors societies, fellowships, and leadership organizations. Such nominations typically ask for a membership fee. Unless a high schooler is nominated for a genuinely personalized reason (other than being within a certain SAT range) and joining is free, toss these offers out with yesterday's grocery store circulars.

RECOMMENDATIONS MATTER

College applicants tend to underestimate the importance of recommendation letters; this is a mistake. According to a recent NACAC survey, over 15% of institutions view recommendations as *highly important* in admissions decisions and another 43% of schools grant them *moderately important* status.[15] In fact, the recommendation letter is often assigned as much importance as your application essays or extracurricular participation.

Why Are They So Important?

Letters of recommendation provide context to a student's application in a way that other credentials cannot. Ideally, a letter of recommendation will further reinforce their strengths as an applicant and reveal positive information not found elsewhere in their application. All other things being equal, a strong letter of recommendation may provide an admissions officer the additional piece of information he or she needs to admit one student over another comparable applicant.

When Should I Ask?

Request early. By November, a student's favorite teachers (who are likely just about everyone's favorite teachers) will be inundated with recommendation requests and will find themselves writing the phrase *It is with great pleasure* over and over until carpal tunnel sets in. When soliciting letters of recommendation, it is important that students submit their requests *as early as possible*, so that their teachers and counselors have ample time to write a well-thought-out and detailed narrative of the student's past contributions and potential as a college student.

Who Should I Ask?

Stay recent. Students should request recommendations from those who have taught, mentored, or counseled them within the past two years. Admissions officers want insight into your child's most recent performance as a high school student, since this is often a good indicator of how they will perform in college.

Stay relevant. Students should be sure to pursue at least one letter of recommendation from a teacher in their area(s) of academic interest (if they have one). For example, if your daughter indicates on her application that she plans to major in engineering, she should ask a science and/or math teacher to write on her behalf. Admissions officers always appreciate the opportunity to read letters that attest to an applicant's abilities in their prospective major. If a student is undecided on a major (as many students are), consider an English or math teacher—knowledge and skills developed in these academic areas are essential to success in any postsecondary field.

Other potential recommenders include a coach, band director, employer, or other extracurricular sponsor with whom they have established a meaningful and productive relationship. However, these professionals should only provide a letter of recommendation in addition to, and not in place of, a letter from a teacher. A parent or other relative should never write on a student's behalf. These people are rarely able to provide an objective, unbiased account of their character and abilities.

What Is Required of Me?

Students should give adequate information. Immediately after making their requests, they should provide all willing writers with a resume and a statement of purpose outlining their academic and other college-related goals. Both will enable recommenders to offer a more comprehensive account of what they bring (i.e., can contribute) to prospective schools.

Should I Send More Letters Than Requested?

Don't go overboard. If a college requires two letters of recommendation, submit no more than three. Admissions officers are charged with wading through an enormous amount of information, so too many recommendations may overwhelm or even annoy a reader. Worse yet, it could send signals of potential desperation and/or insecurity.

UTILIZING YOUR HIGH SCHOOL COUNSELOR

As private college counselors, we are well versed in the criticisms of school-based counseling. *Unavailable, inexperienced, incompetent*—these are the words that some within our industry often use to describe the professionals who work hardest to establish safe and supportive learning environments for our children. Research consistently shows that school counselors improve the academic achievement, health, and psychological and emotional well-being of students—not to mention their college prospects,[16] yet many continue to argue that counselors are becoming obsolete.

We'd like to assert that this argument is not only unproductive, it's untrue. Yes, growing caseloads and increasingly manifold job roles have limited the extent to which many counselors can focus on college planning, making private counseling a progressively attractive solution to many students and families. However, it is important to understand that most school counselors can prove to be powerful advocates during the college application process. In the spirit of full disclosure, here are a few things that a school counselor can do (and that a private counselor cannot do) to help students get into college:

Provide a letter of recommendation. Most colleges still require a letter of recommendation from a school official. At most high schools, this letter is written by a school counselor and is submitted as part of the secondary school report. Counselor-written letters that provide a personal, thorough, and comprehensive account of the student can have tremendous influence on an admissions decision.

Engage a college admissions office. At most high schools, counselors serve as the point of contact when admissions offices have questions or concerns about a student's application. In the case of a *borderline application*, counselors may also provide an additional key piece of information or point of persuasion that moves a student into the *admit* pile.

Offer school-specific information and strategies. How many applicants from their high school have been admitted into certain colleges? Which teachers write compelling letters of recommendation? What courses are sufficiently rigorous and/or draw high praise? It is likely that a school counselor can answer these and other similar questions. In doing so, they direct students to the information, personnel, and activities that improve their college credentials and help them make the most out of their high school experience.

School counselors can still do a lot for college-bound students; however, reaping the college-related benefits of school-based counseling requires that students be proactive. Today's typical school counselor, though competent and hard-working, faces time constraints that preclude them from forging a deep and productive relationship with every student on their caseload. Therefore, students must take initiative, in particular, by:

Starting early and visiting often. Students should introduce themselves to their school counselor as soon as possible, preferably before junior year, and make it a point to provide regular updates about their life inside and outside the classroom.

Staying organized. This is especially important during senior year, as students and their counselor strive to negotiate the deluge of demands associated with the college application process. Staying organized requires that students complete application-related tasks on time and provide their counselor with all of the information they will need to submit a secondary school report, letter(s) of recommendation, and any other school-specific materials—well before the admission deadlines at prospective colleges.

Respecting boundaries. Students should not make same-day requests or demand/expect that their counselor answer emails or phone calls outside of school hours. Being attuned and sympathetic to the many job demands placed upon a school counselor can go a long way in building rapport, as well as mutual commitment to college-related goals.

THE ROLE OF *DEMONSTRATED INTEREST*

Hardly a day goes by where something in the news is not described as *Orwellian*. Whether in reference to the government's latest surveillance efforts or the newest app for your smart phone that is secretly mining your personal information and selling it to advertisers, the term has become nearly inescapable. Its proliferation is a sign of the computerized, information-saturated times in which we live and it's visible in our everyday lives. Amazon.com seems to magically know when we need to order more toothpaste. The UPS driver transporting our Crest 6-pack is being monitored by his employers every time he puts his seatbelt on, backs up the truck, or gets an electronic signature. Of course, it is only a matter of time before drones completely take over package delivery—a change that may be more Asimovian than Orwellian.

In this climate, it should be of little surprise that a flavor of *1984* has entered the college admissions game. So, you ask, what exactly is Dean Big Brother watching? In this case, it's the level of *demonstrated interest* you show toward a college. Are you their pal on social media sites? Did you visit the campus in person? Have you emailed an admissions rep to ask questions or introduce yourself? At the majority of colleges and universities today, this information is being tracked, recorded, and can actually factor into a school's decision about whether to admit or deny an applicant.

The Importance of "Demonstrated Interest" by the Numbers

According to a recent NACAC survey, 20% of colleges and universities consider demonstrated interest as *very important* to a student's application, the highest such distinction on the survey's scale. More ballyhooed application components such as essays and counselor/teacher recommendations actually rated at the same level or lower in terms of importance. With another 34% of institutions assigning *considerable importance* to demonstrated interest, the percentage of schools that strongly value a little attention from applicants is 54%, a higher total than that of class rank, the interview, or extracurricular activities.[17]

This emphasis on demonstrated interest is a relatively new phenomenon. Back in 2003, just 7% of schools identified interest as being a highly important factor and a decade earlier in 1993, the category did not even exist. The growing importance of demonstrated interest can be directly linked to the Common Application and other streamlined tools which have made applying to numerous colleges a fairly easy endeavor.

As students are applying to a greater number of schools, admissions officers are finding it increasingly difficult to determine which applicants are actually committed to attending their institution. And if an institution cannot predict, with reasonable accuracy, who will attend, it is forced to admit more students—an action that can lower both yield (the percentage of admitted students attending) and selectivity, which in turn can have negative effects on a school's desirability, ranking, and/or revenue. As a result, many institutions are now looking to signs of *demonstrated interest* to determine which students are likely to attend and, ultimately, which students they should admit.

What Type of Colleges Are Likely to Emphasize Demonstrated Interest?

Generally, the less selective a school is, the more likely it values being shown some extra love, and private schools tend to value the attention more than publics. Additionally, schools with a lower yield rate value this attribute more than schools with a high yield rate. For example, Loyola University in Maryland, a reputable and moderately selective college, is a common *backup school* among high-achieving students and consistently struggles to improve upon its low yield rate. As such, demonstrated interest is far more likely to be an important factor at Loyola than it is at neighboring Johns Hopkins, a significantly more prestigious school that is a regular favorite among the crème de la crème students or at the state's public flagship, University of Maryland, where in-state tuition rates draw massive numbers of applicants and where government funding is guaranteed.

What Can I Do to Demonstrate Interest?

Email your admissions counselor. At most colleges, there will be one counselor responsible for reviewing applications from students in your region of the country. With some clever Googling, it's usually pretty easy to find the assigned counselor on any institution's admissions website. Once a student finds their counselor, they should send a brief email introducing themselves and describing their interests in the institution. Include a question or two about the admissions process or a particular academic offering, the answers to which cannot be easily found on the institution's website. Remember, keep it brief. They don't need to know your son or daughter's life story or their thoughts on Cartesian dualism—just the fact that they are a high school student who is interested in the school.

Complete an online information request form. Just about every college in the world features a page on its admissions website, where prospective students can request general information, subscribe to the college's blog or admissions newsletter, and/or indicate academic programs/activities that are especially appealing. They'll likely send the student piles of printed materials through snail mail which, whether you carefully peruse or toss directly into the recycle bin, will serve the purpose of communicating interest.

Visit campus. If a prospective college is within a reasonable distance, it is strongly recommended that your teen pays a visit. While there, they should make every effort to attend an information session and schedule an interview or informal meeting with an admissions counselor. Connecting in person with an admissions officer provides students with an opportunity to show their counselor that they are more than just grades and test scores and of course gets them brownie points when they calculate your so-called interest quotient.

Attend admissions events in your area. If an admissions representative from a prospective college visits your student's high school for an information session or college fair, they should make it a point to be there, and be sure to introduce themselves. If they are interested enough in a school to apply, they should definitely be interested enough to meet a rep who has traveled (sometimes across the country) right to their backyard. Afterward, they should remember to send a brief thank you email. Yes, their mailboxes are likely full of perfunctory thank you emails—the email may even be funneled to a special folder exclusively for perfunctory thank-yous. The important thing is—you guessed it—it shows that the student is genuinely interested.

Connect on social media. More schools are offering applicants the chance to create an online admissions profile where they can submit and track their online application, schedule a campus tour, and interact with college staff via Facebook, Twitter, and other social media. Prospective students should take a minute to create an admissions profile at each of their target colleges, and if possible, provide detailed information about their academic and extracurricular interests. It won't take any more time to connect with a college on social media than it did to retweet Katy Perry's latest deep thoughts about eating tacos on the beach (believe it or not, this is an actual message which was retweeted by over 13,000 people).

Don't Go Overboard

It's nice to *like* someone's Facebook post when it resonates with you. It's weird to *like* every single post and picture on their entire account. The line between showing interest and stalking to the point of a full on creep-out is a fine one but there are clear divisions. To put it in movie terms, you want to be more like Hugh Grant buying someone flowers and chocolate in a romcom and less like Robert De Niro in *Taxi Driver*—shirtless, sporting a serial-killer mohawk, and repeatedly screaming, "You talkin' to me?" into the mirror.

Many guidance counselors and students resent the entire concept of *demonstrated interest* and see it as further evidence of the corporatization of college admissions. While this may be so, our recommendation is to just give in and play the game—it's simple enough and won't take too much time. Plus, there's a darn good chance you'll learn more about your prospective institutions through this process, an outcome that will benefit both you and Big Brother.

THE ADVANTAGES OF *LEGACY* STATUS

Colleges love to throw around high-minded words like *meritocracy, access,* and *egalitarianism* when discussing admissions policies. Yet such references to social justice and increased opportunities for the poor ring a bit hallow when you consider that so-called legacy applicants, those who have familial ties to an institution, are still given a sizable edge in the admissions process at the vast majority of elite US colleges and universities.

If a student happens to be interested in attending their parent's alma mater, they will likely find this news encouraging. If not, it's still important to be aware as they enter the admissions process that not every decision to accept or reject is driven solely by merit.

Primary versus Secondary Legacy

The difference between applying to a university that Great Aunt Merle graduated from in 1912 versus a school attended by one or both parents is substantial in terms of the potential impact on a student's admissions prospects. Having a loose connection such as Great Aunt Merle, a grandparent, or a sibling qualifies them as being a *secondary legacy* and can be slightly helpful in the admissions process. A direct parental connection means that they are designated as a *primary legacy* and can be a major boost to their admissions prospects.

Stats on Legacy Admissions

Colleges like to state publicly that legacy status is nothing more than a tie-breaker between equally strong applicants, a *thumb on the scale* is an oft-used phrase. Yet a quick glance at the statistics on legacy admissions suggests that the proverbial thumb in question must belong to Andre the Giant.

A study of thirty elite colleges found that primary legacy students are an astornishingly 45% more likely to get into a highly selective college or university than a non-legacy.[18] Secondary legacies receive a lesser pick-me-up of 13%.[19] One study revealed that being a legacy was equivalent in admissions value to a 160 point gain on the SATs on a 1600 point scale.[20]

The end result of the legacy advantage can be seen on elite college campuses across the country. At Harvard, the admission rate for legacy students is five times greater than for the general applicant pool. Fellow Ivies, Princeton and Yale also admit between 25% and 35% of legacies, three to four times their overall admit rate.[21]

Even elite public universities such as the University of Michigan and UVA grant favor to legacy applicants. However, these two schools differ in how openly they advertise their legacy policies. UVA created its own Admission Liaison Program where children of alumni can attend special events, webinars, and even schedule a one-on-one transcript consultation with the director of the organization at any point throughout high school. In contrast, the University of Michigan's admissions website does not make any reference to legacy status—the only statement about legacy admissions is buried in an FAQ.

Do All Schools Promote This Practice?

It is estimated that three-quarters of all research institutions and liberal arts colleges in the United States factor legacy status into their admissions decisions. This includes all of the Ivies and many other ultra-elite private schools such as Georgetown, Duke, Swarthmore, Middlebury, Amherst, Tufts, and countless others.

A much smaller number of highly selective schools openly oppose granting favor to legacy status. MIT and Cooper Union are both on record as openly opposing hereditary privilege in the admissions process.

Other schools, such as Stanford University and UNC, only take primary legacy into consideration. Interestingly, most elite schools also grant much heavier consideration to a parent who attended their undergraduate school versus a graduate program.

Why Do Schools Do This?

One may ask: Why do schools care if mom or dad graced their campus decades ago? Publicly, institutions typically defend legacy admissions as a way to respect tradition and acknowledge those who helped to lay the foundation on which the university is built. *Intergenerational continuity* is a term that has been thrown around by defenders of the practice.

If your reaction is a skeptical raise of the eyebrow, join the club.

There is little question that legacy schools expect that they will receive greater financial contributions in exchange for keeping things in the family. However, it is interesting to note that one major study found that schools that grant legacy status actually had no fundraising advantage over schools that do not. In fact, two of the eight US schools with the largest endowments are MIT and Texas A&M which banned legacy-based admission over a decade ago.[22]

How to Take Advantage

No matter how you feel about the fairness of legacy admissions, if a student chooses to take advantage, the simplest way to disclose their legacy status is straightforward—just list their alumni connections on the application. On most school's application forms, including the common app, there is a place to list parents' educational backgrounds. If the student is claiming a secondary legacy, they'll have to do so on the individual institution's supplemental forms.

For parents, the more involved with your alma mater you have been since graduation, the more likely your child's legacy is to provide an admissions boost. Admissions offices will look at the alum's history of financial contributions, service on boards, and role as a member of the college's alumni network. While admissions decisions are not made in smoke-filled backrooms, *who you know* can certainly aid your son or daughter's chances of receiving a bulky envelope come spring.

Yet, parents need to be careful that they are tactful throughout this process. Pushy emails and phone calls to admissions reps will come across poorly. An abrasive and overbearing approach will be off-putting to a school and can actually end up hurting an applicant's chances. Keep things positive and know that your student is definitely going to get special consideration at your alma mater.

In the worst case scenario, a thin envelope will arrive and, after the disappointment wanes, your child will select another phenomenal institution to attend, starting a legacy of their very own.

PLAYING YOUR WAY INTO AN ELITE COLLEGE

Ivy League schools and many elite colleges with Division III athletics purport not to grant admissions favor or any edge in scholarship consideration to student-athletes. In related news, Taco Bell claims that their 89¢ tacos are made with 100% sirloin beef.

Since you can't always believe the party line, student-athletes interested in parlaying their physical gifts into selective college admission should be aware of the realities that lie beneath the posture of sports indifference. In truth, if you can shoot, skate, cradle, dribble, sprint, throw, or volley better than 99% of your peers, then you have a significant admissions advantage over your less-coordinated competition.

Athletes recruited by college coaches typically scored 200 points lower on the SAT than the average admitted applicant.[23] While tough to quantify, studies have claimed that athletes are up to four times more likely to be accepted at Ivy League schools than their nonathlete counterparts.[24] There can be a financial advantage as well. Top liberal arts schools may not hand out *football scholarships*, but they may have scholarships under various euphemisms— *leadership*, for example—that may just so happen to go to stellar athletes.

It is worth noting that at many elite schools the percentage of recruited student-athletes relative to the student body is far greater proportionally than at well-known jock schools like Ohio State or the University of Miami. For example, Dartmouth's undergraduate population of around 4,000 students includes over 1,000 varsity athletes.[25] With such skewed demographics, being a jock with a brain can truly be a decisive factor in opening the doors to America's most selective schools. This begs the question: What can scholar-athletes do to exploit this numerical advantage?

Without question, pursuing excellence in the classroom is a must. No amount of gridiron glory is going to get a kid with a 2.3 GPA and a 950 SAT into Princeton. You've got to be, pun intended, *in the ballpark* academically. The recruiting process at top scholarly institutions, while ethically controversial, isn't going to approach the level seen in *Blue Chips*, a 1994 film about a corrupt college athletics department buying basketball recruits with cars, tractors, houses for their families, and suitcases full of money.

National Collegiate Athletic Association recruiting season officially begins the summer before a high school athlete's junior year. However, this time frame is rarely the first time coaches and prospective players communicate. At Division III schools such as Amherst, Middlebury, and Emory, coaches are free to contact you at any time during high school, and at all schools (Division I included) athletes may initiate contact with a coach at any time. We recommend reaching out to coaches early in a student's high school career if they are an athlete interested in attending an academically superior institution.

Getting on the coaches radar early can pay dividends when admissions time rolls around. Remember, even at the Ivies, a lacrosse coach may have more sway than a Nobel Prize–nominated faculty member. Fair or not, it's critical for prospective college athletes to remember that 100% sirloin beef isn't always what it seems.

CAST A WIDE NET: GEOGRAPHIC DIVERSITY AND COLLEGE ADMISSIONS

A recent study revealed that the majority of college-bound students (58%) choose schools within 100 miles of their home, while only 11% opt for an institution more than 500 miles away.[26] In our increasingly mobile society, this finding is somewhat surprising. Although remaining close to home for college can seem the more comfortable and convenient option, there are significant benefits associated with casting a wider net. Most notably, a willingness to travel can lead to improved admissions prospects and better financial aid offers. Why? Because colleges crave geographic diversity.

Like high test scores and low acceptance rates, geographic diversity improves a school's selectivity, as well as its ability to increase enrollment and revenue. All things equal, colleges will almost always favor the applicant coming from a more distant or exotic locale, and not just because the applicant brings a new perspective to campus. For example, assume Denison University, a liberal arts college in the middle of Ohio, is seeking to improve its ranking. Nabbing a highly accomplished student from Columbus or Cleveland might help, but not as much as luring an equally accomplished student from Seattle. A Seattle attendee could introduce the college to an entirely new network of potential applicants, who are more likely to apply to Denison because of its unique institutional qualities, rather than because of its convenient location in the Midwest. As a result, these applicants are less likely to consider Kenyon, Oberlin, Allegheny, and other nearby competitors that *steal away* other prospective students. Ideally, Denison's new Emerald City connection not only generates greater application numbers, it also effects a rise in the college's yield rate, and consequently, its ranking.

Now, not every college wants or needs to improve the geographic diversity of its student body—many selective public flagships, such as UVA and UNC-Chapel Hill, set strict caps on the number of out-of-state students, while Harvard and Yale already attract more qualified Alaskans than they are able to admit. However, if you're an admissions director at a college without

Students coming from faraway or sparsely populated states are likely to gain a slight advantage at these excellent yet geographically homogenous institutions. To create this list, we relied on U.S. Department of Education data revealing the state-by-state distribution of students currently enrolled at every four-year college and university. The schools featured attract far fewer students from outside their region than institutions of similar reputation.

Bucknell University

Butler University

Centre College

College of the Holy Cross

Case Western Reserve University

Clark University

Franklin & Marshall College

Hamilton College

Harvey Mudd College

Lafayette College

Pitzer College

Rensselaer Polytechnic Institute

Rice University

Rollins College

Santa Clara University

Soka University

Trinity University

Union College

University of Rochester

Worcester Polytechnic Institute

Figure 4.2   Great Colleges with Less-Than-Great Geographic Diversity

government mandates or Ivy League prestige, chances are you give admissions and financial aid preference to geographically desirable applicants.

NOTES

1. Francesca Annicchiarico and Samuel Y. Weinstock, "Freshman Survey Part I: Meet Harvard's Class of 2017," *The Harvard Crimson*, September 3, 2013, accessed December 26, 2015, http://www.thecrimson.com/article/2013/9/3/freshmen-employment-demographics-geography/?page=2.

2. National Association for College Admission Counseling, "Effective Counseling in Schools Increases College Access, Research to Practice Brief," 2006, accessed December 26, 2015, http://www.nacacnet.org/research/research-data/Research%20Member%20Only/McDonough.pdf.

3. National Student Clearinghouse Research Center, "Report: High School Benchmarks 2014," October 13, 2014, accessed December 26, 2015, https://nscresearchcenter.org/hsbenchmarks2014/#Results1.

4. Meg Bernhard, "The Making of a Harvard Feeder School," *The Harvard Crimson*, December 13, 2013, accessed January 1, 2016. http://www.thecrimson.com/article/2013/12/13/making-harvard-feeder-schools/

5. For example, see: Espenshade, T. J., Hale, L. E., & Chung, C. Y., (2005), "The frog pond revisited: High school academic context, class rank, and elite college admission," Sociology of Education, 78(4), 269-293.

6. U.S. Department of Education, "The Toolbox Revisited: Paths to Degree Completion from High School through College," last modified March 2, 2006, accessed December 26, 2015, http://www2.ed.gov/rschstat/research/pubs/toolboxrevisit/index.html?exp.

7. National Association for College Admission Counseling, "Factors in the Admission Decision," accessed December 26, 2015, http://www.nacacnet.org/studentinfo/articles/Pages/Factors-in-the-Admission-Decision.aspx.

8. Valerie Strauss, "AP Courses: How Many Do Colleges Want?" *The Washington Post*, January 29, 2010, accessed December 26, 2015, http://voices.washingtonpost.com/answer-sheet/college-admissions/ap-courses-how-many-do-college.html.

9. Susan Hardy, "Study Finds That More AP Classes May Not Be Better," *The University Gazette*, The University of North Carolina at Chapel Hill, January 8, 2013, accessed December 26, 2015, http://gazette.unc.edu/2013/01/08/study-finds-that-more-ap-classes-may-not-be-better/.

10. Zack Budryk, "Should AP Be Plan A?," *Inside Higher Ed*, April 23, 2013, accessed January 1, 2016, https://www.insidehighered.com/news/2013/04/23/new-study-challenges-popular-perceptions-ap

11. College Board, "Institutions Using SAT Subject Tests," accessed December 26, 2015, https://professionals.collegeboard.com/testing/sat-subject/about/institutions#inst_using_SAT.

12. College Board, "2013 College-Bound Seniors Total Group Profile Report," accessed December 26, 2015, http://media.collegeboard.com/digitalServices/pdf/research/2013/TotalGroup-2013.pdf.

13. Ibid.

14. Mary Camille Izlar, "Harvard Summer Program Recommendations Come at Hefty Cost," *Bloomberg Businessweek,* July 17, 2013, accessed December 26, 2015, http://www.bloomberg.com/news/articles/2013-07-17/harvard-summer-program-recommendations-come-at-hefty-cost.

15. Ibid.

16. Andrew S. Belasco, "Creating College Opportunity: School Counselors and Their Influence on Postsecondary Enrollment," *Research in Higher Education,* November 2013: 54(7), 781–804.

17. Melissa Clinedinst, "2014 State of College Admission," National Association for College Admission Counseling, accessed December 26, 2015, http://www.nxt-book.com/ygsreprints/NACAC/2014SoCA_nxtbk/#/28.

18. Elyse Ashburn, "At Elite Colleges, Legacy Status May Count More Than Was Previously Thought," *The Chronicle of Higher Education,* January 5, 2011, accessed December 26, 2015, http://chronicle.com/article/Legacys-Advantage-May-Be/125812/?sid=at&utm_source=at&utm_medium=en.

19. Ibid.

20. Thomas J. Espenshade and Chang Y. Chung, "The Opportunity Cost of Admission Preferences at Elite Universities," *Social Science Quarterly* 86, no. 2 (June 2005): 293–305, doi:10.1111/j.0038-4941.2005.00303.

21. Max Nisen, "Legacies Still Get a Staggeringly Unfair College Admissions Advantage," *Business Insider,* June 5, 2013, accessed December 26, 2015, http://www.businessinsider.com/legacy-kids-have-an-admissions-advantage-2013-6.

22. Delece Smith-Barrow, "10 Universities with the Largest Endowments," *U.S. News & World Report,* October 6, 2015, accessed December 26, 2015, http://www.usnews.com/education/best-colleges/the-short-list-college/articles/2015/10/06/10-universities-with-the-largest-endowments.

23. Gary Gutting, "The Myth of the 'Student-Athlete" *New York Times,* March 15, 2012, accessed December 26, 2015, http://opinionator.blogs.nytimes.com/2012/03/15/the-myth-of-the-student-athlete/.

24. Anneli Rufus, "Your Odds of Getting into College," *The Daily Beast,* September 1, 2010, accessed December 26, 2015, http://www.thedailybeast.com/articles/2010/09/01/college-admissions-15-ways-to-predict-where-youll-get-in.html.

25. Kourtney Kawano, "Athletics and Socioeconomic Status: NCAA and Ivy League Rules Complicate Recruitment," *The Dartmouth,* May 15, 2015, accessed December 26, 2015, http://thedartmouth.com/2015/05/15/athletics-and-socioeconomic-status-ncaa-and-ivy-league-rules-complicate-recruitment/.

26. Niraj Chokshi, "Map: The States College Kids Can't Wait to Leave," *The Washington Post,* June 5, 2014, accessed December 26, 2015, https://www.washingtonpost.com/blogs/govbeat/wp/2014/06/05/map-the-states-college-kids-cant-wait-to-leave/.

Chapter 5

Getting In

Applying

Gregor Samsa went to bed an ordinary, traveling salesman and awoke the next day a giant, hideous insect. *The Metamorphosis* chronicles this absurdist tale of a young man who, out of nowhere, is left irrevocably stuck going through life as grotesque, oversized vermin. Surprisingly, things don't end well.

Unlike poor Gregor, at a certain point during their senior year of high school, your son or daughter will undergo a significant change that is, quite fortunately, far less creepy. Instead of shapeshifting into a human-size cockroach, they will go to bed one night a high school student and awake the next morning a full-blown *college applicant*. Yet, just like becoming a repulsive human-size bug, a major mindset adjustment will be necessary.

In reality, even the strongest student will encounter a perilous gauntlet of admissions-related choices that require strategic thinking and an understanding of the rules of a very different game. To help you and your child shift gears, we move from looking at how *high school students* can bolster their college prospects to how *college applicants* can best position themselves to win acceptance at the college of their dreams.

QUESTIONS TO CONSIDER BEFORE APPLYING EARLY DECISION

In the early 1990s, the University of Pennsylvania was struggling to keep up with their fellow Ivy League universities and found themselves frequently relegated to *backup plan* status among the nation's top students. Their institution's location in less-than-idyllic West Philadelphia and the "sounds like a state school" name contributed to their relative woes. In an effort to net more big fish, the University of Pennsylvania offered prospective students a bargain of Mephistophelean proportions—make a binding commitment to us months before the regular admissions cycle begins and we'll offer you significantly improved odds of acceptance. Those who fondly recalled hearing their grand-mothers utter the axiom "a bird in the hand is worth two in the bush" quickly shook hands on the deal.

Nonbinding forms of the early application process have been around since the 1950s, but as we neared the 2000s, hundreds of schools began to see the advantage of locking in members of their freshman class as early as possible. This was, however, not without controversy. By 2007, in response to cries that Early Decision (ED) put minority and low-income applicants at a disadvan-tage, schools like Princeton and Harvard did away with the practice. Yet, the number of ED applicants at other premier schools persisted and has continued to rise year after year. In the 2014–15 admissions cycle, Johns Hopkins saw an increase of 17%[1] from the prior year, while just about all of the Ivies saw an increase in the 15–16 cycle.[2]

This phenomenon does not only occur at the nation's most elite institutions like our examples above. Many less-selective institutions offering an ED plan continue to experience record volumes of fall applications. Because it has become so common to apply ED, we see more students select this option in a way that is uniformed and ultimately harmful to their college selection process. To help students avoid making a similar mistake, we cover the five questions they should be able to answer with 100% confidence before pulling the trigger on an ED app.

1. Have I Adequately Vetted My First-Choice School?

This is the first question anyone considering applying ED needs to ponder, and ponder hard. Have you visited the campus, taken a full tour, and had the chance to ask questions of current students as well as admissions reps? Have you done sufficient homework on other, comparable institutions to make sure you aren't missing out on any even better opportunities? Perhaps most impor-tantly, have you sat down with your parents and calculated the four years of tuition, fees, and living expenses at your ED school? Planning the financial end is absolutely critical for anyone, which leads us to our next question. . . .

2. "Are College Costs a Significant Concern?"

ED admission into a college precludes you from comparing financial aid offers. You will be receiving only one award, which may or may not be enough to sufficiently cover your college-related expenses. Most schools promise to give equal consideration to early admits for both need-based and merit aid, yet this is simply not in line with reality, especially with regard to merit aid.

Remember, institutions dangle merit aid to lure exceptional students, ones who might otherwise elect to attend a more prestigious school, to their flock. Your ED college has little incentive to award a generous merit aid package, given that they have already secured your commitment to attend. Even if they do offer some degree of aid, it may not be the number you expected. To be safe, if you anticipate needing substantial financial aid, think twice applying ED. Early Decision is a binding enterprise and backing out, even with financial justification, is not a pleasant road to travel down.

3. "How Likely Is It That My Desires Might Change During Senior Year?"

Senior year can be a time of significant growth and change. A commitment you make in the fall may seem far less appealing months later. An inspirational AP English teacher may steer you away from the engineering path you felt so strongly about in October. Perhaps you'll learn about a lesser-known college that sounds like it was built just for you. Conduct a serious self-assessment of your personality before submitting your ED application. Are you someone whose academic and career desires stay consistent over time or do your interests tend to change as you engage in new experiences? Will you genuinely enjoy attending college 2,500 miles from home or are you someone who ultimately likes to see the family on a regular basis?

Settling on a college is a huge decision in so many ways, and one that many students are not ready to make when their first day on campus is still 10 months away.

4. "Is My Application as Strong as It Can Be?"

Unlike colleges with (nonbinding) Early Action (EA) admission policies, schools employing ED typically accept or reject (rather than defer) the majority of applicants. Thus, if an ED school is top on your list, it's important that you *sell yourself* at the highest possible point. ED applicants sell themselves based on where they stand at the end of the all-important junior year (unless they opt for ED II—more on this in a moment). If you feel you've maxed out your SAT/ACT score, possess a GPA that is adequately high, and have no regrets about the rigor of your courses from 9th through 11th grade, then you may be an ideal ED candidate.

If you are more in the late-bloomer category (i.e., you thought 9th grade was still middle school and forgot to study . . . for an entire year), you may need senior year in order to maximize your potential and show colleges what you can really do. In that case, ED may not be the best choice.

5. "How Much Will Applying Early Decision Really Help My Chances at Admission?"

On the surface, a look at ED versus Regular Decision (RD) acceptance rates makes it appear as though applying ED is a *huge* advantage. Middlebury's 2014–15 ED admit rate was 33% compared to 15% overall. Dartmouth admitted 28% of ED applicants and just 10% of those who waited until January. All of the other Ivies admitted ED students at approximately 2 times the rate of everyone else.[3]

Applying ED does give applicants an edge at top schools; however, the stats above are misleading for several reasons. For one, students applying ED to elite schools tend to be more qualified, on average, than students in the RD pool. In addition, many selective colleges admit the bulk of their student-athletes through ED—these applicants have already been reviewed and selected ahead of time. ED is also a time when many legacy students are brought aboard as well as those with a special skill or skills (i.e., the juggling, fire-breathing cello virtuoso). Remove these applicants from the ED pool and advantages associated with applying early shrink greatly.

With all these considerations in mind, an applicant should think carefully before surrendering their free agency in exchange for an acceptance. Schools across the selectivity spectrum are not going to *reach* for a student well below their mean; it is students on the bubble who are most likely to receive a boost.

Ultimately, if a student has considered every variable and ED still sounds like a good idea, then they should go ahead and move forward with that *bird in the hand*. However, if they are feeling less than sure, take time to check out those bush-dwelling feathered friends—sweet, old cautious grandma may philosophically disapprove but, in the end, they'll be more likely to end up picking the best college for them.

EARLY DECISION II

An increasing number of highly selective institutions have initiated a second round of binding admission programs, giving students another chance to

Early Decision vs. Regular Decision

Institution	Early Decision (%)	Regular Decision (%)
Amherst College	35%	13%
Bates College	42%	23%
Boston University	42%	34%
Bowdoin College	28%	13%
Brown University	18%	8%
Carleton College	37%	21%
Carnegie Mellon University	33%	24%
Claremont McKenna College	27%	9%
Colby College	50%	26%
Colgate University	44%	24%
College of William and Mary	50%	27%
Columbia University	20%	6%
Cornell University	28%	12%
Dartmouth College	28%	10%
Duke University	26%	10%
Emory University	39%	25%
Grinnell College	52%	27%
Hamilton College	36%	25%
Harvey Mudd College	17%	14%
Haverford College	49%	23%
Johns Hopkins University	33%	9%
Macalester College	51%	36%
Middlebury College	33%	15%
New York University	34%	36%
Northwestern University	35%	11%
Pomona College	19%	11%
Rice University	20%	15%
Smith College	58%	41%
Swarthmore College	36%	15%
Tufts University	39%	15%
University of Pennsylvania	25%	8%
University of Richmond	39%	31%
University of Rochester	69%	36%
Vanderbilt University	23%	12%
Vassar College	43%	21%
Wake Forest College	48%	33%
Washington and Lee University	41%	17%

Source: The College Board

*Most recent year for which admissions data is made available

Figure 5.1   Admission Rates—2014–15: ED versus RD

commit to a college before acceptance while bypassing many of the potential drawbacks cited in our last section. Unlike traditional ED (I) programs, ED II allows students to wait until later in the admissions cycle to declare their allegiance to a particular school.

Why Do Colleges Offer Early Decision II?

Colleges offer an ED II option primarily as a means to improve their yield rates, which as mentioned previously, is an important indicator of desirability and one that can have significant influence on a college's ranking. Effectively, ED II offers institutions a second chance to grab guaranteed enrollees.

Why Would a Student Apply Early Decision II?

There are two reasons, in particular. First, a student may be denied at her first-choice college—to which she applied ED—but has a clear second favorite and wants to improve her odds of admission at that institution. Second, a student may apply ED II to take advantage of the flexibility that a later deadline offers. For example, ED II applicants have more time to improve their standardized test scores, solidify their college preferences, and assess their financial need. Students applying ED II also have an opportunity to submit strong grades earned during their senior year.

When Exactly Is Early Decision II?

Most application deadlines for ED II fall on January 1, at or around the same time as RD deadlines. ED II applicants usually receive a decision in mid-February.

Aside from Timing, What Other Differences Exist Between Early Decision I and Early Decision II?

There are *none*, really. Both offer potential advantages in the admissions process. However, both plans are also binding, meaning that you *must* attend if admitted.

THE CASE FOR APPLYING EARLY ACTION

For those not ready to commit to the binding contract of an ED application, EA and rolling admissions can offer many of the same benefits with a good deal more flexibility.

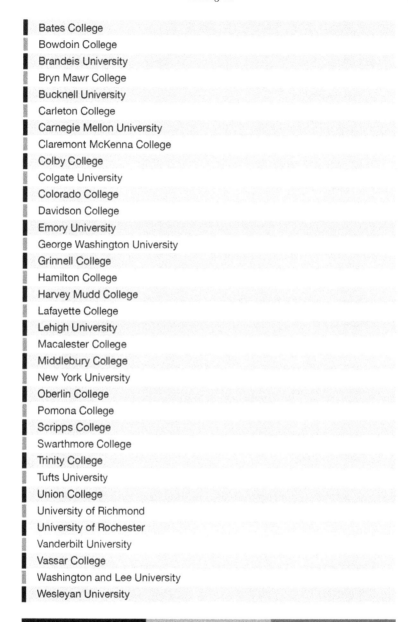

Bates College
Bowdoin College
Brandeis University
Bryn Mawr College
Bucknell University
Carleton College
Carnegie Mellon University
Claremont McKenna College
Colby College
Colgate University
Colorado College
Davidson College
Emory University
George Washington University
Grinnell College
Hamilton College
Harvey Mudd College
Lafayette College
Lehigh University
Macalester College
Middlebury College
New York University
Oberlin College
Pomona College
Scripps College
Swarthmore College
Trinity College
Tufts University
Union College
University of Richmond
University of Rochester
Vanderbilt University
Vassar College
Washington and Lee University
Wesleyan University

Figure 5.2   Colleges Offering ED II

Early Action vs. Regular Decision

Institution	Early Action (%)	Regular Decision (%)
Bentley University	57%	36%
Boston College	41%	32%
California Institute of Technology	19%	9%
Case Western Reserve University	45%	33%
Georgetown University	20%	16%
Georgia Institute of Technology	31%	35%
Harvard University	21%	3%
Massachusetts Institute of Technology	9%	7%
Princeton University	19%	5%
Sewanee: University of the South	77%	43%
Stanford University	11%	4%
Tulane University	37%	11%
University of Chicago	12%	7%
University of Miami	50%	29%
University of North Carolina–Chapel Hill	32%	17%
University of Notre Dame	36%	14%
University of Virginia	30%	30%
Villanova University	41%	60%
Yale University	16%	5%

Source: The College Board

*Most recent year for which admissions data is made available

Figure 5.3   Admission Rates—2014–15, EA versus RD

EA comes in two varieties: restrictive and nonrestrictive, and knowing which category your institutions of interest fall under is an essential first step. Colleges offering restrictive or *single choice* Early Action (REA) prohibit applicants from applying EA or ED to any other institution, unless that institution happens to be public. For example, students applying to Stanford REA may still apply EA to Georgia Institute of Technology and the University of Virginia, given that both institutions are publicly controlled. Nonrestrictive EA means that you are free to apply to as many schools as you like, just as during the normal cycle. Typically, students will receive a decision from EA schools in mid-December rather than having to wait until early April with their regular admission peers. Yet, the potential solace of enjoying Christmas break with an acceptance under their belt is only a secondary reason to go down this road.

One of the distinct advantages of applying EA is that a student's odds of admission may be increased. At some selective schools, the difference between EA and regular acceptance rates are substantial enough to suggest that EA applicants are given a slight edge. For example, Harvard accepts 21% of their EA applicants versus just 3% of the regular applicant pool. Other uber-selective schools such as Yale and Princeton also seem to grant significant favor to EA applicants.

If increased admissions odds aren't enough to entice your kid into considering EA, perhaps our financial argument will carry more weight. Quite simply, more merit aid money is stacked in schools' coffers in the fall than will remain by the time the regular April deadline rolls around. Therefore, scholarship offers can be more generous to EA applicants than those applying as part of the normal cycle. Further, unlike with ED, EA applicants have the advantage of being able to apply to any other school they please if the offer of aid is less than satisfactory. This, of course, means that schools have more of an incentive to make aggressive offers to desirable applicants.

Even high school seniors who need an additional semester to beef up their transcript and/or test scores are encouraged to at least consider applying EA, particularly if the school(s) to which they are applying defer, rather than reject, the majority of EA applicants. Students applying EA to these institutions may still reap the above-mentioned benefits while taking comfort in the fact that even if their credentials don't pass muster the first time around, they will be reevaluated again as part of the regular admission pool.

Ultimately, EA offers much of the benefit and none of the downside of more binding alternatives.

GOING TEST OPTIONAL

An iconic year, even by the standards of its iconic decade, 1969 teems with momentous events in America's cultural history: the moon landing, Woodstock, the Amazin' Mets, and the start of American withdrawal from Vietnam. That same year, events quieter, although within the narrower scope of college admissions history, of no less magnitude, unfolded in the small, coastal town of Brunswick, Maine. There, the newly minted, fresh-faced Dean of Bowdoin College, Roger Howell Jr., all of 33 years old, made a bold decision—he would eliminate the SAT as an admissions requirement for his school.

Howell explained in his inaugural address that he preferred that Bowdoin focus on the *human quality of its students* in the admissions process. It was a concept that very much fit the spirit of the times. Yet unlike other 1969 debuts such as *Sesame Street*, the ATM, and the Abbey Road album, test-optional admissions was not a trend that swept the nation like wildfire. In fact, the second domino's much-delayed drop took place in 1984 when Bowdoin's fellow-Mainer, Bates College, jettisoned its standardized test requirements. After Bates, things fell quiet for decades until all of a sudden in the mid-2000s when anti-SAT sentiment reawakened and quickly reached a fever pitch.

Given its humble beginnings, it is fairly astounding that there are now 850 test-optional schools in the United States, including highly selective liberal arts institutions such as Wesleyan, Bryn Mawr, Smith, Dickinson, and Pitzer. There are also many elite schools that have become *test flexible* such as Middlebury, Colby, and Hamilton. Understanding the implications of these policies on your admissions and financial aid prospects is important.

Why Colleges Go Test Optional

Institutions eliminating or de-emphasizing standardized tests often cite a lack of confidence in the SAT's and ACT's ability to predict college success and/or a desire to improve campus diversity. However, studies have shown that test-optional polices may not be increasing the enrollment of underrepresented students.[4]

Pure-intentioned or not, test-optional schools gain the benefit of not having to claim the SATs of their presumably lower-scoring students. Applicants who do not submit scores typically have scores that are significantly lower than those who elected to include scores in their application. Therefore, test-optional schools can boast artificially higher-average SATs for admitted students, which makes them appear more selective.[5]

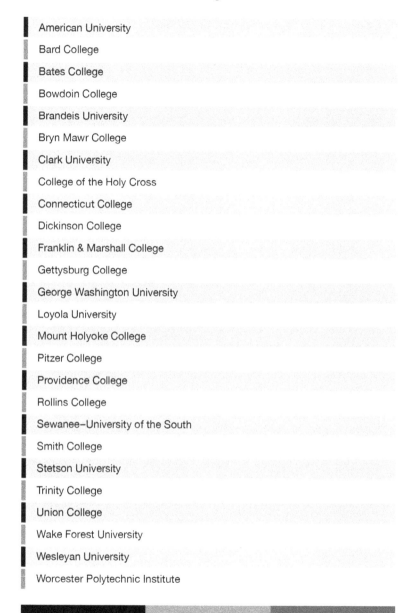

American University

Bard College

Bates College

Bowdoin College

Brandeis University

Bryn Mawr College

Clark University

College of the Holy Cross

Connecticut College

Dickinson College

Franklin & Marshall College

Gettysburg College

George Washington University

Loyola University

Mount Holyoke College

Pitzer College

Providence College

Rollins College

Sewanee–University of the South

Smith College

Stetson University

Trinity College

Union College

Wake Forest University

Wesleyan University

Worcester Polytechnic Institute

Figure 5.4   The Most Selective Test-Optional Colleges

Don't Confuse Test Optional and Test Flexible

There are a number of selective colleges, including Hamilton, Colby, and NYU that do not require the SAT or ACT, but still require applicants to submit results from one or more other exams, such as AP or IB exams and SAT Subject Tests. Before developing an admissions strategy, make sure that you are familiar with the exact testing requirements at each prospective college and that you learn whether the submission of test scores is truly optional. These policies are ever-evolving so it is important to stay on top of the most current policy information. For example, Bryn Mawr became test flexible in 2009 but switched to full-blown test optional in 2014.

There are also institutional variations of test-optional policies. Lewis & Clark requires test-optional applicants to submit a portfolio containing, among other things, an analytical writing sample as well as an example of quantitative or scientific work. The University of Mary Washington only allows standardized tests to be excluded from one's application if that individual has a high school GPA of 3.5.

Should You Go Test Optional?

It's not enough to simply compare standardized test scores against those of the average incoming student. Students should also take a serious look at other components of their application. Determine whether their grades, essays, and/or extracurricular record can truly distinguish them as an applicant and compel their prospective colleges to vote *yes*. These application materials will be even more heavily scrutinized now that their admissions officers are without an essential piece of information, which although biased, can still provide for meaningful comparisons between them and the rest of the applicant pool.

Impact on Merit Aid

Some test-optional colleges still award merit aid on the basis of standardized test scores, at least in part. If an applicant is needy and/or cost conscious, make sure they understand the financial implications of withholding your test scores. For example, Dickinson, Gettysburg, and Goucher are three selective test-optional schools that still require test scores for merit-based scholarships. We advise you to contact the admissions offices at each prospective test-optional college to determine whether merit aid is tied to standardized test performance, and if so, to what extent.

Bottom Line

If a young person, for one reason or another, cannot achieve SAT/ACT scores that are commensurate with their ability as a student, then exploring the test-optional route makes good sense. However, unless you possess a blank check to cover their four years of study, due diligence on each test-optional/flexible school to which they apply is essential.

WHAT ESSAY TOPICS SHOULD I AVOID?

We would never unequivocally tell an applicant that any proposed college essay topic is off limits. Great writers can take the most mundane, banal, and generic subject matter and transform it into a captivating composition. However, in our experience reading thousands of college essays, we are able to say with confidence that students are wise to steer clear of the following five topics—lest they fall victim to some all-too-common pitfalls.

Drugs, Sex, and, Well, Just Those Two . . .

While students are not auditioning to become an altar boy/girl, there are certain risqué topics that are unlikely to be viewed in a positive light by an admissions committee. On occasion, we've seen students aim for shock value by incorporating stories of sexual encounters or drug use into their essays—99% of the time this is an awful idea.

There are of course tactful ways to address these subjects if they are central to revealing who the student is. One could easily talk about their sexual identity without writing an abridged version of *Fifty Shades of Grey*. Likewise, if a story arc of addiction and recovery is an essential part of a student's past, it may be a worthy topic to tackle. However, drugs or alcohol should never be casually discussed. It sounds like obvious enough advice, but you'd be surprised . . .

Travel Experiences

This is a common go-to topic for many students. If done well, recounting a trip to a foreign country, whether for leisure or volunteer work, will reveal something deeply personal and meaningful about you. Unfortunately, this is rarely executed well.

Too often, students, even fantastic young writers, waste precious application real estate on fanciful descriptions of Peruvian landscapes or generic observations about impoverished denizens of a Central American village. If your son writes about a trip to Haiti and chronicles the culture of the Haitian people, then the essay is not really about him—it might as well be a homework assignment for a World Cultures elective.

An admissions officer is not going to emerge from reading an essay like this thinking, "What a worldly chap!" In reality, they are likely to feel like they just read a page from the J. Peterman catalogue of *Seinfeld* fame.

Remember, students should talk about something that happened to *them*, where *they* are at the heart of the action. Colleges want to know who they are and how they view the world—the essay may be their only chance to provide a college with this type of insight and the travelogue is rarely an effective vehicle.

Grandiosity

Many applicants are naturally inclined toward over dramatization, hyperbole, and enhanced self-importance in their essays. This is natural for two reasons: (1) even students with perfect SATs still have a teenage brain and (2) they wrongfully assume that this is required to impress admissions officers.

Writing an essay that is compelling doesn't mean that they need to have wrestled a puma, grown up in a cult, or discovered a new galaxy at age 7. A great college essay can take place on a grand stage, but it can just as effectively take place in everyday life. There is a ready supply of dramatic tension and conflict in the course of a typical day.

Parents can help their children in the brainstorming and editing stages by providing them with an adult sensibility and a mature, grounded perspective. Many overinvolved parents believe that they are helping their child's essay by rewriting it in the style and tone of the *New York Times*. This is a mistake. Admissions officers do not want to read Nicholas Kristof's version of the high school experience—they want it in a student's real teenage voice. Yet, parents can help and be of great assistance by reminding their child to tone down their all-too-eager-to-impress natures. For example, a change in school lunch menu policy instituted by a student council president should not be compared to the New Deal. A photographic expose` in the school newspaper highlighting the poor condition of the football team's locker rooms should not lead to comparisons to Jacob Riis. A discovery in robotics club should not . . . well, you get the idea.

Sports Glory

(In a John Facenda voice) . . . "On a crisp and dreary autumn day, a JV football field was the setting of a clash of titans, middleweight monsters of the gridiron, and there I stood, ready to perform the most challenging of the athletic arts, that fickle mistress known as . . . punting."

Ask any admissions officer how many compelling sports-themed essays they've read in their entire careers. The answer will likely be somewhere between zero and one. Not even the spawn of Grantland Rice himself or herself could breathe life into this black hole of a topic.

The caveat here is that an essay can, of course, involve athletics as the backdrop to something deeper and more personal. Competition and training undoubtedly provide ample opportunity to show more about an applicant's character, ability, sportsmanship, reaction to adversity, and ability to contribute to a larger cause. Just make sure something more revealing is being communicated than the fact that they once netted a hat trick against a rival or drained a last second three-pointer despite a sprained ankle. If they're that great at a given sport, chances are a coach has already recruited them.

The Stream-of-Consciousness Essay

Okay, so this isn't exactly a topic, per se, but more of an ill-fated genre that we've seen attempted before. Applicants will throw formality to the wind and spew out a string of stream-of-consciousness thoughts. "If it worked for James Joyce, why not me?" Unfortunately, such works typically read more like a crazy email written by a jilted lover at 3 am than *A Portrait of the Artist as a Young Man.*

Writing in an authentic voice does not mean scribbling down some stream-of-consciousness thoughts 24 hours before the application deadline. There is a popular myth that Abraham Lincoln jotted down the Gettysburg Address on a napkin on his way to the battlefield. In truth, he spent over two weeks crafting the speech and went through five full drafts. All of that labor for a 272-word document about half the length of a college essay! The more time that a student dedicates to their essay, the better the product will be.

Final Thoughts

Again, all of the above topics could be done in a masterful way and end up a beautiful essay, but based on our experience the probability of this occurring is less than strong. The basic rules for writing a stellar college essay vary little from the general guidelines for producing any strong piece of written work: be authentic, tell a story that is personal and compelling, and diligently edit, revise, and polish your product. If students follow all of these steps, they will naturally steer clear of the stumbling blocks and hazards chronicled above.

HOW SHOULD I APPROACH THE *WHY US?* ESSAY?

Many colleges and universities require students to compose an essay on why they wish to attend their school. While it is a relatively generic and rather dull question, students should not be lulled into delivering an equally generic and dull answer. They should refrain from offering superlatives without specific evidence to back up their praise. Imagine an admissions officer, at the end of a long day's work, getting ready to digest his or her 37th "Why this college?" answer of the day. Picking up the next essay, the officer learns that this student wants to attend their school because it is *great* and *has a stellar reputation*—common descriptors that could be applied to any institution. Yawns ensue. After being reminded for the 37th time in a day of their school's *U.S. News and World Report* ranking, they take another sip of espresso and move on to the next file. At best, that student's essay plays little to no role in the eventual admissions decision.

On the other hand, a student could say that University X is *great* because Professor Anderson's research on the human genome inspired them to study biology, and they are impressed by the *stellar reputation* of their one-of-a-kind undergraduate research initiatives. The student goes on to lavish praise on the school's state-of-the-art laboratories that were completely revamped in 2012, with further renovations scheduled for 2016. In expressing their individual passion for biology, they paint a picture of how attending University X would tie in to their academic and career aims . . . Now, that student has earned the admissions officer's attention.

Remember, admissions officers want to see that a student has done their homework on their institution and has demonstrated serious interest in actually attending their school. They also want to get to know the student further through their essays in a way that cannot be communicated by transcripts and standardized test scores. Students should not just go through the motions when explaining why they want to attend a school. They should make sure their essay is personalized, passionate, and specifically tailored to each school to which they apply. If they can't accomplish this in a sincere way, they might want to rethink why a given school is even on their application list in the first place.

ARE *OPTIONAL* STATEMENTS REALLY OPTIONAL?

Too many students fail to complete optional parts of an application, and severely hinder their admissions prospects in the process. Optional statements demonstrate interest and provide an additional opportunity to showcase attributes that cannot be captured via a grade or test score. On the other hand, not completing the optional essays can sink their application to an elite school faster than the infamous "Ninja Rap" sunk Vanilla Ice's rapping career.

Many students hatch what they believe to be a plan for the perfect crime—write a generic enough essay that can be used for every school to which they apply, one that broadly addresses most prompts but directly answers none. Trust us, admissions officers can spot these attempts at playing application Mad Libs in their sleep.

> My involvement with the student newspaper has fueled my desire to attend _____ University/College, so that I can take advantage of excellent offerings in the Department of _____. The academic rigor at your institution is unparalleled and I would be proud to call myself a [*mascot name here*] for life.

Going this route, students might as well just fill in the blanks with *snot* and *butt* like they did with their Mad Libs back in 5th-grade. It might at least elicit a smile from an admissions officer.

What to Do

Students—reference specific academic programs at each prospective college, talk about the details of your college tour, and highlight a conversation you had with one (or two) of the school's current students. Check out the school's webpage, social media, and any recent news stories about exciting developments around campus. Anything you can do to demonstrate knowledge of each prospective school and genuine interest will help your admissions cause.

Not Always "Why This College?"

The "Why this college?" prompt is just one of a multitude of optional essay variations inhabiting the oft-overlooked bowels (another good 5th-grade Mad Libs word) of the college application.

As an alternative, Duke offers students a chance to address the following:

Duke University seeks a talented, engaged student body that embodies the wide range of human experience; we believe that the diversity of our students makes our community stronger. If you'd like to share a perspective you bring or experiences you've had to help us understand you better—perhaps related to a community you belong to, your sexual orientation or gender identity, or your family or cultural background—we encourage you to do so. Real people are reading your application, and we want to do our best to understand and appreciate the real people applying to Duke.[6]

If a student is gay/bisexual, has a non-Caucasian ethnic background, or grew up on a hippie commune, they'll likely be able to address this question in a compelling manner without too much consternation. Yet, if they resemble one the first 43 presidents of the United States (white, male, and financially comfortable), they'll have to get a bit more creative. Unless, of course, they look like Martin Van Buren, our eighth and most mangy president, in which case they'll need all 250 words just to explain their overgrown sideburns.

The University of Pittsburgh offers a full-blown smorgasbord of optional essay topics, nine in total, from describing an influential person in your life to sharing a talent that was otherwise not noted on your application. There is literally a topic for every conceivable applicant and while not explicitly stated, it is fully expected that students will avail themselves of the opportunity.

Bottom Line

For serious applicants, completing optional essays are about as optional as brushing your teeth. Likewise, leaving optional fields blank on college applications, especially at competitive institutions, will undoubtedly decay a student's prospects of winning the admissions game.

As the immortal poet John Keats once said:

Kickin' it up, hour after hour,
Cause in this life there's only one winner,
You better aim straight so you can hit the center.

Actually that was Vanilla Ice along with a bunch of mutant amphibians, but you get the point.

NAILING THE ALUMNI INTERVIEW

Walk into any Starbucks, Barnes and Noble, or public library around the holiday season and at least a few tables will be occupied by teen/middle-aged dyads, with the older member asking things like, "Why our college?"

or "What's your favorite activity?" Alumni interviews are *not* an overwhelmingly important part of the college application process, but they do count and a successful meeting can provide a slight boost to a student's admissions prospects.

Prep and Practice

Students should develop intimate knowledge about their prospective school well in advance of the interview—frantically checking their phone for university factoids at stoplights while driving to their interview won't cut it. Their knowledge of the institution needs to be deeply engrained so that they're able to talk naturally and substantively about it.

Alumni interviewers like it when they learn something new about their alma mater from an interviewee. Students should want to be the guy/gal who tells their Stanford alumni rep that their engineering department is so cutting edge that they recently developed gecko-like gloves that allow people to climb glass walls like superheroes (true story). They should be the guy/gal who explains to their Kenyon College interviewer that they were impressed that out of 42 college and universities in Ohio, Kenyon grads finish with the second-lowest debt sum.

Equally important is that your child develops an intimate familiarity with their own resume. They should be prepared to discuss their courses, activities, interests, and objectives going forward, as questions asked are likely to focus on the areas in Figure 5.5.

Students should reflect on Figure 5.5 and other similar questions beforehand. Avoid going into an interview cold. Students can ask their counselor to conduct a mock interview and provide feedback, if possible. They'll likely gain a helpful pointer or two and feel less nervous on interview day.

Remember the Little Things

Typically, the alumni interviewer will contact an applicant to suggest a time to chat. Unless they are scheduled for pancreas surgery or are testifying before congress (or something less random but equally important), students should accept whatever date and time they are offered. It's important to acknowledge that this adult's time is valuable; hence, a teenager saying that he or she can't meet after school on Tuesday because they have a Halo 5 tournament at their buddy's house is not recommended.

A few tips for students: Shake hands with your interviewer. Say *please* and *thank you*. Offer a *bless you* if he or she sneezes. Send a follow-up note or

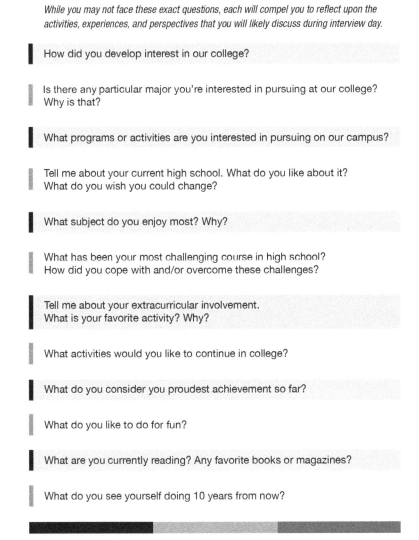

While you may not face these exact questions, each will compel you to reflect upon the activities, experiences, and perspectives that you will likely discuss during interview day.

How did you develop interest in our college?

Is there any particular major you're interested in pursuing at our college? Why is that?

What programs or activities are you interested in pursuing on our campus?

Tell me about your current high school. What do you like about it? What do you wish you could change?

What subject do you enjoy most? Why?

What has been your most challenging course in high school? How did you cope with and/or overcome these challenges?

Tell me about your extracurricular involvement. What is your favorite activity? Why?

What activities would you like to continue in college?

What do you consider you proudest achievement so far?

What do you like to do for fun?

What are you currently reading? Any favorite books or magazines?

What do you see yourself doing 10 years from now?

Figure 5.5   Common Alumni Interview Questions

email expressing your appreciation. As is true in all of life's arenas, a little politeness and courtesy can go a long way.

Show Enthusiasm

Right before the student is a real-life human being who spent four years at one of their prospective colleges. Hopefully, they will be naturally bursting with questions. Ask an alum about their experiences and how their college has contributed to the person he or she is today. Inquire about the college's alumni networks and/or solicit advice regarding what a first-time college student might do to ensure a successful college transition. At the same time, acknowledge that the interviewer may be far removed from his or her college experience. Avoid questions about class size, course offerings, and specific professors.

Whether or not a given college places significant weight on the assessment of their alumni interviewers (some schools do more than others), the process of chatting with a knowledgeable individual should be a positive and enlightening experience. Your son or daughter should be their most polite, inquisitive, and knowledgeable self and the interview will take care of itself.

THE MOST COMMON APPLICATION MISTAKES

1. Typos

Let's start with the most obvious mistake—the dreaded typo. In life, they happen. Autocorrected texts can turn your *dear friend* into your *dead friend* and bad grammar can mean the difference between "knowing your crap" and "knowing *you're* crap." Students should always reread their application, then reread it again, then ask everyone they know to read it. Because when it comes to grammar or dandruff in a 1980s perm, you never get a second chance to make a first impression.

2. Be Professional

That partystud1@hotmail.com account has served your son well ever since 6th grade. While others in his social group traded in their hotmail accounts for gmail eons ago, he's held steady. He's not partystud 2, 34, or 79—he's partystud1. We fully encourage students to keep their goofy/offensive/nonsensical email accounts and use them without shame . . . except when they are emailing prospective colleges.

Explain to your son that his safest bet is to open a new account that is as close to his legal name as possible: FirstName.LastName@whatever. com. If his name is Mike Jones you might have to add a 6 digit number after your name but that's okay. And tell your son not to worry, partystud1 may have to lie dormant for a few months, but he'll entertain himself—he's partystud1!

3. Beating a Dead Horse

Of course, we're using a cliché here and not referring to actual postmortem equine abuse (tip: that wouldn't look good on an app either). Admissions officers do not like to read the same thing over and over. In other words, don't weave the same tale of overcoming adversity through field hockey into every essay topic.

Real estate on an application is as valuable as Park Place. Don't treat it like Baltic or Mediterranean Avenue (even if hotels are cheaper to build and it's all part of your grand plan to be a Monopoly slumlord). Students should use every open space on an application to reveal something new and important about who they are. That's what it's there for.

4. The Never-Ending Activity Page

"Oh, you organized a potato sack race at your family reunion when you were ten? Welcome to Stanford, young man!"

Perhaps this absurd, never-gonna-happen scenario is the fantasy driving applicants who submit activity pages and resumes longer than that of the average head of state. Keep resume/activity lists *short but sweet* (less than one page, if possible). Colleges know that no matter how accomplished your 18-year-old may be, they're still a teenager. The great majority of resume-worthy achievements lie ahead.

5. Keep Mom and Dad on a Leash

Speak to any group of college admissions officials and tales of overly involved parents abound and make no mistake, excessive parental intervention can harm a student's admissions chances. Emails and phone calls to the admissions office should come exclusively from students, who are the applicant—not their parents. An application should not show any traces of mom's or dad's handwriting or middle-aged writing styles.

LOWER THE RED FLAG: HOW TO AVOID INCONSISTENCIES IN YOUR COLLEGE APPLICATION

In the adult world, it is fairly common, almost expected, for one's resume to exaggerate their past achievements. A babysitting gig can easily become experience *managing an energetic group of young associates* and an office filing job demonstrated your ability to *promote synergy and vertical integration for data-management systems.* These examples are not lies in the sense that they are not conjured from thin air, but are rather comically souped-up versions of the truth.

Compare that to famous examples of adults who have achieved notoriety for flat-out fabrications. Frank Abagnale of *Catch Me If You Can* fame managed to work in high-profile professions such as physician, lawyer, and airline pilot without possessing a single credential. MIT's dean of admissions, Marilee Jones, was exposed in 2007 of not actually having earned any of the three degrees she claimed on her resume. Amazingly, she had been at MIT for 28 years and had even been bestowed an award as their best administrator.

In the college admissions realm, you'd be surprised how often students, in an effort to make themselves stand out, go a little too far in exaggerating their accomplishments and end up putting forth contradictory or incompatible information. For example, if a student's resume claims that they had a lead role in *The Glass Menagerie* but their drama instructor's recommendation lauds them for their admirable work as a stagehand, suspicions will inevitably arise. This is one of many ways applicants can stretch the truth and risk setting off an admissions official's BS-alarm.

Write the Essays Yourself

One of the bigger hot spots for eyebrow-raising contradictions comes on the essay section. A student with a low writing score on the ACT whose admissions essay is composed with Hawthorne-level prose will raise more red flags than a Kyrgyzstani color guard (their flags are red—Google it!).

Regardless of a student's literary bona fides, admissions officers expect their essay to be written in a 17- or 18-year-old voice, not a 40-year-old voice, unless of course they are a middle-aged applicant, in which case writing in a teenage voice would be quite strange. Leave the *quarter* words resting in the pages of SAT study guides and stick with language of the small change variety. We're not saying students should dumb anything down, but if an admissions officer comes across an essay littered with words like *lugubrious* or *perfidy*, they are going to assume that a student's essay was written by either a paid essay coach or the ghost of a nineteenth-century crime reporter.

Of course, students should get feedback and editing assistance from adults throughout the essay-writing process. Just make sure that as they incorporate advice on grammar, flow, sentence structure, and so on, they do not accidentally incorporate someone else's voice as well.

Be Honest about Your Extracurricular Involvement

Students should not exaggerate their level of volunteer work, or extracurricular experience or the number of weekly hours that they spent engaged in such activities. The notion that they somehow volunteered at a nursing home 20 hours per week, while playing three varsity sports, holding down a job, and editing the school newspaper can be invalidated through basic math.

There is no reason to be less than 100% honest about what a student did in their spare time during high school. Some folks, short on activities, panic at the sight of so much blank space on their extracurriculars section that they resort to grossly embellishing or completely inventing clubs, sports, jobs, and the like. This phenomenon is seen way too often in admissions offices around the country—the applicant from the Great Plains region who founded a spelunking club, the do-gooder who alleges to have volunteered more hours than that exist in a week, and the teen who claims to fluently speak three languages but seems to have trouble remembering any of them during an admissions interview.

Your Interests Should Match Your Past Pursuits

This last topic is not an issue of dishonesty but rather sheer incongruity. Some candidates try to claim academic and career interests that are not at all supported by the rest of their application. If you claim to be passionate about political science and yet passed up the chance to take AP Comparative Government & Politics senior year in favor of a massive block of study halls, you have some 'splaining to do. This is not to say that the above scenario cannot represent a sincere and compelling true story. Maybe a student had no interest in history until they watched the film *Lincoln* this past October, which then led them to clear out the history/politics section at Barnes and Noble, igniting a passion that fueled their search for the nation's top poli-sci programs, and forever changed their life course. No problem. Just be sure to chronicle that unique journey in the application.

Falsifying any part of the application will likely cause an applicant more harm than a mere blemish or two. Believe it or not, an admissions officer does not want to see a supernaturally well-rounded applicant who claims to have filled every waking moment with some type of extracurricular activity and even volunteered for a sleep study at a research institute just to cover those embarrassingly lazy non-waking moments. Colleges want to see a real human being capable of communicating their passions and actual life experience. Be genuine. In the world of college admissions, an honest stagehand is always a more marketable applicant than a fraudulent lead player.

ABOUT THAT *D* IN FRESHMAN ENGLISH

If a student's high school career has been an uninterrupted parade of top-notch grades, near-perfect standardized test scores, and saintly behavior, then those folks can stop reading . . . Except they probably won't since perfectionists like to finish every single thing they start, right?

Academic blemishes come in all shapes and sizes, from bombing sophomore year entirely to a lone C minus breaking a string of trips to the honor roll. On the nonacademic front, perhaps a student was disciplined for a fight, had a series of unexcused absences, or was caught plagiarizing an essay (did you really think your overuse of the word *moribund* wouldn't set off red flags?).

No matter the severity of the stain, our advice for beginning the cleansing process is the same—deal with it head on.

Students can use the essays, short response questions, or *Additional Information* section as a chance to explain the story behind that semester or grade that is not like the others. Maybe they found out they had a learning disability or ADHD. Maybe their parents were getting separated. Or maybe the reason is unspectacular but gives insight into them as a human being—a bout of depression, a philosophical crisis, or full-blown ennui.

Students should solicit recommendations from those who are familiar with their flawed past and can speak to their growth process. Colleges expect that in their rigorous and challenging environment they will experience a setback or two over the course of four years. How students responded to adversity in their life may impress an admissions officer every bit as much as if they had sailed through high school under storm-free blue skies. After all, research is showing that *grit* may be a better predictor of success in college than raw ability.[7]

We always tell clients that we all are men, in our own natures frail, and capable. Of our flesh; few are angels. Okay, we admit it—that was Shakespeare. Like we said, nobody's perfect.

DISCIPLINARY VIOLATIONS: TO REPORT OR NOT REPORT

Early 1990s television is littered with examples of teens who gained acceptance to their dream school in spite of a laundry list of high school transgressions. In an effort to eclipse her Uncle Jesse's legendary senior prank of decades past, *Full House's* D.J. Tanner somehow rents an industrial-size crane which she and her classmates use to lift the principal's convertible onto the roof of the school. Later that evening, as rain starts to pour down, D.J. panics that the car's leather interior will be ruined and recruits Uncle Jesse to hot-wire the vehicle so they can put its top up. Unfortunately for D.J., a cop catches them in the act. Several convoluted plot twists later, everything is resolved and this foray into auto theft does not stop D.J. from getting into Berkeley.

Saved by the Bell's Zack Morris must have been the master of handling his high school misdeeds through his college admissions process. Despite kidnapping Valley's mascot, making fake IDs, driving drunk, surreptitiously photographing scantily clad teenagers for his Girls of Bayside calendar and, of course, routinely torturing the hapless Mr. Belding, Zack still gets into fictional California University.

The point of this journey down sitcom memory lane is that one's college prospects are not necessarily doomed by doing something stupid in high school. Of course, since filling out a disclosure statement on a college application, while a titillating subject for television, was never the subject of an episode of *Full House* or *Saved by the Bell*, the question remains — how did D.J. and Zack successfully address these misdeeds on their college applications?

By the Numbers

Let's start by qualifying what types of disciplinary blemishes are most common. The vast majority of infractions in high school are for relatively minor infractions: cutting a class, cell phone use during school, disrespecting a teacher, or an excessive public display of affection. To quantify this, the *New York Times* reported that at the University of South Carolina, 7% of applicants self-reported an infraction during high school. Of those students, 87% were of the *typical kid* nature as listed above, 13% involved more serious offenses such as cheating, fighting, or misdemeanor criminal acts like theft.[8]

The number of applicants reporting more serious criminal activity such as vehicular homicide or armed robbery were in the single digits. We're going to assume that your issues do not involve ski masks, demands for unmarked bills, or getaway cars and are more garden variety high school mistakes.

Don't High Schools Automatically Report That Stuff Anyway?

Given the stakes are so high, one would assume that some governing body would have laid out clear and explicit rules for how and when high schools disclose discipline records to prospective colleges. Sadly, this is not the case. Roughly 40% of high schools always send along discipline records to institutions of higher education, another 25% sometimes disclose such infractions.[9]

Whether or not the fight a student got into as a 15-year-old accompanies their otherwise unblemished transcript comes down to luck. Ultimately, unless they are at one of those rare schools where counselors are mandated to report every misdemeanor down to chewing gum, a guidance counselor will likely have the decision-making power whether or not to disclose the incident.

How College Admissions Offices Use This Information (or Don't)

According to a recent study, over three-quarters of colleges and universities in the United States request discipline data on applicants, and out of those schools, almost 90% weigh this factor in making admissions decisions.[10] Unfortunately, only a small percentage of colleges actually have a clear written policy on how disciplinary matters are to be factored into admissions decisions, thus, as with the high school counselor situation, those who voluntarily disclose are subject to the whims of the given official reviewing their application.

Our Advice

College admissions officers universally advise that students be completely forthright about any missteps in their past. People make mistakes, and 99% of admissions officers are not going to judge students solely on their worst moment, especially if that moment is not so severe that they would worry about the safety of others on campus. Students should use the disciplinary disclosure area on the application to thoroughly explain the circumstances around their disciplinary/legal issue. They should talk about how they learned from the incident and experienced growth and maturation as a result. If they are sincere and thoughtful, there is a great chance that checking *yes* on the disclosure form will not hurt their admissions chances whatsoever.

Far worse than self-disclosing an incident and having the chance to explain it is when an admissions officer finds out about the incident through other means—then the applicant just looks plain dishonest. For example, if an admissions professional is told about the incident off the record by a counselor or finds out about the incident through a Google search (the student got caught drinking on their 18th birthday and graced the local paper's police blotter), his or her admissions chances are likely shot.

For Those Who Do Not Like Our Advice

Given how arbitrary this system is at both the high school and college levels, it's understandable that an otherwise honest applicant might not be thrilled to follow our "honesty is the best policy" advice. We get it and there are circumstances in which a student may choose not to disclose—but they have to be smart about it. Let's say that back in 9th grade your daughter's essay on *Romeo and Juliet* was identified as being partially plagiarized when her teacher ran it through turnitin.com. In reality, she didn't mean to take another's work, but she improperly cited some source material in one paragraph. Labeling her as a *cheater* at age 18 for a genuine mistake made at 15 doesn't sit right with you. You worry that even with this explanation, she might lose a spot at a highly selective school to an applicant with similar credentials and no alarmingly lengthy disclosure statement.

Here's what she should do: talk openly and honestly with her counselor. She can tell them how she feels and ask two questions: (1) Will this incident be automatically reported as part of my school records? (2) Do you feel it is necessary to report this incident on my application? If the answer to both of these questions is a clear-cut *no*, then feel free to move forward without fear and let the past be just that.

"Did I Do That?"

The lessons of 1990s television on the subject of high school behavioral incidents do not end with D.J. Tanner and Zack Morris. Perhaps the most encouraging case is that of Steve Urkel who was still able to get into MIT regardless of causing property damage just about everywhere he went and essentially stalking (by almost any legal definition) Laura Winslow for nearly a decade. While the details of his disclosure statement are unknown, we suspect, that Urkel may have simply laid all of the blame on his smooth-talking alter ego, Stefan Urquelle.

Unless a student, like Urkel, invented a DNA serum named *cool juice* at some point in their high school career and has a legitimate doppelganger-related excuse, we recommend either (a) being completely honest with potential institutions and providing a thoughtful explanation that demonstrates personal growth or (b) being completely honest with your guidance counselor and formulating a plan that best fits the unique circumstances.

NAVIGATING THE ADMISSIONS PROCESS WITH A LEARNING DISABILITY

The college admissions process can be stressful enough for the average family. However, college-related anxieties are often compounded when learning needs are present. In our experience, we have found that the two most frequent sources of consternation revolve around the disclosure of a learning disability and the procurement of learning accommodations. The following information should help assuage fears on both fronts.

Disclosure

It is important to know that admissions and disability offices are not allowed to discuss prospective students, so revealing a student's learning issues to a disability office, in particular, will not impact their admission prospects. That said, the consequences of alerting an admissions office to their disability will vary across colleges. Some uber-selective institutions are not particularly accommodating to LD students. However, negative consequences should ultimately prove irrelevant because any college assigning admission penalties to LD students would not present a good fit anyway.

At other institutions, disclosing a learning disability can actually bring advantages. For example, a learning disability may explain a relatively low grade or test score or provide applicants an opportunity to showcase their hard work and/or to discuss how they overcame learning-related challenges. In these cases, LD students can increase their odds of admission.

More often than not, we advise students to disclose their learning disabilities if they feel compelled to do so and to discuss within their application how their experiences as an LD student have made them more adaptable, more resilient, and more capable of adding diversity to a particular college.

Accommodations for Testing

Public school students identified with a disability or medical condition that impacts learning are supported throughout their K-12 experience via one of two legal documents: an Individualized Education Program (IEP) or a less-comprehensive 504 Service Agreement. Extended time on school-based assessments is a relatively commonplace accommodation for students with learning disabilities, traumatic brain injury, emotional needs, or ADHD. However, it is under the purview of the companies who run the SAT and ACT to decide if these school-based accommodations are truly necessary for their exams.

The Application Process

On both the SAT and ACT, students with special needs can apply for 50% extended time or even 100% extended time in extreme cases. The application is made through the high school's guidance department, which is responsible for providing documentation that demonstrates the need for extra time. A counselor will fill out a form giving a condensed account of the child's history. When were they identified with a disability? How long has extended time been provided through their IEP or 504? Has there been a recent reevaluation by a school psychologist to confirm the continued need for extended time?

The vast majority of initial applications are approved, with the College Board giving the thumbs-up to roughly 92% of those who apply and the ACT with a slightly more stringent 85%.[11] Those numbers ultimately end up even more favorable, as many of those initially denied resubmit with additional documentation and eventually triumph.

Both testing companies will most heavily scrutinize instances where a student was not identified with a disability until high school or when the provision of extended time was added at the 11th hour to an existing IEP or 504. Each is aware that having an extra 90 minutes or more can constitute a significant advantage, and want to make sure that savvy students and their families aren't trying to game the system.

If You Are Approved

Get ready for a long day of testing. In the case of 50% extended time, students will be enduring 5 full hours of analogies, exponents, and meticulous bubbling with a number-two pencil. Students in the extended time room who finish early must nevertheless stay for the duration of the testing block. This, however, is but a small price to pay for those who genuinely need the extra time.

Accommodations for College

Students with significant learning disabilities *must* consider learning support services as one of the most important factors in their college search. There are many colleges and universities that offer minimal to almost no assistance. On the other end of the spectrum, there are schools that will allow students to take exams orally, grant extended time, and provide free tutoring. Some institutions even offer structured programs specifically tailored for students with disabilities.

Securing Support

During the K-12 experience, students with disabilities are guaranteed appropriate accommodations through IDEA, a federal law. IDEA does not apply to postsecondary schools, therefore the only mandate that schools are required to follow comes from the Americans with Disabilities Act, legislation that lacks teeth in the educational arena compared with IDEA.

Accommodations are granted on a case-by-case basis and are almost entirely at the discretion of the college's Office of Disability Services. To improve a student's case, it is essential that disability documentation be current and conclusive—a specific diagnosis should be provided and recommended accommodations should be clear.

Before You Apply

Consider the student's unique circumstances and educational needs, and then do your homework on which institutions might present a solid fit. Afterward, speak directly with the coordinator(s) of disability support services (titles sometimes vary) at each prospective school to learn about eligibility requirements. A student should seek guidance from parents, but make the call themselves, if possible.

If a student has a disability, the development of self-advocacy skills is paramount to succeeding in college. Every student should understand the nature of their disability and be able to articulate its impact on his or her learning process. In a public high school, it is incumbent upon the teaching staff to address the student's needs and make accommodations. Those tables turn 180 degrees in college as the onus now falls squarely on the student's shoulders.

Parents, as you assist your teen through the complexities of the application and transition process, make sure not to lose sight of the larger task—helping your child to assume ownership of his or her education. After all, being granted accommodations is one challenge. Taking advantage of them is quite another.

IS THERE ANYTHING STUDENTS CAN DO AFTER BEING DEFERRED?

There's a reason the National Hockey League forever did away with the tie back in 2005—it's an outcome that is antithetical to the natural human desire to sort out winners and losers, to see results in black and white terms, to know definitively where one stands. Unfortunately (or perhaps, fortunately), the Early Admission/Early Decision process in college admissions frequently results in the ultimate act of indecision—the deferral. While better than an outright rejection, being deferred can leave students feeling helpless and lacking further agency in the quest to win acceptance. This is simply not the case.

Students—below are 5 things that you can and should do upon being handed the admissions equivalent of a 1–1 tie.

1. If you haven't already done so, draft a letter to the admissions counselor assigned to your area, which reiterates why the college is particularly suited to your interests and goals, and, if applicable, discusses any accomplishments that have occurred since the submission of your application. If the college is your top choice, be sure to state so. Also make sure that your letter strikes an upbeat and appreciative tone—this shows resilience and leaves a positive impression.
2. Solicit a letter of recommendation from someone who is able to offer a different and fresh perspective on your candidacy. For example, if you've already submitted a teacher recommendation from a math or science teacher, consider sending a letter of recommendation from your English instructor. Alternatively, ask an extracurricular sponsor or work supervisor who can attest to your abilities and work ethic outside of the classroom.
3. Seek opportunities to earn additional recognition. If you're a writer, send an article to your local newspaper; if you're an artist, explore opportunities to exhibit your work; if you excel in math, enter a competition. Securing a competitive scholarship, distinguished award, or similar honor can often aid borderline applicants.
4. If you have not yet visited your first-choice college, consider doing so. A campus visit offers you an opportunity to talk with students and current staff, meet face to face with your admissions counselor, and further acquaint yourself with the offerings of a particular college. It may also improve your admissions prospects.
5. Study hard. First-semester grades are extremely important for deferred applicants and provide you with one last opportunity to exhibit scholastic promise and a trend of academic improvement. It is also important to note that a number of competitive colleges are willing to review January SAT and/or February ACT scores in their regular admissions processes, so if you're not satisfied with your current scores and believe improvement is possible, consider registering for one final test.

Even if you dutifully adhere to the above advice, it's important to remember that your first-choice school may still reject you in the regular admissions cycle. In 2015, MIT deferred 4,535 early admission students and later accepted only 248 of that cohort.[12] Historically, Dartmouth ultimately accepts only 5% of its deferred ED applicants.

Receiving a deferral is by no means a defeat, but it is critical that students line up a solid back-up plan as they wait for a final decision. Remember, there are countless institutions that can offer a top-notch education. If deferrals turn into a *yes* later on, that's fantastic. If not, keep in mind that students still have a plentitude of excellent choices before them.

IS IT POSSIBLE TO GET OFF OF THE WAITLIST?

After battling through the epic journey of the college application process, with all its emotional twists and turns, the torturous anticipation, the potential heaven of acceptance or hell of rejection, judgment day has finally arrived. They tear open the envelope and frantically scan the letter for a telling phrase. They have been "offered a spot." So far so good. Then, the dreaded words appear . . . "on the waitlist." *Ugh.* Welcome to admissions purgatory.

The Good News . . .

Colleges do not place students on the wait list to soften the blow of rejection or to spread false hope. The waitlist exists as a useful tool that provides institutions with a safety net against tough-to-predict yield rates. A growing number of top-tier schools have opted to drop ED, which makes pinpointing how many accepted students will actually enroll an even more unpredictable science. Thus the percentage of students plucked off the waitlist varies greatly from year to year. For example, in the last decade the number of applicants accepted off of the Brown University waitlist has fluctuated between 0 and 196 students.[13] It's quite possible that you will luck into a good year for waitlisters.

The Bad News . . .

Of course, the odds are not exactly forever in a student's favor. Stanford's waitlisted students stand somewhere between a 0% and 5% chance of receiving an offer, depending on the year. Acceptance rates for those waitlisted by juggernauts like Johns Hopkins, Princeton, and Middlebury average under 4%.[14]

Bottom line, in a good year, chances may be half-decent. In a bad year, odds are more on par with a participant in The Hunger Games.

What You Can Do . . .

The number-one thing students can do while on the wait list is communicate clearly, firmly, and respectfully to the admissions office that, if offered, they will accept a spot at the school. Admissions officers like knowing that they have students who will enroll if called upon.

A sincere letter to the admissions office and an occasional check-in from a guidance counselor will suffice. Waitlisted students who obsessively pepper the dean of admissions' inbox with crazed inquiries typically do not do themselves any favors. Remember, colleges are looking for the next productive member of their freshman class, not the next stalker.

Of equal importance to expressing a student's intentions is, not surprisingly, maintaining a strong academic performance. Spring grades, another teacher recommendation, or a recent unique accomplishment can still sway an admissions committee.

The student will still want to submit a nonrefundable deposit at their first-choice school to which they were accepted. There are no bonus points awarded for declaring that if they do not get off of the Tufts waitlist, they'll skip college altogether and become a street performer.

If the call off of the waitlist never comes, allow them to grieve as they must, and then move on and get ready to thrive at their second-choice school. After all, the second-choice school surely has a waitlist full of people stuck in their own purgatory who can only dream of being in your child's shoes.

HOW CAN A STUDENT WITHOUT ELITE CREDENTIALS GET INTO AN ELITE COLLEGE?

Two caveats, before we dish out the advice. First, you've no doubt come to see by now, we do not believe that attending an elite institution constitutes the only pathway to professional success and a rewarding college experience. Yet, we also recognize that elite schools can provide an edge in certain professional fields and that, in some instances, those schools may represent a good *fit* for certain students.

Second warning . . . there is no magic button to press or secret handshake to master, which results in an acceptance letter to a college that might be a bit out of a student's league. There are, however, strategies that can increase their odds.

1) The Transfer Plan

Students might consider starting off at a less-selective school, racking up a couple of semesters on the dean's list, and then transferring into the college of

The following competitive colleges typically accept a relatively high number of transfer applicants and/or possess transfer admission rates that are higher than their freshman admission rates.

Boston College

Boston University

Brandeis University

Colby College

College of William and Mary

Cornell University

Davidson College

Georgia Institute of Technology

Macalester College

New York University

Rensselaer Polytechnic Institute

Smith College

University of California, Los Angeles

University of Michigan

University of North Carolina at Chapel Hill

University of Notre Dame

University of Virginia

Vanderbilt University

Washington University

Wesleyan University

Figure 5.6   Selective and Transfer-Friendly Colleges

their dreams. Many elite schools have lower admission standards for transfer students than for high school applicants, although acceptance rates typically vary greatly from year to year based on enrollment needs.

If a student's prospects of getting into, say, Notre Dame out of high school are on par with Rudy Ruettiger's at the beginning of classic sports film *Rudy*, their best bet may be working toward a transfer to South Bend after freshman year. Notre Dame, along with selective schools like the University of Virginia, the University of North Carolina, and Wesleyan University are all known to be consistently transfer-friendly.

2) The Less-Popular Major Maneuver

Colleges have *institutional needs* to consider during the admissions cycle. This can work to a student's advantage as the following example demonstrates:

> Applicants to Prestige College's Italian program have dwindled in recent years. Applicant X took four years of Italian culminating with a high score on the AP Italian Language and Culture exam. Unfortunately, Applicant X's SATs are in the lower quartile for accepted students at Prestige College and their overall GPA, thanks to a slow start freshman year of high school, isn't quite up to snuff either.

Now, Applicant X wants to study business at Prestige College but knows he will likely be rejected from that program, so he considers selling his background in another interest, Italian, to get accepted. If the plan works, Applicant X could decide to transfer into the business program a semester or two after matriculating, provided he earns good grades.

Of course, the only reason such a plan would have a prayer for success is the demonstrated interest and proficiency in Italian previously shown by Applicant X. If his only stated experience with Italian was enjoying Paul Newman's Sockarooni pasta sauce, the college would have easily sniffed out the scheme, which, not coincidentally, would have smelled like diced bell peppers and garlic.

It's also worth noting that this strategy isn't viable at all colleges, as not all colleges consider choice of major as a significant factor in their admissions process. Generally, larger universities with a relatively high number of majors and distinct undergraduate divisions/schools—UC Berkeley, Carnegie Mellon, and Cornell, for example—are likely to assign more emphasis to an applicant's desired program of study.

3) Enroll in the College of General/Liberal/Continuing Studies

If a student is not opposed to living off campus, studying part-time, and/or learning among nontraditional students, this could be their ticket to a prestigious undergraduate degree. Several highly competitive colleges offer alternative undergraduate degree programs that allow students with less-than-elite credentials to benefit from the resources and brand of a topflight institution. These institutions include, among others, Columbia University's School of General Studies, University of Pennsylvania's College of Liberal and Professional Studies, and Harvard University's Extension School.

Before pursuing any of these options, however, it is important to understand elite institutions distinguish between students enrolling in traditional and alternative programs, not only during their undergraduate years, but after college as well. In addition to learning about the level of access *alternative* students have to university faculty and facilities, it's also important to determine whether they will have access to the same career-related services and alumni networks, and whether the degree/diploma you receive will be identical to (i.e., as marketable as) that of students graduating from more traditional programs at the same institution.

NOTES

1. Jill Rosen, "Johns Hopkins Welcomes First Members of Its Class of 2019," *The Hub*, December 12, 2014, accessed December 26, 2015, http://hub.jhu.edu/2014/12/12/early-decision-class-of-2019.

2. Jon Victor, "Early Apps Increase at Peer Schools," *Yale Daily News*, December 11, 2015, accessed December 26, 2015, http://yaledailynews.com/blog/2015/12/11/early-apps-increase-at-peer-schools/.

3. Jennie Kent and Jeff Levy, "Early Decision vs. Regular Decision Acceptance Rates," September 2015, accessed December 26, 2015, https://www.iecaonline.com/PDF/IECA_Library_ED-vs-RD-Acceptances.pdf.

4. Andrew S. Belasco, Kelly O. Rosinger, and James C. Hearn, "The Test-Optional Movement at America's Selective Liberal Arts Colleges: A Boon for Equity or Something Else?," Educational Evaluation and Policy Analysis, (2015), 37(2), 206–23.

5. Lynn O'Shaughnessy, "The Other Side of 'Test Optional,'" *New York Times*, July 20, 2009, accessed December 26, 2015, http://www.nytimes.com/2009/07/26/education/edlife/26guidance-t.html.

6. Scott Jaschik, "Duke Asks the Question," *Inside Higher Ed*, September 2, 2014, accessed December 26, 2015, https://www.insidehighered.com/news/2014/09/02/duke-u-adds-voluntary-admissions-question-sexual-orientation-and-gender-identity.

7. Marguerite Del Giudice, "Grit Trumps Talent and IQ: A Story Every Parent (and Educator) Should Read," *National Geographic*, October 14, 2014, accessed February 29, 2016, http://news.nationalgeographic.com/news/2014/10/141015-angela-duckworth-success-grit-psychology-self-control-science-nginnovators/.

8. Rebecca R. Ruiz, "Disclose Disciplinary Infractions, Admissions Officials Say," *New York Times,* October 27, 2011, accessed December 26, 2015, http://thechoice.blogs.nytimes.com/2011/10/27/infractions/.

9. "Education Suspended: The Use of High School Disciplinary Records in College Admissions," Center for Community Alternatives, May, 2015, accessed 1/3/2015, http://www.communityalternatives.org/pdf/publications/EducationSuspended.pdf

10. Ibid.

11. Joie Jager-Hyman, "Receiving Testing Accommodations for Learning Disabilities," *The Huffington Post,* February 7, 2014, last modified April 9, 2014, accessed December 26, 2015, http://www.huffingtonpost.com/joie-jagerhyman/receiving-testing-accommo_b_4740601.html.

12. "Admissions Statistics," accessed February 29, 2016, http://mitadmissions.org/apply/process/stats.

13. Agnes Chan, "Waitlist Admissions See Huge Jump for Class of 2019," *The Brown Daily Herald,* September 10, 2015, accessed December 26, 2015, http://www.browndailyherald.com/2015/09/10/waitlist-admissions-see-huge-jump-for-class-of-2019/.

14. Akane Otani, "At Top Schools, a Spot on the Wait List May as Well Be a Rejection," *Bloomberg Businessweek,* April 28, 2015, accessed December 26, 2015, http://www.bloomberg.com/news/articles/2015-04-28/at-top-schools-a-spot-on-the-wait-list-may-as-well-be-a-rejection.

Chapter 6

Planning the Financial End

Paradigm shift is one of those pop-business buzzwords that tends to be among the most overused phrases of the twenty-first century. These days, every time an office manager replaces the old breakroom coffeepot with a Keurig, it's a *paradigm shift*. Whenever a grad student decides to do a Prezi instead of a PowerPoint, it's a *paradigm shift*. We could go on and on but you get the point—it's an absurdly overused term.

Thus we ask that you do not take it as a hyperbole when we label the new reality we are about to set forth as a genuine paradigm shift. While it might not exactly be as earth-shattering as the heliocentric model, the discovery of genetic inheritance, or the mass production of the automobile, it does represent a radical change in thinking about a process that impacts millions of lives each and every year. Amazingly, this change in thinking is so simple and supported by such a preponderance of evidence that you don't have to be a luminary on the level of Copernicus, Mendel, or Henry Ford to stumble upon it. Ready? Here it is: *Prospective colleges need students more than students need them.* Simple, sweet, and absolutely true. Higher education is a *buyer's* market.

As this chapter unfolds, we will show you how this shift in thinking leads to the adoption of a consumer mindset to the college selection and admissions process. In aiming to make you the most informed college consumer, we will show you, among other valuable insights, that the sticker price has little correlation with what families actually pay, how to take advantage of inefficiencies in the financial aid system, and how your child can shave tens of thousands of dollars off of their future college tuition while they're still in high school.

But first, we will provide hard evidence that students, not colleges, are in the driver's seat.

Excess Supply

Contrary to common belief, most college admissions officers will not spend this fall sifting through a surplus of qualified applicants, rejecting student after student with straight A's and perfect SAT scores. In reality, the majority of admissions folks will be frantically trying to meet their enrollment goals as the supply of quality higher education continues to outpace (eligible) student demand. Simply put, higher education is, despite what media headlines suggest, more of a buyer's market than ever before. Consider the following findings:

- 58% of admissions directors surveyed in 2015 had not met their enrollment goals for the previous year.
- Over half of admissions directors were *very concerned* about meeting enrollment goals for the 2015–2016 admissions cycle.[1]
- More than 30 percent of admission directors spent their spring and summer months recruiting students who had already committed to attending other colleges—a practice that is effectively banned by the National Association for College Admissions Counseling.[2]
- Many private colleges now send out revised (i.e., increased) aid offers to previously admitted students who have yet to commit to their school.[3]

Although the above findings inspire fear among every college administrator outside of the Ivy League, they should have the opposite effect on college applicants and convey a few admissions-related truths.

1. The Application Process Does Not End in November

The rise of Early Decision, Early Action, and priority/VIP applications does not indicate a more competitive admissions process wherein applying early is an absolute must; it reflects an increasingly competitive and desperate four-year college sector that is willing to adopt almost every strategy under the sun to increase applications and enrollment yield. Although meeting a November deadline can offer advantages at a number of *Early Decision* and *Early Action* colleges, using the months of December and January to solidify a student's college preferences and improve their applications is appropriate, given that the overwhelming majority of institutions *need* to accept students meeting their admissions criteria, regardless of whether they apply by the early or regular decision deadline.

2. There Is a Lot of Money to Be Won

In an effort to boost attendance and meet enrollment targets, many colleges have devoted an increasing share of their budgets to attracting desirable students via the offering of merit-based (i.e., non-need-based) financial aid. Using merit scholarships to lure high-achieving or high-scoring students can improve a college's ranking and eventually its desirability, ultimately fueling enrollment. And because *high-achieving* and *desirable* are relative terms, students don't have to be academic superstars to earn merit money. A number of reputable schools now offer sizable merit awards to *B* students.

3. If You're a Good High School Student, You Can Attend a Great College

There are many reputable institutions that failed to meet their enrollment goals within the past couple years, and each was recruiting good (not necessarily great) students well into the summer. Here are a few:

- Beloit College
- Clark University
- Colorado State University
- Drexel University
- Hofstra University
- Lawrence University
- Lewis & Clark College
- Loyola University of Maryland
- New College of Florida
- Reed College
- SUNY at Binghamton
- University of Arizona
- University of Florida
- University of Maryland, College Park
- Wheaton College, Massachusetts

This list and the survey highlighted above offer indisputable evidence that higher education is indeed a buyer's market. This fact should compel students to adopt an admission strategy that is based on confidence, rather than worry, and take comfort in the fact that any applicant with an open mind and decent transcript can attend an excellent college at an affordable price.

THE PRICE IS *NOT* WHAT YOU PAY

If you've ever noticed a sudden, unexplained rise in your cable bill, you've probably experienced something like this: After calling the cable company and enduring twenty straight minutes of deafeningly loud advertisements for the latest sequel to *Horrible Bosses*, you finally get an operator on the phone. You express your displeasure and threaten to switch to another company. Without hesitation, the representative immediately pitches you a new *limited time offer* that includes more channels for less money than you were originally paying. This offer wasn't listed on the website or advertised anywhere, but must simply be reserved for irate customers with one foot out the door.

The lesson here is that cable companies are not exactly beacons of transparency—unfortunately, and this may surprise you—neither are colleges. Most college-bound students and their families eye the list price of a prospective school when deciding if it is a financially viable option. Yet, in the modern higher education marketplace, the list price and the net price, that is, what the average student actually pays, frequently have little to do with one another. Grasping the difference between the stated and actual tuition costs can revolutionize the way you shop for colleges and can greatly expand a student's economically sound postsecondary options.

Don't Believe the Sticker Price

If you shop for colleges the way you shop for other high-expense items, automobiles for example, you would be doing yourself a disservice and greatly limiting your options. While car dealers, like cable companies, are not exactly known for their straightforward pricing methods, we still enter a dealership with a general idea of what we can afford. If our budget allows us to target preowned Toyotas with a list price of 14K and nothing a penny higher, then we can be pretty darn sure that even if we are the best negotiator in the entire world, the 40K Lexus in the same showroom is not going to be realistic option for us. Evaluating college costs, however, could not be a more different ball game.

Let's look at the example of Beantown Barbara, a Massachusetts resident and accomplished high school student who would love to attend a selective private college, but is being told by her middle-class parents that this is off the table unless she wants to take out massive loans. Barbara had been interested in high-caliber schools like Northwestern University in Chicago, IL, Vanderbilt in Nashville, TN, or even Tufts, the prestigious college right in her own backyard. Her SATs and grades are likely good enough to gain acceptance at all three, but she and her family are turned off by the Lexus-level pricing, as each school costs in excess of $40,000 per year in tuition alone. Wanting to avoid accumulating unnecessary undergraduate debt, Barbara decides that UMass, with an in-state tuition rate of 14K, is probably her best bet.

Unbeknownst to Barbara and her family is the fact that Northwestern, Vanderbilt, and Tufts, through generous merit and need-based aid opportunities, actually have average net prices *equal to* UMass. Amazingly, all three private schools have an average net price (again, what students actually pay) of under $20,000 (including tuition, fees, room and board), approximately one-third of their respective sticker prices. That doesn't mean that Beantown Barbara would have been offered exactly that price. It could have been higher but it also could have been lower; either way, it would have been worth applying and finding out.

Net Price by Income

We will move a few states westward for a moment for our next example. As a high school student in Ohio, Buckeye Bob finished in the top 10% of his class and kicked butt on his last attempt at the ACT. His dream is to attend a selective private university somewhat close to home. Bob shares with his parents that his top choices are Oberlin, Kenyon, and Denison. Bob's parents beam with pride until they see the sticker price of these schools—all over $60,000.

Bob's parents are solidly middle class, earning $67,000 a year in combined family income. They assume that they are caught in no man's land, earning too much income to qualify for government grants but not enough to cover the steep tuition costs at a private school. Discouraged, Bob looks at Ohio's state school options. He knows that he'll be fine attending a school like Ohio State, Cleveland State, or the University of Akron, but he wishes there was some way he could have a shot at his true best-fit schools.

Fortunately for Bob, his guidance counselor understands the concept of net price at private schools like Oberlin, Kenyon, and Denison. These institutions tend to be generous with aid and take income strongly into consideration. While Oberlin's annual cost of attendance is approximately $66,000 per year, the actual price students pay sharply declines as you go down the income ladder.

The average family whose income exceeds $110,000 pays around 40K. Families making between 75 and 110K get a sizable discount, with the average falling just below $26,000. Those with an income level in the 48–75K range, like Buckeye Bob's family, pay under $18,000 in tuition. At Denison, families in that income range pay a little over $17,000. Kenyon College's average net price for a student like Bob comes in even lower at roughly $11,000.[4]

Most of the state schools in Ohio cost somewhere in the neighborhood of 10 grand per year. Most likely, a university like Ohio State will still cost Bob less than his dream schools, but the revelation about net price may still have moved a school like Oberlin from a complete fantasy to a potential reality.

Don't Forget to Select a Quality Financial Safety School

Discovering the concept of net price should lead students to radically alter the way they go about selecting target colleges—they should feel freed up to aim high and dream big. However, it is crucial to also come up with backup plan that is a sure thing from a financial end. Most college-bound students are aware of the importance of having a *safety school*, an institution where obtaining admission is pretty darn close to a statistical guarantee. However, for anyone without unlimited funds, selecting a *financial safety school* may be of equal importance.

No one likes to consider doomsday scenarios, but if you thoughtfully selected a quality financial safety school, you can now breathe a little easier as you await financial and merit aid notifications from your top-choice schools. In our examples above, UMass and Ohio State would have made perfectly good financial safety schools (assuming that they were also *safeties* from an academic standpoint) because they were affordable (even at 100% of the list price) and not schools that our sample students found undesirable. In picking a financial safety school, don't just pick a random school that happens to be relatively inexpensive. Target a school that you would genuinely like to attend, considering for location, availability of majors of interest, extracurricular activities, etc.

Understanding that the list price and the net price are two very different concepts will help to broaden the college search and may just put a student's dream schools within financial reach. Don't believe us? Call your cable

Net prices depend on other factors in addition to family income, such as a family's assets and a student's academic or extracurricular accomplishments; however, the figures indicated below should still provide a decent approximation of what you can expect to pay at some of the nation's most competitive private colleges. For example, at Amherst College, students with a family income of less than $30,000 pay an average of $1,936 per year; students with a family income between $48,000 and $75,000 pay an average of $10,016; and so on. Prices include tuition, fees, room, board, and other college-related expenses.

Institution	Published Price	Net Price < $30k	Net Price $30-48k	Net Price $48-75k	Net Price $75-110k	Net Price > $110k
Amherst College	$67,172	$1,936	$8,389	$10,016	$20,930	$40,162
Boston College	$65,620	$15,622	$17,159	$23,085	$31,577	$47,078
Carnegie Mellon University	$65,895	$23,362	$24,802	$28,057	$31,540	$43,299
Colgate University	$64,800	$7,134	$9,867	$12,384	$20,466	$32,798
Davidson College	$62,894	$9,479	$8,341	$10,963	$19,302	$36,869
Emory University	$63,058	$18,204	$17,610	$24,192	$30,192	$44,920
Grinnell College	$61,098	$10,120	$10,432	$16,199	$24,219	$24,381
Harvard University	$69,900	$3,897	$2,977	$5,405	$13,604	$36,946
Johns Hopkins University	$66,646	$11,547	$8,574	$14,927	$25,131	$41,745
Middlebury College	$63,456	$7,537	$9,671	$13,076	$19,052	$38,912
Northwestern University	$68,060	$15,481	$15,436	$17,920	$26,969	$41,946
Pomona College	$63,670	$4,712	$5,169	$6,964	$15,107	$32,232
Rice University	$58,283	$7,799	$8,123	$10,187	$20,344	$35,553
Stanford University	$65,177	$3,516	$4,260	$6,240	$12,679	$40,323
Tufts University	$65,900	$10,325	$10,238	$19,711	$26,268	$44,777
University of Chicago	$66,765	$8,112	$8,408	$12,579	$23,131	$40,545
University of Notre Dame	$64,775	$12,176	$10,245	$16,583	$22,897	$37,946
University of Richmond	$61,370	$8,599	$11,497	$17,475	$22,645	$41,215
University of Rochester	$65,346	$15,555	$15,140	$19,815	$24,682	$38,527
Vanderbilt University	$63,532	$7,411	$6,793	$9,047	$16,926	$32,971

Source: U.S. Department of Education

For a complete list of colleges and their net prices, please visit *www.collegetransitions.com/net-price-by-institution*

Figure 6.1 Institutional Net Price (By Family Income)

company today and start enjoying the full gamut of premium channels for a fraction of the price.

ESTIMATING COLLEGE COSTS: THE POWER
OF A NET PRICE CALCULATOR

The Genesis of the Net Price Calculator

To address the problem of price obfuscation, the feds passed a bill in 2011, which requires institutions of higher education to post a *net price calculator* (NPC) on their university website. While the required components of these calculators are clearly delineated by the government, enough wiggle room exists for some schools to still offer less-than-helpful estimation tools. We present a guide for distinguishing between helpful and less-helpful calculators and offer tips for using this tool in formulating an application strategy.

Good versus Bad NPCs

If you are able to input all of your data into a school's NPC in less time than it takes to read a Garfield comic, then you are highly unlikely to unlock useful financial information (Yes, even one of the longer, semi-dramatic Garfield strips, i.e., when Odie mistakenly gets taken to the pound). The rule of thumb for the time it should take to plug in your data is 15-20 minutes. Have documents related to family income, assets, and investments by your side—if an NPC is going to tell you anything accurate, this information will all be required.

Visit the Net Price Calculator before Applying

There is no reason for a student to waste money and precious time completing an application for a school that even in the best-case aid scenario is well beyond their financial reach. The worst strategy a student can employ is to base their entire college list on pure financial guesswork. Therefore, we urge students and families to visit the NPCs of prospective colleges before, rather than after, a student decides to submit an application.

Use Net Price Calculators as a Guide

If you play around with the merit aid section of an NPC, you will see how altering certain variables will affect the net tuition price. For example, running the numbers for both a 1290 and a 1350 SAT score may give you two very different estimates. The 1290 a student has in the bag as they enter their senior year might be more than enough to ensure acceptance at their top-choice school; therefore, they see little reason to retake the SAT another time. Yet if the NPC on the school's site tells you that an extra 60 points will cut *five grand* off the tuition, it's probably time for that student to bury his or her nose back in those test-prep guides.

To find net price calculators for a prospective college, simply google the institution's name and *net price calculator*. Or, visit the Department of Education's Net Price Calculator Center at https://collegecost.ed.gov/netpricecenter.aspx.

WINNING NEED-BASED AID

You likely vowed to start planning for your son or daughter's education back when he or she was only a baby. Your intention was to open a 529 Plan and stash away a little extra cash each month until it matured into a six-figure sum. With that money plus an athletic scholarship—I mean, your kid *was* a peewee soccer MVP at the time—you would be sitting pretty by the time it came to pay that first tuition bill. Unfortunately, life got in the way of these best-laid plans, and now you're scrambling for practical short-term advice on how to finance the education of their dreams.

Unless you happen to stumble upon a 1985 Delorean fully loaded with a flux capacitor (in which case you should pull a Biff and bet on future sports events), you're not going to be able to go back in time and execute that long-term savings plan. But that certainly doesn't mean that all is lost. In this section, we offer tips for navigating the financial aid process, as well as a few short-term strategies you can employ to maximize your chances of receiving a sizable award.

Fill Out the FAFSA!

For those with significant financial need, the federal government continues to be the largest source of student aid. Each year upward of 65 billion dollars, money that comes in the form of Pell Grants, work-study programs, and educational tax breaks, is awarded to families. Additionally, the feds loan out 95 billion dollars with far more favorable terms than private lenders.[5] That's over 160 billion dollars handed out each year for higher education, a sum greater than the gross national product of all but 57 countries in the world.[6] The bottom line is that there is a substantial amount of federal money available, so filling out a FAFSA is certainly worth your time.

This seems like obvious enough advice, yet each year over one million families fail to file a FAFSA solely because they do not believe that they would meet the income requirements for aid (hundreds of thousands of others fail to fill out the FAFSA for other reasons).[7] This includes many middle-class and upper-middle-class families who, due to the funky, almost nonsensical formula for awarding aid, may have actually received an award had they simply taken the time to complete the form.

Changes Are Coming

To encourage higher filing rates and a more equitable application process, the federal government has recently taken steps to simplify the FAFSA. As of fall 2016, applicants are able to file the FAFSA on October 1, a full three months earlier than in years past, and complete the form using tax data from two years prior. Proponents of FAFSA simplification assert that these changes will encourage more students to apply before a college's financial aid deadline—thus receiving priority consideration for scholarships and other institutional funds—and will allow families to more accurately estimate how much aid they're likely to receive *before* applying to a particular college. Under the previous system, families had to wait until January to file the FAFSA and often did not know their aid eligibility until after the application process had concluded, which prevented many from choosing and applying to colleges where they were likely to receive the most aid.

Understand the Expected Family Contribution

After submitting a FAFSA, you will be assigned an Expected Family Contribution (EFC); this is the amount the federal government deems appropriate for you to pay each year toward tuition, room and board, books, and so on. However, receiving a low EFC doesn't mean it is time to pop the champagne corks and pick any college you want. The EFC is only a guideline that schools may or may not adhere to. In fact, only a relatively small number of competitive and well-funded institutions can meet the full financial need of all admitted students.

The CSS Profile

Many of these well-funded colleges comprise a group of nearly 300 schools that also require the CSS Profile, a form primarily used to assess an

The colleges and universities listed below report meeting 100 percent of demonstrated financial need for their full-time undergraduates. Not surprisingly, the most generous colleges also happen to be the most selective.

Amherst College	Georgetown University	Trinity College
Barnard College	Grinnell College	Tufts University
Bates College	Hamilton College	University of Chicago
Boston College	Harvard University	University of North Carolina-Chapel Hill
Bowdoin College	Haverford College	University of Notre Dame
Brown University	Macalester College	University of Pennsylvania
Bryn Mawr College	Middlebury College	University of Richmond
California Institute of Technology	Mount Holyoke College	University of Southern California
Carleton College	Northwestern University	University of Virginia
Claremont McKenna College	Oberlin College	Vanderbilt University
Colby College	Occidental College	Vassar College
Colgate University	Pitzer College	Washington and Lee University
College of the Holy Cross	Pomona College	Washington University
Colorado College	Princeton University	Wellesley College
Columbia University	Rice University	Wesleyan University
Connecticut College	Scripps College	Williams College
Cornell University	Smith College	Yale University
Dartmouth College	Soka University of America	
Davidson College	Stanford University	
Duke University	Swarthmore College	
Franklin and Marshall College	Thomas Aquinas College	

Figure 6.2   Colleges with Great (Need-Based) Financial Aid

applicant's eligibility for institution-based (rather than government-based) aid. Unlike the FAFSA, the CSS Profile charges a filing fee—$25 for the first school and $16 for every additional school.

You may grumble about the fees associated with CSS Profile submission, yet it might turn out to be the wisest investment since Asa Griggs Candler's $2,300 purchase of the Coca Cola recipe back in 1888. Random references to nineteenth-century business transactions aside, the CSS Profile can produce its own lucrative results, but families may find that the questions about their financial lives are far more invasive than those on the FAFSA. This is due to the fact that the CSS Profile allows schools to apply their own Institutional Methodology. Questions may arise on topics such as family medical costs, retirement accounts, detailed business records for the self-employed, and other financial matters that are likewise outside the purview of the FAFSA.

Meet (Priority) Deadlines

In order to maximize your eligibility for federal, state, and institutional funds, it is essential to file the FAFSA, CSS Profile, and other required financial aid documents on or before a college's *priority* financial aid deadline, which can be different from deadlines set by federal and state agencies. For example, the federal government requires students to file a FAFSA on or before June 30 in order to receive federal funds. However, waiting until June 30 to file a FAFSA would likely prevent these same students from receiving institutional-based aid at their target school, as the overwhelming majority of selective colleges have priority financial aid deadlines that come much earlier, typically between February and April. Every year, thousands of families fail to meet these institution-set deadlines, leaving otherwise guaranteed money on the table.

Now that you have a better idea of which forms need to be filed and when, let's take a look at several quick and easy strategies to maximize your aid eligibility.

Defer Your Year-End Bonus

To understand why you should postpone the receipt of a year-end payout, you first need to understand an important term in the financial aid world, known as the *base income year*. The base income year, or base year, is the calendar year that precedes the academic year for which financial aid is being sought.

For example, a high school senior seeking aid for the 2018–2019 academic year would have 2016 as his or her base year. The base income year largely determines a student's financial aid eligibility as a college freshman and also often influences the amount of aid he or she is awarded during subsequent years. Thus, if possible, a family should take steps to minimize *the appearance of* earnings during this period.

Certainly, it would not make any financial sense to go to extreme measures to reduce your income such as quitting your job or refusing a raise. However, if you are due to receive a lump sum payment, such as a company bonus or retirement/pension account withdrawal, you may want to look into deferring the receipt of that money until you are outside the aforementioned window of time.

Move Assets from Child to Parent

Now, we're not advocating going all Macaulay Caulkin's dad on your kids and spending their summer job earnings on a bedroom Jacuzzi. This one actually comes down to simple math. According to financial aid formulas, parent assets are calculated at 5.65%, while student assets are assessed at a much higher rate—between 20% and 25%. In other words, for every $1000 in a son or daughter's bank account, a family's EFC will increase by least $200. If that same $1,000 was in a parent's name, the family's EFC would only increase by a little more than 50 bucks.

Use Savings to Pay Down Debt

The world of financial aid punishes you for having large stacks of available cash; yet it does not credit families for having high-interest debt on a credit card or auto loan. Thus, paying off these types of consumer debt before submitting the FAFSA can kill two birds and greatly improve your chances of getting more aid. It may just be the most lucrative shifting of funds you can do not involving the Cayman Islands and a banker in a white suit.

Additional Strategies

There are numerous other long-term and short-term strategies that families can adopt to improve their financial aid prospects. However, a detailed account of all of these strategies is beyond the scope of this book. If you're interested in learning more, here are a couple great resources:

- *Paying for College Without Going Broke*, written by Kalman Chany;
- *Finaid.org*, a comprehensive financial aid information website developed by Mark Kantrowitz.

PAYING FOR COLLEGE: HOW TO WIN MERIT AID

At the risk of sounding like Matthew Lesko, the question mark suit-clad lunatic of early 2000s infomercial fame, *colleges want to give you free money!!!*

Okay, so schools aren't exactly looking to send cash to any freeloader with a self-addressed stamped envelope, but each year billions upon billions of dollars are indeed handed out by institutions for the purpose of luring desirable students onto their campuses.

The Top Factors in Netting Merit Aid

As usual, it starts with the good ol' meat and potatoes of the application—strong test scores and a high GPA. Some colleges, especially larger institutions, literally have formulaic scholarship tables that tell students how much money they're likely to get from them. Trinity University in Texas is just one of a slew of schools that take much of the suspense out of the merit aid process through such means. Applicants at Trinity with a 1250 SAT and a 3.75 GPA will qualify for an award of 17K per year. Raise that to a 1350 and a 4.0 and the award is 23K per year.[8]

Maximizing Your Chances

Students traditionally approach the admissions process from a place of desperation, "Please, please accept me!" This isn't exactly the best mindset for a consumer in any marketplace . . . and yes, students as college applicants are in fact consumers. When students realize that many admissions officers feel an equal desperation to land a student like them, the tables suddenly turn. The focus is now on constructing a college list comprised of *good-fit* schools that are likely to reach deep into their coffers for a student with a great academic profile.

Strategic targeting of schools is critical in the merit aid chase. The Ivies and other uber-selective colleges rarely award scholarships based strictly on merit, primarily because they don't have to—these schools attract plenty of students with remarkable credentials *and* bank accounts, and as such,

Institution	Cost of Attendance	% Receiving Merit Aid	Average Award*
Case Western Reserve University	$61,950	52%	$22,009
Davidson College	$62,894	12%	$27,020
Duke University	$67,399	16%	$13,689
Emory University	$63,058	14%	$17,796
George Washington University	$66,310	31%	$18,307
Grinnell College	$61,098	21%	$18,473
Lafayette College	$61,390	16%	$25,737
Northeastern University	$63,330	40%	$20,784
Rensselaer Polytechnic Institute	$66,172	31%	$17,440
Rice University	$58,283	16%	$22,478
Rhodes College	$57,714	56%	$19,113
Southern Methodist University	$67,565	55%	$19,568
Tulane University	$66,518	35%	$22,660
University of Notre Dame	$64,775	30%	$14,793
University of Rochester	$65,346	31%	$13,573
University of Richmond	$61,370	22%	$33,520
University of Southern California	$67,212	34%	$21,460
Vanderbilt University	$63,352	30%	$16,325
Wake Forest University	$64,478	40%	$30,763
Washington and Lee University	$61,235	19%	$45,042

A Sample of Highly Competitive Colleges Awarding Significant Merit Aid

*Does not include need-based aid
Source: The College Board; CollegeData.org

For a comprehensive list of colleges and their average merit awards, please visit *www.collegetransitions.com/merit-aid-by-institution*

Figure 6.3 Selective and Generous: A Sample of Highly Competitive Colleges Awarding Significant Merit Aid

award almost all of their aid according to financial need. However, dozens of equally reputable yet slightly less-selective institutions will open their pockets to high-achieving students. George Washington, Tulane, and Wake Forest University are just a few of the many prominent colleges that strategically use merit aid to increase their institutional rank and profile.[9]

In general, applicants should look for schools where they are close to the 75th percentile for SAT scores and GPA/class rank. Don't be deterred by the sticker price of private colleges in this process. In general, private schools offer larger merit aid packages that can knock their tuition below that of seemingly cheaper state schools students may have been considering.

Keeping Your Merit Aid

When merit aid is offered there is typically a stipulation that students must maintain a certain GPA to be able to renew the scholarship beyond freshman year. The exact number fluctuates from school to school. For example, Drexel University requires that students maintain a 2.75, Hofstra a 3.0, while Rutgers demands a more stringent 3.25. The only other common requirement is that students remain full-time, carrying a full credit load.

TEST YOUR WAY TO A LOWER TUITION

Widely considered one of the best documentaries of the 2000s, *The King of Kong* takes you deep within the surprisingly fascinating subculture of competitive retro video gaming. The film tells the story of two middle-aged men competing to obtain the world record in *Donkey Kong*, a rudimentary arcade game from the early 1980s, with such cutthroat ferocity that you would think millions of dollars or perhaps even eternal life was at stake—in reality, only bragging rights are on the line. They stay up in the wee hours, nestled in their garages, trying desperately to unlock additional points and outdo their competitor. So, you ask, what in the heck does this have to do with students testing their way to lower tuition?

Most people approach endeavors in life, whether we're talking about *Donkey Kong* or the SAT/ACT, as challenges to be conquered and then quickly moved on from. If a college-bound junior scores well on their SAT/ACT and feels that that score will be good enough to secure admission at the schools that they are interested in, they typically refocus themselves on their coursework, extracurricular activities, and life outside of school. While this approach is completely understandable, students who take the *King of Kong* approach to standardized tests often make out with, well, a whole lot of quarters. It costs about $55 to retake the SAT or ACT, but it's important to understand that 55 bucks plus hours of dedicated preparation can be worth thousands upon thousands of dollars in merit aid money.

Guaranteed Scholarships

Many public and private schools offer guaranteed scholarships to students who meet defined criteria, usually in the areas of GPA and SAT/ACT scores. For example, Hartwick College, a private liberal arts school in New York, offers five different scholarship levels, the highest of which grants $26,000 per year to students with an A average and at least a 1260 SAT/28 ACT score. West Virginia University (WVU) is a public institution and has a range of scholarships for students with GPAs ranging from 3.0 to 3.8 and SAT scores from 1030 to 1340. At WVU, the amounts awarded to nonresidents are much greater than scholarships for West Virginia residents, who already enjoy a greatly reduced in-state tuition.

Other schools do not offer a 100% guarantee on these scholarships, but still state minimum SAT/ACT requirements for consideration. One such school is the University of Kentucky, which requires applicants to their top scholarship to have an unweighted 3.8 GPA and a 1440 SAT/34 ACT score. While students possessing the requisite credentials are not guaranteed the awards as in the cases above, winners receive quite a bounty including full tuition, room and board, a stipend, a new iPad, and cash to use while studying abroad.

Other Merit Aid

Even at colleges where scholarship criteria is not explicitly laid out, SAT/ ACT scores play a huge role in determining which applicants receive offers of merit aid. Remember, the point of non-need-based merit aid from an institutional standpoint is to offer enough of a discount to attract top students. There are two metrics that will clue students in about their chances of scoring merit aid at a given college or university. The first is the percentage of students at that school that receive merit aid, numbers which are readily accessible at col- legetransitions.com. The second is to look at the 75th percentile of SAT/ACT scores for accepted students, also easy to track down online or in literally any college guidebook. If a student's score falls at or above that number and a given school is known for being relatively generous with merit aid, chances are that they will get a substantial offer.

Test-Optional Schools Still Reward High SATs

Remember, just because a school is willing to admit an applicant without consideration of SAT scores, they are still less likely to award a scoreless applicant merit aid. Some test-optional institutions explicitly state on their websites that they will not take the submission of standardized test scores into consideration when making merit aid decisions. In our experience, regardless of such proclamations, strong scores always impact award decisions. Even test-optional institutions are still concerned about their rankings in *U.S. News* and will dish out merit aid to reel in candidates with exceptional standardized tests scores.

Second (or Third) Time Is a Charm

Students typically take the SAT or ACT for the first time in the spring of their junior year. Those who elect to retake the test a second or third time, especially the following fall, improve their overall score by an average of 40 points.[10] It makes sense that students would receive a natural boost for two reasons: (1) it's not their first rodeo, they know the routine, the timing of the test, the format, etc. and (2) they've been exposed to more relevant academic material in the classroom since the last sitting. And these advantages don't even account for the biggest difference of all—students have an entire summer to learn the secrets of the SAT/ACT backward and forward.

Study Hard

Registering for a test-prep course or one-on-one tutoring can pay dividends, particularly if a student benefits from the structure of formal instruction and/or lacks the discipline to develop and follow a test-prep regimen. However, if they are truly self-motivated and committed, burying their nose in a prep book can prove just as effective. Students should take practice test after practice test while simulating the conditions they will encounter on test day. Afterward, they should read the detailed explanations provided on the questions they get wrong. Trust us—it works.

Your Dedication Will Pay Off

The only thing that masterfully maneuvering Mario up a series of platforms to depose an oversized ape will get you is a good reputation among a couple dozen socially awkward grown men. However, obsessive dedication to the SAT/ACT, even just for a brief spurt of time, can earn students and their family significant tuition discounts, money that will impact not only a young person's undergraduate years but their adult years as well.

START EARLY AND SAVE BIG: THE BENEFITS OF EARNING COLLEGE CREDIT DURING HIGH SCHOOL

Too many talented students pass up opportunities to earn college credits during their high school years for just a tiny fraction of what they will pay later in freshman tuition. Understanding the options that may be available to students at their high school is step one. Step two is exploring the policies of each of the prospective colleges with regard to awarding postsecondary credits earned prior to matriculation. What follows is an overview of Advanced Placement (AP), International Baccalaureate (IB), College-Level Examination Program (CLEP), and dual enrollment options and how they have the potential to save students tens of thousands of dollars at almost any college or university in the United States.

Advanced Placement (AP)

Advanced Placement tests cost approximately $90 a pop and can earn students between three and eight college credits a piece. AP exams are offered in May, typically at or near the end of an AP course; however, *students don't have to enroll in an AP class to register for an AP exam*. In fact, an increasing number of high schoolers without access to AP coursework are opting to take the tests, as are students who have access to AP coursework in their respective schools but who cannot fit a particular class within their schedule.

The rise in AP test-taking seems justified, given that the returns for good performance are nothing short of astonishing. The average private college costs over $31,000 per year in tuition.[11] That's for 30 credits, which translates to over $1,000 per credit. In this example, passing just one AP test can save between 3 and 8 thousand bucks. You'll be hard-pressed to get that kind of return on a $90 investment if Gordon Gekko or heck, even Nostradamus, was your financial advisor.

Most schools accept AP credits with open arms although the minimal level of performance varies. Boston University, like many selective institutions, only accepts scores of 4s and 5s on the AP exam and, in some cases, a distinction is made between the two. In evaluating AP Biology scores, BU will award 8 credits for a 5 on the AP exam and 4 credits for those who scored a 4.

Yet many colleges, even selective ones, award credits for a 3 on an AP exam in all or at least some subjects. The University of Chicago will award some level of credit for a 3 in physics. The University of Wisconsin–Madison will grant three credits for each score of 3 on an AP exam and will typically offer even more credits for scores of 4 or 5. To learn about AP credit policies at prospective colleges, visit the College Board website at https://apstudent.collegeboard.org/creditandplacement/search-credit-policies.

Ultimately, whether your kid is eyeing a less-selective or super-prestigious college, it pays to take AP exams. Not only are there significant admission-related benefits for doing so, but the financial rewards can be immense.

International Baccalaureate (IB)

International Baccalaureate courses are very popular outside of the US, but a growing number of American high schools now offer students a chance to earn college credit through the IB program. Unlike with AP, IB tests require students to have completed an IB course prior to sitting for the exam. However, not all schools in the United States will offer credit for singular IB test scores but rather require the completion of a comprehensive IB diploma.

The IB diploma takes teens two years to complete and requires courses in six disciplines. While the AP curriculum allows students to play to their strengths, the IB diploma program takes a more holistic approach and forces students not only to master traditional subjects like experimental science and math but also to learn a foreign language, write an essay, complete a community service project, and pass tests in every single content area. IB exams are scored on a 1-7 scale with 4 generally being considered as passing (like a 3 on the AP).

It's a common misconception that IB credits are not widely recognized by colleges and universities in the United States. While this was a fairly accurate assessment a handful of years ago, today almost 1,700 American postsecondary schools now award credit for IB.[12] As with AP, individual schools' policies vary and need to be explored on a case-by-case basis.

The University of Florida will give you 3-4 credits for a score of a 4 and 6-8 credits for anything above a 5. The prestigious Barnard College will award 30 credits for the IB diploma if the aggregate score of all six tests is a 30. Caltech will not give credit for any IB coursework; however, they do not grant credit for AP either.

College-Level Examination Program (CLEP)

CLEP exams are a lesser-known option for earning college credits, and students can do so by paying a relatively small fee of $80 and demonstrating sufficient knowledge in one of 33 different areas. Administered by the College Board, the same company who runs AP and the SAT, CLEP exams are accepted by over 2,900 colleges and universities.[13]

Since there is no accompanying course for CLEP exams, students are pretty much on their own in terms of preparation. Pick up a CLEP study guide for ten bucks, get a sense of the material covered, take a sample test, and if they feel like they have a firm grasp on the material, give it a try. The best time to do this is typically right after completing high school coursework that is relevant to the exam. Maybe they just finished an honors economics course and feel like they understand the material at a *college level*. A student's knowledge gained in the classroom plus their self-directed independent study should be a solid recipe for success on the CLEP.

Even though the vast majority of institutions will award credit for strong test scores, it is especially important to check the policies of individual schools related to CLEP. Many schools will only accept exams that they feel directly match up to a component of their own core curriculum. At Elon University, only 6 of the 33 CLEP exams can be substituted for undergraduate credit. At Denison, a small liberal arts school in Ohio, CLEP scores must be at or above the 75th percentile in order to receive credit. The University of North Carolina—Charlotte is more generous and accepts all but a few CLEP tests with much lower required scores than the previous two schools.

Dual Enrollment

Rather than a simulated college atmosphere, as with AP or IB, dual enrollment is an option that affords teens the chance to actually immerse themselves in a college environment while they are still in high school. Most commonly, the participating postsecondary school will be a community college or local branch campus of a larger state university. Students typically utilize dual

enrollment opportunities to either knock out core courses that will be requirements at their prospective colleges or to sample an academic offering that
may be unavailable at their high school (i.e., a less commonly studied foreign
language or computer science course).

Numerous studies have found that participation in dual enrollment aids
college readiness and persistence. If that isn't reason enough to consider this
option, taking college courses during high school can, as with AP, IB, and
CLEP, lop off a sizable portion of their freshman bill.

Finding out whether one's future college will accept dual enrollment credits is relatively easy—a simple Internet search will usually do the trick. There
are a few schools that have more stringent policies. Rice University will consider previously earned college credits but not if they appear on a high school
transcript as dual credit. On the other hand, the University of Texas at Austin
does accept credits earned in this manner. As a general rule, public schools
are far more open to honoring dual enrollment credits than private schools,
especially of the elite variety.

Final Thoughts

A great many students pursue a rigorous college-level course of study in high
school purely from an admissions-driven mindset. We encourage teenagers
to expand their thinking, considering the enormous financial advantages that
can be obtained as they simultaneously complete challenging coursework
that will prepare them for a successful college experience. Spending time on
such pursuits will be far more valuable than one of the favorite pastimes of
less-informed college bargain hunter—the wild goose chase of searching for
private scholarships.

THE TRUTH ABOUT PRIVATE SCHOLARSHIPS

In the early 1970s, the US auto industry received warnings from economic
experts—if they continued to focus on the wrong thing, Japanese car companies would soon put them out of business. Detroit's Big 3 of GM, Ford, and
Chrysler were told that if they remained attached to producing oversized,
inefficient American-style models, they would be surpassed by the compact,
fuel-efficient cars being made by the Japanese if the price of gasoline were
to drastically increase.

Laughing off these dire warnings, US auto execs continued with business as usual. Over the course of the decade, due to a changing atmosphere in the Middle East, the price of oil skyrocketed and the American car companies crumbled. If you've ever seen Eminem's *8 Mile* or an episode of *Hardcore Pawn*, you know how things turned out in the Motor City.

It's easy to become fixated on details that are new, shiny, and fun (like a '72 Corvette) and ignore others that are counter to our belief system. Such is the case with how prospective college students seek financial aid. For whatever reason, students and parents alike spend an inordinate amount of time seeking out private scholarships from employers, nonprofits, and local organizations and not enough time investigating where the bulk of aid money actually comes from.

The Shocking Numbers

Let us quickly disabuse you of this notion through simple numbers. In the 2014–2015 academic year, roughly $180 billion in total student aid was awarded to undergraduate students. The overwhelming majority of student aid comes from the federal government, representing roughly half of all aid awarded. Institutional aid from colleges and universities is the second largest source, accounting for $40 billion and state governments give just over $10 billion of total aid. Only 6% of the total aid handed out comes in the form of employer and private scholarships, a number that doesn't quite support all of the hype.[14]

Unclaimed Money?

Many parents mistakenly believe the popular notion that millions of dollars of private scholarship money goes unclaimed each year so they spend precious time scouring through scholarship websites, books, and other sources chasing this pot of gold. While there is some truth to the idea of unclaimed private college money, the fact also remains that many of those scholarships are inaccessible because the qualifying requirements are so limiting.

For example, there may be a scholarship at a regional university specifically aimed at a student from a particular county, with a high school GPA of 3.5 or higher, who is majoring in interior design. If no incoming student meets these criteria, the scholarship may go unclaimed. If the scholarship is claimed, however, funds are likely to be awarded for only one year, not four—unlike federal, state, and institutional scholarships/grants, private scholarships are rarely renewable.

Private Scholarships Can Hurt Your Financial Aid Package

It is also important to note that since the federal government requires postsecondary institutions to consider private scholarships when calculating financial aid, outside scholarships can actually *reduce* your original aid package. Let's say, for example, that a family's EFC is $17,000 and the cost of the college is $30,000. In order to meet this cost, the college offers $13,000 in its financial aid package to assist the family.

Now let's say that the student wins a $3,000 scholarship from a local employer. In this instance, most schools would then reduce their respective financial aid offers by $3,000. Hopefully, these reductions target loan awards, rather than grant awards, although that isn't always the case at every school. All in all, private scholarships have very little impact on the *bottom line* for students requiring need-based aid since scholarships often lead to a reduction in their original financial aid award. For affluent students who do not require aid, however, scholarships will undoubtedly impact out-of-pocket costs by reducing the amount they owe.

By no means do we want to discourage students from applying for private scholarships; we just encourage them not to dedicate an excessive amount of time to these often fruitless pursuits. On the subject of common mistakes parents and students make, we turn next to wallet-killing obsession with out-of-state public schools.

THE OUT-OF-STATE SIRENS' SONG

In Greek myth, the Sirens, half-woman/half-birdlike creatures crooned such sweet melodies to passing sailors that they would abandon ship, become so enraptured with the Sirens' song that they would completely forget to eat, eventually starving to death. Flagship state schools such as the University of Michigan, the University of Virginia, Penn State, and those in the University of California system have never caused any seafaring gents to die of hunger, but their name recognition, desirability, athletic prowess, and status as *research* institutions have lured many out-of-state applicants to unwisely pay hefty tuition bills, while passing up better-value opportunities at private colleges.

Let's look at a few examples. Annual, out-of-state costs at the University of Michigan run close to 60 grand, roughly double what Michigan residents pay. UCLA charges nearly $25,000 more to those who hail from outside the Golden State. Penn State, a bargain for PA residents, climbs to approximately

$50,000 for outsiders, and after accounting for need-based and merit-based aid, proves as more expensive than Franklin & Marshall, Lafayette, or Lehigh—three highly competitive colleges in the same state. That's right, on top of the steep nonresident markup, prestigious public schools of this ilk rarely offer significant financial aid packages and rely on out-of-staters who can and will pay the maximum tuition. This practice is far from nefarious.

Public institutions have been hit hard with budget cuts in recent years and do not sport the gargantuan endowments of many private schools. Out-of-state students capable of paying the full bill have become a desirable source of revenue. The less admirable side is that students from out of state sometimes have an admissions edge if they have the funds behind them. This is not exactly a shining example of egalitarianism. None of this is to argue against attending any of these terrific schools if students have done their homework and feel they've found an ideal fit. Flagship universities offer worldwide name recognition, gigantic alumni bases for networking, and the excitement of 100,000-seat football stadiums on Saturdays.

However, for those with finite financial resources (i.e., most of us), students may find an equally strong private school that is far more likely to offer a sizable financial aid package. If they're in need of funds yet give into the allure of a flagship school, a student may not end up on an island, withering away, listening to a bunch of mutant bird-women harmonize, but they are almost guaranteed to end up with a more cumbersome than necessary tuition bill.

CAN YOU REALLY PAY IN-STATE TUITION AT AN OUT-OF-STATE UNIVERSITY?

In an effort to dodge the aforementioned price hike of an out-of-state school, many parents inquire about, ahem, *alternative methods*.

To most of us, the concept of in-state tuition is a straightforward proposition—government-subsidized public institutions offer a lower tuition price to residents of their state. Families can elect to take advantage of the in-state tuition or pay a sizable premium for an out-of-state public school. Pretty cut and dry, right? Not anymore. Savvy parents have figured out how to exploit legal loopholes that allow their children to enjoy an in-state discount at an out-of-state school. With the four-year difference between the out-of-state and hometown tuition price entering the six figures at some state schools, the stakes of this new game could not be higher.

What Are the Rules and How Do Students Bend Them?

Every state has unique rules and loopholes that might open the door to being awarded in-state status. The most common strategy that crafty families employ involves trying to establish residency in the state where they hope to attend college and taking some form of a *gap year*. If students are going to go this route, they'll need to show evidence that they weren't just playing the system (even if that is precisely what they are doing). They need to get a driver's license in their chosen state, find a job, and pay income taxes. In most cases, awarding or withholding in-state status is still completely at the school's discretion, and they do not shy away from rejecting students whose profile raises red flags.

Establishing independence from one's parents is another huge hurdle. Many states require any student under a certain age (often 23 or 24) to prove that they have been financially independent from their parents for at least two years. Otherwise, residency is viewed as reverting back to their parent's home state, even if a student has physically resided elsewhere for a long period of time.

On the more extreme end, some students have even gone as far as to arrange sham marriages with people who reside in the state where they wish to attend school. Establishing residency, at that point, is a breeze, even if the rest of your life would likely be a freak show (and also a Lifetime movie).

Hired Help

For-profit organizations are springing up to assist families with this process and, according to many college officials, are toeing the line between opportunism and criminal deception. For upward of ten grand, an organization will help you put together a petition for in-state tuition. Such substantial documentation is required that these applications can end up literally being hundreds of pages long. No information is publicly available as to how successful these agencies are at delivering the goods.

More Legit Avenues

If a student comes from a military family or is the child of a recently discharged veteran, he or she may qualify for in-state tuition as an out-of-state student. The recently passed Veterans Access, Choice, and Accountability Act of 2014 allows dependents of recently discharged veterans to claim in-state tuition at public schools in all 50 states. Individuals currently serving in the military (and their dependents) do not qualify for the nationwide tuition benefit, but due to other legislation, still quality for lower rates. Virginia, Texas, Ohio, and dozens of other states have passed bills offering in-state tuition to out-of-state military families.

In addition to passing legislation benefiting military families, many states have arranged reciprocity agreements with each other, providing lower tuition to students residing in neighboring states. For example, member states of the Midwest Student Exchange Program allow out-of-state students to receive a tuition rate no higher than 150% of the in-state rate. The Western Undergraduate Exchange which includes the popular higher education destination points of Arizona, California, and Colorado have the same 150% cap, but require students to apply for consideration.

In some instances, such pacts will allow students right on the border of one state to attend. The University of Louisville's agreement with certain bordering Indiana counties is one such example.

We believe that, in the absence of extenuating circumstances, the effort and/or money spent to try to procure out-of-state tuition through questionable means would be better spent researching other affordable public and private options and pursuing merit aid and scholarships. There are simply too many outstanding institutions across the United States to warrant engaging in a *The Sting*-style *long con*. However, if a student is part of a military family or if their state is part of one of the consortiums that offers discounts, then in-state or reduced tuition is an excellent avenue to explore.

Crossing state borders is only one far-from-home option in the quest to find a higher education bargain. For all the would-be globetrotters out there, many values exist if students are willing to cross international borders.

GOING ABROAD FOR COLLEGE

Pursuing an undergraduate degree abroad may sound like an extravagance reserved for the jet-setting upper-class, yet going to college in a foreign country can actually make excellent economic sense for the more cost-conscious prospective college students. As we write, there are 27,000 American students pursuing degrees abroad at a host of locations around the world. The United Kingdom, Canada, and France are the three most popular destinations, but many other countries including Brazil, Germany, and several Scandinavian nations also offer appealing educational options for American students.

Do I Need to Speak a Foreign Language?

The polyglot answer is *nyet*, *non*, and *nein*. Studying abroad does not require speaking multiple languages or even being bilingual. Three-quarters of these students elect to study in English-speaking countries but many non-English-speaking countries, Germany, for example, now offer courses and even entire academic degree programs fully in English.

Tuition-Free or Reduced Options

The idea of spending 50 grand per year is a foreign idea (pun intended) in many places around the world. German universities are completely state funded and are 100% tuition free. Universities in France, Sweden, Finland, and Norway also allow US students to enroll at little or no cost.

Not every nation is so benevolent with higher education services that students can attend sans tuition, but most countries at least have lower average tuition than the United States. The average tuition for international students studying in the United Kingdom is around 18K.[15] Canada's rates for US students are in the same ballpark (or shall we say ice rink?), which while a bargain by American standards, is actually three times the rate for natives.[16]

Can I Still Get Loans?

Believe it or not, students wishing to complete four years at a foreign university may still be eligible for federal financial aid. While not every international postsecondary institution participates in US federal loan programs, over 800 schools worldwide do. Roughly half of these 800 are German-based universities, but locations also stretch to locales such as New Zealand, Argentina, and the Czech Republic

Consider Cost of Living

In many cases, the cost of living while studying abroad will be similar to or less than the cost of living on a college campus in the States. However, there are exceptions. For example, American students studying in Australia and the United Kingdom would likely incur higher (non-tuition) expenses than they would staying closer to home. Some destination points will cost you *a lot* more. To give you an idea, in Norway's capital city of Oslo, a can of soda will cost you the US equivalent of $3.43.[17] One can only imagine the cost of a meal plan.

Earning Acceptance

Generally speaking, foreign universities assign more weight to the hard facts of an application—such as rigor of course load, GPA, and SAT scores—and place less emphasis on extracurricular involvement. So, while simultaneously heading the debate team, entering Ukrainian dance competitions, founding a nonprofit, and lettering in three varsity sports is extremely impressive, don't expect it to improve a student's admission prospects at Cambridge or Oxford, for example.

Earning Your Degree

Many foreign schools offer less-structured learning time than American universities, which means a greater degree of self-motivation and discipline will be involved from the jump. Many students going abroad will be expected to assume responsibility for their own learning, as well as navigate course requirements and exams, often without the aid of a syllabus or reading list. Of course, if students have the internal drive and independent mindedness to seek out an academic program thousands of miles from home, chances are they can adjust to the differences of a foreign university system.

Three-Year Bachelor's?

In 1999, a number of European nations signed what was known as the *Bologna declaration*, which among other less interesting things, legitimized the 3-year bachelor's degree. In the years since, additional nations have jumped on board making this abbreviated option pretty standard. Other countries such as Australia and India are not part of the Bologna club but still offer 3-year full undergraduate programs. Students hailing from the United States do need to be careful when pursuing this option, however, as some American graduate schools will not admit holders of so-called Bologna degrees or will do so only conditionally.

Traveling to a foreign land to pursue an undergraduate degree is not for everyone. Yet for adventurous, open-minded young people, the willingness to consider schools outside of American borders can open up intriguing academic possibilities at potential bargain prices.

Popular Undergraduate Destinations for U.S. Students

The following colleges and universities attract their fair share of high-achieving American undergraduates. Each of these excellent institutions also sports a significant American alumni network and may prove significantly more affordable than U.S. schools of comparable quality.

Institution	Location
King's College	United Kingdom
McGill University	Canada
Queen's University	Canada
Trinity College	Ireland
University College London	United Kingdom
University of Glasgow	United Kingdom
University of Edinburgh	United Kingdom
University of British Columbia	Canada
University of St. Andrews	United Kingdom
University of Toronto	Canada

Figure 6.4   Going Abroad: Popular Undergraduate Destinations for US Students

FINAL THOUGHTS

The advice dispensed in this chapter was crafted to assist just about any student, regardless of academic/career interest, in selecting a college that will provide value in addition to a first-class higher education experience—even those who haven't the first clue what they wish to do when they grow up. Chapter 7 will take things a step further, offering guidance for career-focused teens who are motivated to ultimately enter a targeted professional field.

Creating a postsecondary plan for a student who aims to one day enter med school can be quite different from planning for a student who dreams of one day being an elementary school teacher. Issues of prestige, undergraduate financial planning, and major selection are explored for the nine professions that our students most frequently desire to enter.

NOTES

1. Scott Jaschik, "Pressure from All Sides: The 2015 Survey of Admissions Directors," *Inside Higher Ed*, October 1, 2015, accessed December 6, 2015, https://www.inside-highered.com/news/survey/pressure-all-sides-2015-survey-admissions-directors.

2. Scott Jaschik, "More Pressure Than Ever: The 2014 Survey of College and University Admissions Directors," *Inside Higher Ed*, September 18, 2014, accessed December 6, 2015, https://www.insidehighered.com/news/survey/more-pressure-ever-2014-survey-college-and-university-admissions-directors.

3. Ry Rivard, "Summer Scramble," *Inside Higher Ed*, May 21, 2014, accessed December 28, 2015, https://www.insidehighered.com/news/2014/05/21/colleges-miss-enrollment-targets-step-their-summer-recruitment.

4. U.S. Department of Education, Institute of Education Sciences, National Center for Education Statistics.

5. College Board, "Trends in Student Aid 2014," accessed December 6, 2015, https://secure-media.collegeboard.org/digitalServices/misc/trends/2014-trends-student-aid-report-final.pdf.

6. World Bank, "GDP Ranking," last modified December 16, 2015, accessed December 27, 2015, http://data.worldbank.org/data-catalog/GDP-ranking-table.

7. Mark Kantrowitz, "Reasons Why Students Do Not File the FAFSA," January 18, 2011, accessed November 11, 2015, http://www.finaid.org/educators/20110118nofafsareasons.pdf.

8. https://new.trinity.edu/admissions-aid/financial-aid/academic-merit-scholarships-first-year-students.

9. Nick Anderson, "Colleges Often Give Discounts to the Rich. But Here's One That Gave Up on 'Merit Aid,'" *The Washington Post*, December 29, 2014, accessed December 21, 2015, https://www.washingtonpost.com/local/education/

colleges-often-give-discounts-to-the-rich-but-heres-one-that-gave-up-on-merit-aid/2014/12/29/

a15a0f22-6f3c-11e4-893f-86bd390a3340_story.html.

10. College Board, "Retaking the SAT," accessed September 17, 2015, https://professionals.collegeboard.com/testing/sat-reasoning/scores/retake.

11. College Board, "Average Published Undergraduate Charges by Sector, 2015–16," Trends in Higher Education, accessed December 6, 2015, http://trends.collegeboard.org/college-pricing/figures-tables/average-published-undergraduate-charges-sector-2015-16.

12. International Baccalaureate, "The IB by Country," accessed December 28, 2015, http://www.ibo.org/country/US/.

13. College Board, "CLEP: Getting College Credit," accessed December 6, 2015, https://clep.collegeboard.org/overview/collegecredit.

14. College Board, "Total Undergraduate Student Aid by Source and Type, 2014-15," Trends in Higher Education, accessed December 6, 2015, http://trends.collegeboard.org/student-aid/figures-tables/total-undergraduate-student-aid-source-and-type-2014-15.

15. David Matthews, "International and Postgrad Fee Survey, 2014," *Times Higher Education*, August 21, 2014, accessed February 29, 2016, https://www.timeshigher-education.com/features/international-and-postgrad-fee-survey-2014/2015207.article.

16. "University Tuition Fees, 2015/2016," *The Daily*, September 9, 2015, accessed February 29, 2016, http://www.statcan.gc.ca/daily-quotidien/150909/dq150909b-eng.pdf.

17. Shivika Jindal, "Most Expensive City in the World–Oslo, Norway," February 13, 2014, accessed December 6, 2015, http://richglare.com/expensive-city-world-oslo-norway/.

Chapter 7

College Advice for the Career Minded

So You Want to Be a . . .

Speak with enough successful professionals and you'll likely come across a few folks who stumbled into their success after a relatively aimless, meandering youth. They drifted through high school, maybe even undergrad, and then, voila, they were one of the leading orthopedic surgeons in the world. For some, professional success springs from humble or directionless beginnings. Yet, it's fair to say these folks are the exception, not the rule.

Many who enter professional fields like medicine, law, engineering, teaching, or computer programming were driven from a relatively early age to pursue activities related to their desired field. Sometimes a career path manifested itself in high school, for others they were destined for certain careers since they could talk—think of the future engineer somehow jerry-rigging a pile of Duplos into a working combustion engine as a toddler.

Back in chapter 1, we cited alarming statistics regarding both rising student debt and the shocking number of degree holders working jobs that did not require a college education, many of whom are now suffering long-term financial consequences as a result. Look no further than a statistic released in 2015 revealing that 37% of Uber drivers possessed college degrees and nearly 11% held graduate degrees.[1] Again, as we said before, there is absolutely nothing wrong with choosing to work in a field that doesn't require any higher education. What is undesirable is accruing massive student loan debt at an expensive private college and then ending up in a lower-wage, limited-benefits job—especially when this circumstance could have easily been avoided with just a small dose of planning back in high school.

In such a challenging economic climate, we feel that a resource guide is needed to more effectively guide young people toward a style of college planning that properly accounts for long-term financial and career-related realities. In the absence of such advice, it's simply too easy for parents and students to develop tunnel vision in the college selection process where practical and down-the-road factors fall by the wayside; it's also easy to sign up as an Uber driver.

Whether your child has been sure of their future field since they were in Huggies or is just beginning to lean toward a certain profession as a high school senior, our "So You Want to Be a . . . " chapter is designed to help all career-minded high school students think intelligently about their postsecondary journeys. In this chapter, we will look at the financial, academic, and personal factors that college-bound students and their families should consider when exploring some of the most popular professions: doctor, lawyer, engineer, software developer/programmer, teacher, financial analyst, psychologist, professor, and journalist. We also highlight the colleges that send the highest percentage of students to top jobs and graduate schools in these professional fields, and by doing so, reveal whether attending a prestigious undergraduate school can actually help one's job prospects.

SO YOU WANT TO BE A DOCTOR . . .

Should I Be a Pre-Med Major?

This may come as a surprise, but the acceptance rate to medical school among those who majored in the biological sciences is actually less than that of humanities, math, or social science majors.[2] Translation: Students are genuinely free to pursue any academic major on the road to med school.

That being said, if you choose to pursue your dream of majoring in a foreign language, there will be a laundry list of prerequisites that you will have to squeeze into your academic schedule. Most medical schools require two to four semesters of biology, two semesters of both organic and inorganic chemistry, physics, and math (including calculus). If you can balance a non-premed major and these demanding courses, go for it. If you start accidentally labeling hydrolytic enzymes in French on your biology final, it may be time to consider a more focused course of study.

Gain Experience in the Field

Not only will gaining experience in the field help you decide if a medical career is right for you, it will help you build a resume demonstrating passion and a lifetime commitment to the profession. Selecting a college with ample research opportunities for undergraduates can be advantageous, as can involving yourself in clinical work and medical-related community service. In fact, the majority of US medical schools cite these activities as *important* or *very important* to their admission decisions.[3]

Do I Need to Attend a Prestigious Undergraduate School?

Earning admission into medical school requires, above all, a high undergraduate GPA and MCAT score, regardless of your undergraduate institution; however, the competitiveness of your alma mater can indeed have influence, especially at the most prestigious medical schools. For example, Harvard Medical School insists that it "is looking for people with broad interests and talents, not for students from particular academic institutions." Yet, an analysis of where current HMS students attended college would suggest otherwise.

Using data from the business networking site, LinkedIn, we were able to identify the undergraduate backgrounds of 385 Harvard Med students, who comprise more than half of the school's MD candidate population. Surprisingly, more than 70 percent earned undergraduate degrees from a college or university identified as *elite*.[4] The most commonly represented institutions included Yale, Duke, MIT, Stanford, and, of course, Harvard.

Similar analyses of other top medical schools yielded very much the same results, indicating that undergraduate prestige does matter. For example, of the nearly 260 Stanford MD candidates with a LinkedIn profile (more than half of Stanford's current MD student population), a whopping 60 percent earned bachelor's degrees from one of 12 undergraduate institutions: Stanford, MIT, Duke, Johns Hopkins, or one of the eight Ivy League colleges. Keep in mind there are over 2,000 four-year colleges and universities in the United States.

Of course, Stanford, Harvard, and other elite medical schools may admit a disproportionately high number of Ivy League students, not because of the name on their undergraduate diplomas, but because they possess abilities and/ or talents that are actually superior to candidates from other, less-competitive institutions and which enabled them to secure a spot at a top college in the first place. However, the lack of undergraduate diversity among elite med school students is too glaring to ignore; and in light of several recent studies suggesting that the overwhelming majority of high-achieving students do not in fact attend an Ivy League or other elite college, it would seem fair to conclude that elite medical institutions do give at least some preference to

Using student-level data provided by LinkedIn, we were able to identify the colleges and universities sending the highest percentage of graduates to a top-ranked medical program. Results are listed in alphabetical order and suggest that undergraduate prestige does matter within the field of medicine.

Undergraduate Institution

Amherst College

Bowdoin College

Brown University

Columbia University

Cornell University

Dartmouth College

Duke University

Harvard University

Haverford College

Johns Hopkins University

Massachusetts Institute of Technology

Pomona College

Princeton University

Rice University

Stanford University

Swarthmore College

University of Pennsylvania

Washington University

Williams College

Yale University

....

The medical schools incorporated into our analysis:
Columbia · Duke · Harvard · Johns Hopkins · Stanford · University of California, San Francisco · Chicago · Penn · Washington University · Yale

Figure 7.1   Top Feeders to Elite Medical Schools

graduates of highly selective institutions, irrespective of their GPA or MCAT results.[5]

Interestingly, the results of our analysis also suggest that certain elite medical schools, such as Stanford and Duke University, give preference to their own undergrads, perhaps in part because they have an intimate familiarity with the rigor of the program, but also because these schools have a vested interest in seeing their own alumni advance to the highest rungs of the medical profession. For example, a Duke undergraduate who goes on to attend Duke medical school is more likely to become an alumni donor, and given her MD from Duke, is more likely to land a coveted position within the medical field, thus bringing greater revenue and prestige to the university.

What If I Can't Get Admitted into a Prestigious College?

Ultimately, attending a highly selective undergraduate institution can improve one's medical school prospects, but it is not the only pathway to a medical career. There are nearly 150 accredited MD-granting institutions in the United States, and another 30 plus accredited institutions granting doctorates in osteopathic medicine—most accept students from a wide array of undergraduate institutions, and nearly all produce physicians who achieve success within their respective specialties. It is also important to note that job security, employment prospects, and earnings are almost always strong for medical school graduates, *regardless of which medical school they attend*. This is not the case in other desirable professions, such as business or law, where a significant percentage of students attending less than prestigious graduate schools fail to secure jobs and salaries that are commensurate with their level of education.

However, if you remain determined to attend an elite medical school but don't quite have the credentials to attend an elite college, you might consider these slightly less-selective institutions, all of which have strong pre-med offerings, and despite their absence from our top feeders list, still have excellent track records of placing graduates into the best MD programs:

- Baylor University
- Boston University
- Case Western Reserve University
- Clark University
- College of the Holy Cross
- University of California, San Diego
- University of Pittsburgh
- University of Washington

Plan the Financial End

Eighty-six percent of medical students emerge from school with debt to their name. The average debt load is close to 180K.[6] The good news is that, unlike with law school, just about everyone who makes it through med school will end up with a six-figure career, yet doctors' salaries vary greatly by specialty area. While primary care physicians bring home a median compensation of $241,000, cardiologists and orthopedic surgeons make more than twice that amount.[7]

It's important to remember that becoming a medical doctor can involve up to 14 years of higher education meaning that you will be missing out on as many as ten post-undergrad, income-generating years. While this represents a pretty significant opportunity cost, those with a burning desire to join the medical field will find the rewards well worth the sacrifice.

Related Careers

If you want a career in health care but don't want to spend the time or money pursuing a medical degree, consider these other popular professions, seen in Figure 7.2.

SO YOU WANT TO BE A LAWYER . . .

Should I Be a Pre-Law Major?

The American Bar Association does not recommend a pre-law course of study for future barristers in college. In fact, they have decreed publicly that there is no *right* major. A look at law school admissions data reveal that history, economics, math, science, and philosophy majors all have far superior rates of admission into law school than those with a pre-law or criminal justice background.[8] Essentially, if law school is your desired next step, then you

---

If you want a career in healthcare but don't want to spend the time or money pursuing a medical degree, consider these other popular professions:

Profession	Median Pay	Expected Job Growth (2014-2024)	Entry-Level Degree
Cytotechnologist	$71,277	14%	Bachelor's
Medical Sonographer	$62,540	24%	Associate's
Nurse Practitioner	$95,350	31%	Master's
Physician Assistant	$95,820	30%	Master's
Radiation Therapist	$80,090	14%	Associate's

Figure 7.2 Popular Health Care Professions

have a license to pursue whatever subject you find intellectually stimulating as an undergraduate. The operative phrase there is *intellectually stimulating*. To be adequately prepared to ace the LSAT and handle the rigor of law school, you'll want to steer clear of phys ed, advanced crocheting, or bowling industry management.

Make Sure You Actually Want to Be a Lawyer

To picture the day-to-day experience of most attorneys, start by imagining your favorite oozingly earnest Sam Waterston closing statement from *Law & Order* . . . Okay, ready? Now subtract all of the glamour, drama, and high-minded ideals. Substitute in 90-hour workweeks, endless mountains of paperwork, and a cutthroat and highly stressful work environment.

Okay, maybe that was a bit harsh but if you examine surveys of those presently in the field, a less-than-rosy picture of the job emerges. Over half of those practicing law today say they wish they had chosen a different career.[9] Equally bleak is the fact that depression, substance abuse, and even suicide are more prevalent in the legal field than in any other profession.[10] We're not saying there aren't lawyers who have wonderful and fulfilling careers, but you'll want to do your research to make sure there is an area in the field that genuinely excites you.

Gain Experience in the Field

Jumping straight from your college graduation into law school might make you feel like the star of your five-year high school reunion ("Man, that guy/gal has got direction!"), but it could cost you the chance to do your due diligence. We recommend spending some time working in a legal setting before cutting that first hefty law school tuition check. Whether it's in the summer or after graduation, there is no better method of career counseling than actually seeing the real deal up-close.

Does Going to a Prestigious Undergraduate School Help?

Getting into a reputable law school, where job opportunities are plentiful, is first and foremost a numbers game. In general, so-called tier-one law schools are looking for students with outstanding GPAs and LSAT scores. These are, after all, the primary metrics used by *U.S. News* to rank the top law programs. The prestige of one's undergraduate institution is less of a factor, but still appears to play an important role.

Using LinkedIn data, we were able to identify the undergraduate back-grounds of approximately 60 percent of all students enrolled in law schools that are ranked among the top 15 by *U.S. News*. Although degree holders from elite colleges are not as pervasive as they are at the nation's top medical schools, their numbers still far exceed their representation among four-year college graduates. Of the nearly 8,700 students currently enrolled at a top-15 law school and for whom we were able to collect education data, more than 38% earned degrees from an undergraduate institution that was rated as *Elite*, while approximately 63% graduate from one of 73 colleges defined as *Elite* or *Extremely Selective* (see the Appendix to learn how we rank colleges by selectivity). Harvard, Yale, and UC Berkeley sent the highest number of graduates to elite law schools, and are included among our other *top feeders*.[11]

Although our analysis suggests that undergraduate prestige does matter, it also indicated that graduating from an uber-selective college was not the only way to earn entry into a top law program. According to our estimates, close to 30% of all elite law school attendees graduate from an undergraduate school accepting more than half of all applicants. In addition, there were a number of reputable yet slightly less-competitive schools that sent a significant share of graduates to the nation's best law schools, including the following:

- American University
- Fordham University
- Furman University
- George Washington University
- St. Olaf College
- University of Florida
- University of Georgia
- University of Pittsburgh

In fact, given the overriding importance of GPAs and LSAT scores, it is safe to assume that there can be potential advantages associated with attend-ing a *slightly* less-selective institution, particularly if you are able to earn a higher GPA than you would at a more exclusive school. For example, a student with a 3.7 from George Washington University may present as more competitive than a 3.4 student from nearby Georgetown.

Ultimately, if you are an aspiring lawyer and in the midst of choosing an undergraduate institution, perhaps it's best to keep in mind what Michigan's top-ranked law school wrote about the role of college prestige, which likely summarizes the stance adopted by other prestigious law programs:

Using student-level data provided by LinkedIn, we were able to identify the colleges and universities sending the highest percentage of graduates to top-ranked law schools. Results are listed in alphabetical order and suggest that the selectivity of one's undergraduate institution may have influence in the law school admissions process.

Undergraduate Institution

Amherst College

Barnard College

Brown University

Claremont McKenna College

Cornell University

Dartmouth College

Duke University

Georgetown University

Hamilton College

Harvard University

Haverford College

Middlebury College

Pomona College

Princeton University

Stanford University

University of California, Berkeley

University of Pennsylvania

Wesleyan University

Williams College

Yale University

The law schools incorporated into our analysis:
Columbia • Cornell • Duke • Georgetown • Harvard • NYU • Northwestern
Stanford • UC Berkeley • Univ. of Chicago • Penn • Univ. of Virginia
Univ. of Michigan • Univ. of Texas • Yale

Figure 7.3   Top Feeders to Elite Law Schools

While the strength of an undergraduate institution is certainly a factor we consider in the admissions process, our commitment to maintaining the excellence of our student body does not limit the wide range of educational institutions from which our students hail. There most assuredly is no accredited school whose graduates we would be simply unwilling to admit.[12]

Plan the Financial End

Two key things to remember here:

1. Law school is extremely expensive.
2. Not every lawyer makes a ton of money.

Just about everyone who successfully works their way through medical school will go on to a lucrative career. This is simply not true of law school, where, quite frankly, there will be winners and losers. Your performance relative to the rest of your class matters, and those at the bottom 50th percentile of their class rarely, if ever, waltz into six-figure jobs. Those with a passion for less lucrative sectors of the profession such as family law, civil rights, or public interest also need to be particularly thoughtful in this area.

The average law school graduate comes out over $100K in debt.[13] There is, of course, good debt and bad debt. Overpaying for a high-end undergraduate education and then paying big bucks for a lower-end law school is likely to leave you with bad debt. If you have a choice between attending an elite college for undergrad or an elite law school (and not both), go with the elite law school every time.

What Kind of Law School Should I Aim for?

Unlike our approach to undergraduate admissions, we do not place as large of an emphasis on *fit* when it comes to law schools. Of course, fit matters to the extent that, for example, candidates interested in a career in government may find better prospects at a DC-area law school. Yet, it is important to acknowledge the reality that law school and the legal field itself are hypercompetitive and prestige is of paramount importance.

If you're going to go to law school, aim for a top-shelf institution. Tier 3 and 4 law school graduates too often face a chilly job market and are saddled with burdensome debts. If, after looking over your law school prospects, you conclude, like Groucho Marx, that you wouldn't join any club that would have you as a member, it may be time to explore other professions.

Profession	Median Pay	Top 10%	Entry-Level Degree
Arbitrator/Mediator	$57,180	>$121,050	Bachelor's Degree
E-Discovery Professional	$75,800	>$175,000	Bachelor's Degree
Law Librarian	$58,467	>$88,000	Master's Degree
Political Scientist	$104,920	>$153,960	Master's Degree
Sports/Entertainment Agent	$64,200	>$188,000	Bachelor's Degree

Figure 7.4   Careers Related to Law

Related Careers

College-bound students with interests in law, policy, and/or criminal justice should understand that becoming a lawyer is not their only career option. In reality, there are dozens of potentially fulfilling and financially rewarding occupations for which having a legal background is desired, if not required.

SO YOU WANT TO BE AN ENGINEER . . .

Many Types of Engineers

There are more than 25 different areas of study within the engineering discipline including but not limited to civil, mechanical, biomedical, chemical, electrical, geological, architectural, industrial, aerospace, software, and nuclear engineering. Naturally, these varying fields can involve very different courses of study. However, all engineering disciplines share certain core competencies that must be mastered in order to enter this highly competitive profession.

Do You Have an "Engineering Mind?"

Because engineering degrees dominate lists of top-paying bachelor's degrees, a good number of high school students (and their parents) understandably elect to explore it as a career option. Here's a word of warning on that subject: this is rarely a skill set that appears suddenly in late adolescence when it's time to select a college major—for most, it is evident from early childhood.

From a very early age, those with an *engineering mind* can often be found taking things apart and putting them back together. Some may enjoy repairing machinery or electronic equipment, teaching themselves computer programming, or tinkering with inventions. In essence, these individuals possess both a passion and an aptitude for figuring out how things work. This combination of innate ability and zeal is essential in a discipline that requires a high level of perseverance and diligence.

Fact: Engineering Programs Are Challenging

The attrition rate for engineering students in unparalleled. A gulp-worthy 50% of freshmen engineering students eventually drop out or change majors.[14] The primary reason why students drop out of engineering programs is a lack of preparedness for the high level of rigor. Beyond the sheer challenge of the material is the time commitment required. The average engineering major spends 20–25 hours studying outside of the classroom, more than any other major.[15] However, students at top engineering programs at schools like MIT and Caltech have the lowest freshman dropout rates, in large part because their classes are comprised exclusively of students who took the most rigorous curriculum available to them in high school.

What Courses Should I Take in High School?

No matter what type of engineering you plan on studying, it's a good bet that impeccable math skills will be required. Plan on taking AP Calculus and AP Statistics while in high school. Not surprisingly, advanced science courses are also a must—chemistry, biology, and physics of the honors or AP variety are recommended. Nationwide, only 63% of public high schools offer physics and just 50% have a calculus course.[16] If these courses are unavailable in your school, seek out opportunities online or at a local community college.

Partaking in any computer science program offered by your high school is also strongly recommended for all would-be engineers. Some schools offer computer-aided design and AP Computer Science. All engineers need to be tech-savvy and formal training in high school can give you an edge. It's also wise not to neglect English. Engineers in today's marketplace are often required to be strong writers and communicators. Soft-skill areas such as adaptability and collaboration are also great assets for anyone entering the world of engineering.

Do I Need to Attend a Prestigious Undergraduate School?

The engineering field is more egalitarian than others—most employers are more interested in what you can produce than the selectivity of your undergraduate college.

An examination of starting and mid-career salary data from over 300 engineering schools supports this reality and reveals a pretty level playing field and a general lack of correlation between prestige and pay.[17]

For example, Stevens Institute of Technology in Hoboken, New Jersey, is ranked by *U.S. News* as the 76th best engineering program.[18] Its graduates have an average starting salary of $66,800 and an average mid-career salary of $120,000. Compare that to MIT, ranked first overall, where graduates enter the field with an average salary of $74,900 and enjoy an average mid-career salary only $4,000 more than a typical Stevens grad.[19]

We're not making the argument that Stevens Institute of Technology and MIT are on equal footing; we are merely highlighting the fact that the choice between attending a highly selective and moderately selective engineering program is not likely to determine the amount you are compensated for your work.

The selectivity of your undergraduate institution, however, may determine *where* you work. Although there appears to be little, if any, relationship between the name on your diploma and numbers on your paycheck, undergraduate brand can still have an influence on the companies to which you have access. The following *Top Feeders* list shows that if you want to work as an engineer for some of America's most sought-after employers, having a degree from a selective institution can certainly help your chances.

Consider a Dual Degree Program

If you are determined to attend an elite engineering school, yet don't have the credentials to matriculate right away, a dual degree engineering program is an avenue worth exploring. This format allows students to earn a bachelor's degree at any one of a host of participating colleges in three or four years and then, if a minimum GPA is earned (typically a 3.3 or better), matriculate into a prestigious engineering program. For instance, Columbia University's highly selective engineering school partners with almost 100 liberal arts colleges across the country, from Ivy-caliber institutions like Middlebury to Marietta College in Ohio, which has a 70% acceptance rate. Students apply to Columbia during their junior year, and if accepted, spend the next two years earning a BS in engineering. Washington University and Dartmouth College also offer prestigious dual degree engineering programs.

Job Outlook

In making a case for STEM education, politicians frequently bemoan our country's *shortage* of engineers. These speeches leave the impression that anyone with a bachelor's in engineering will have 15 job offers before his or

Using publicly available data provided by the business networking site, LinkedIn, we were able to estimate which schools, after adjusting for average student enrollment, feed the highest number of bachelor-degree recipients to employers that engineering majors most commonly rate as "ideal." The list features a number of elite institutions, but also included are several excellent yet less selective colleges where students with good but not stratospheric credentials can earn admission. Schools are listed in alphabetical order.

Institution	Top Employer	Runner-Up
California Polytechnic State	Lockheed Martin	Boeing
California Institute of Technology	Boeing	NASA
Carnegie Mellon University	Boeing	General Motors
Cornell University	Lockheed Martin	Boeing
Georgia Institute of Technology	Lockheed Martin	Boeing
Harvey Mudd College	SpaceX	Boeing
Massachusetts Institute of Technology	Boeing	NASA
Penn State University	Lockheed Martin	Boeing
Purdue University	Boeing	General Motors
Rice University	Shell	ExxonMobil
Rensselaer Polytechnic Institute	General Motors	Lockheed Martin
Stanford University	Lockheed Martin	Boeing
Texas A&M University	Lockheed Martin	Shell
University of California, Berkeley	Boeing	Lockheed Martin
University of California, Los Angeles	Boeing	NASA
University of Illinois	Boeing	Ford Motor Company
University of Michigan	General Motors	Ford Motor Company
University of Southern California	Boeing	NASA
University of Texas at Austin	Lockheed Martin	ExxonMobil
University of Washington	Boeing	Lockheed Martin

The companies incorporated into our analysis:

Boeing · ExxonMobil · Ford Motor Company · General Electric
General Motors · Lockheed Martin · NASA · SpaceX · Shell · Tesla · Walt Disney

Figure 7.5   Top Feeders (Engineering)

her graduation cap flies into the air. It's true that an engineering degree of any variety is typically about as sound an educational investment as exists, however, some engineers, such as those in the naval and mining fields, actually suffer from higher unemployment rates than the general labor pool.[20]

The ten-year job outlook for engineers varies greatly by branch and, of course, is always subject to change based on technological developments, environmental factors, and shifting political landscapes. For example, the Bureau of Labor Statistics (BLS) predicts that openings for civil engineers will grow significantly through 2022 due to the nation's aging infrastructure and need to replace roads, tunnels, bridges, and dams.[21]

From aging structures to aging humans, the need for biomedical engineers should be in demand over the coming decades as the elderly population in the United States continues to need more and more medical care.[22] Likewise for petroleum engineers, ever-increasing oil prices and an older-than-average workforce should lead to healthy job growth.[23] However, the oil and gas industry is notoriously boom or bust and so it is very difficult to project with any certainty.

Bottom Line

Explore engineering as an area of study if you have an aptitude *and* passion for the related subject matter. Don't try to read the industry tea leaves when selecting a branch of engineering to study; pick a specialty area that is of high interest and within your academic wheelhouse.

Earning an engineering degree from any school, no matter the level of prestige, requires an exceptional level of commitment and fortitude. Those who conquer the academic challenges and enter the marketplace with a bachelor's in any engineering field will be well positioned to earn substantial compensation relative to other degree holders.

SO YOU WANT TO BE A SOFTWARE DEVELOPER/ ENGINEER/PROGRAMMER . . .

What's the Difference Between a Software Developer, Engineer, and Programmer?

These terms are sometimes used rather interchangeably which can lead to confusion. While there is a degree of overlap in terms of job duties and educational requirements, *software developers*, *engineers*, and *programmers* all have unique job duties and educational requirements.

Programmers' primary duties center around creating and inputting code. Most programmers have computer science degrees; others are self-taught. In a Venn diagram, the ability to code would overlap for both programmers and those termed software developers. Typically, the job title of software developer goes to someone who is a generalist, well versed in a number of systems and languages but not necessarily an expert in any one (like a programmer). Developers lead teams of programmers, possess strong communication skills, and help connect employees with expertise in different areas to work toward a bigger-picture goal.

Here's where things get unnecessarily confusing . . . some software engineers hold the title of software developer. However, the designation of engineer carries some weight and your average engineer would not enjoy being grouped as a *developer* with individuals lacking a degree in engineering. By definition, engineers explore the practical applications of scientific and mathematical principles as related to the creation of software. They, like developers, are looking at the big picture of a project, but with a lens more focused on science than art.

Do I Need to Attend a Prestigious Undergraduate School?

Indeed Google, Apple, and other premier tech companies do recruit heavily from the usual suspects: Stanford, MIT, Carnegie Mellon, etc. However, a school's proximity is also of great importance.

For example, Redmond, Washington-based Microsoft, plucks the majority of their employees from places such as nearby University of Washington, Washington State, and Western Washington University. Apple, located in the heart of Silicon Valley, draws a large portion of its workforce from nearby San Jose State and Cal Poly.[24]

As with the engineering profession at large, entering the field of software development is more about what you can *do* than the name on your diploma. That said, a computer science major from an elite school that also possesses an exceptional skill set will be at a premium on the job market and will also have an inside track to the most desirable companies in the tech industry, as the following *Top Feeders* list demonstrates.

What Courses Should I Take in High School?

It should come as little surprise that math is going to be of paramount importance. Taking a rigorous algebra, trigonometry, geometry, and pre-calc/calc

There is certainly no shortage of high-school students with Silicon Valley dreams—as companies like Apple, Facebook and Google continue to capture the world's attention, the number of computing-related majors continues to rise. If you want to break into the increasingly competitive tech industry, it's good to know which schools can pave the way. The colleges listed below are those that, after adjusting for average student enrollment, graduate the highest number of bachelor's degree recipients in computer science and computer engineering, who eventually go on to work at the nation's premier tech companies. Data used to create this list were drawn from the business networking site, LinkedIn. As demonstrated below, elite privates, public flagships, and California-based institutions are well-represented among this group of top feeders.

Institution	Top Employer	Runner-Up
Brown University	Google	Microsoft
California Institute of Technology	Google	Microsoft
Carnegie Mellon University	Google	Microsoft
Cornell University	Google	Microsoft
Georgia Institute of Technology	Google	Microsoft
Harvey Mudd College	Google	Microsoft
Massachusetts Institute of Technology	Google	Microsoft
North Carolina State University	Cisco	IBM
Purdue University	Intel Corporation	Microsoft
San Jose State University	Apple	Cisco
Santa Clara University	Cisco	Apple
Stanford University	Google	Apple
University of California, Berkeley	Google	Apple
University of California, Los Angeles	Google	Microsoft
University of California, San Diego	Qualcomm	Google
University of Illinois	Google	Microsoft
University of Michigan	Microsoft	Google
University of Southern California	Intel Corporation	Google
University of Texas at Austin	IBM	Microsoft
University of Washington	Microsoft	Amazon

The companies incorporated into our analysis:
Adobe · Amazon · Apple · Cisco · Facebook · Google · IBM · Intel LinkedIn · Microsoft · Oracle · Qualcomm

Figure 7.6   Top Feeders (Tech Companies)

class is a must, but none of these branches of mathematics translates directly to computer science.

If possible, find a way to take a discrete mathematics class. Discrete math is the foundation of modern-day computer science and includes topics such as combinatorics, probability, number theory, logic, and graph theory. While discrete math is a staple of most high school math competitions, it is not always offered by schools due to the fact that its content is not the primary focus of high-stakes state standardized tests or the SAT. You may have to take a summer course at a local college or study the subject on your own, but the rewards will be ample.

Of equal *duh* status is to partake in any and every computer course offered by your school. AP Computer Science is immensely beneficial but is only available at fewer than 5% of American high schools.[25] Roughly 40,000 high school students in the United States take the AP Computer Science exam each year compared to over 400,000 who take AP Calculus.[26] As with discrete math, ambitious students should seek to enroll in computer science coursework online or at a local college.

What Should I Major in?

Appropriate fields of study for entry into this profession include computer science, computer engineering, computer information systems, or mathematics. Regardless of your major, it'll be of benefit to be well versed in a variety of programming languages such as C++, CSS, Python, PHP, Java, and JavaScript. Opportunities to complete independent research projects and obtain internships during your four years of study will also be key in showing employers that you have the practical experience and knowledge needed to land your first job.

Salary Expectations

Software engineering is a well-compensated field, with the national average salary right around 90 grand. This is a rare career where the starting salary for a bachelor's degree holding individual reaches almost $70,000 per year. Experienced engineers/programmers/developers working for major multinational corporations such as Amazon, Oracle, and Intel will achieve average salaries in the low-six figures.[27]

Computer programmers without the *engineer* title attached to their name will typically earn close to 50K out of college and will average out at around

70K. Those who go on to become IT managers or take on other administrative duties can bring home salaries in excess of 100K.[28]

Job Outlook

Jobs in software development are projected to grow at 22%, faster than the average occupation, through 2022.[29] In addition to the continually growing world of mobile applications, this field will also benefit from the expansion of information technology in the health care field as well as increased investment in electronic security for government and private networks.

Bottom Line

Jobs in the software development field, whether you are an engineer or a programmer are stable, well compensated, and projected to grow significantly moving into the future. Those who are knowledgeable, experienced, and efficient will see a tremendous return on their educational investment whether they attend a selective tech powerhouse or a state school.

SO YOU WANT TO BE A TEACHER . . .

Does Going to a Prestigious Undergraduate School Help?

Breaking into the teaching field is numerically a very different endeavor than landing a job in the highly selective worlds of law, medicine, engineering, etc. There are presently 3.7 million people making their living as primary or secondary school teachers in the United States. Almost 85% of those 3.7 million educators are employed by their respective states in the public system, while the remaining few hundred thousand individuals staff private and parochial schools.[30]

If school districts, even top-notch ones, only accepted candidates from elite colleges and universities, the majority of the country's classrooms would be left unsupervised. A resume that boasts a prestigious undergraduate school may certainly catch the eye of a hiring official, especially from a desirable suburban district where breaking in is extremely competitive. However, even in these districts, a distinguished alma mater is far from a prerequisite.

Of more importance is the proximity of your college. Public institutions are often the best feeders into the most desirable schools and districts within their respective states. For example, in Pennsylvania, where teacher salaries are relatively high and pensions are relatively generous, many schools draw a high percentage of their employees from Penn State, University of Pittsburgh, and other less-selective state institutions, such as Millersville and West Chester Universities. Students attending these schools have an inside track to PA jobs because they are more likely to meet requirements for state licensure, secure local student teaching opportunities (which often to lead to employment), and benefit from strong alumni representation/networks within PA school districts. In general, if you know where you want to spend your teaching years, it's best to concentrate your college search on nearby schools, particularly those that are in-state and at least moderately selective.

Teacher Salaries

The widespread belief that teaching is, across the board, a low-income profession is a bit too broad and is ultimately misleading. In reality, teacher salaries vary greatly by type of school (public vs. private), region of the country, and type of community (urban vs. suburban vs. rural).

The overall average salary for a public school teacher in the United States comes in at just over $53,000.[31] However, in certain geographic pockets such as the Philadelphia, Chicago, New York, and San Diego suburbs, teachers at the top of the pay scale bring in six-figure salaries. Scarsdale School District in New York has the highest median teacher salary in the country at $137,000.[32]

Private school teachers will make significantly less than their public school counterparts. Charter schools, which continue to spring up in urban areas across the United States, also typically offer lower pay than public schools.

As with salary, benefits bestowed upon teachers have great variability on a state-by-state basis. There are 28 states who currently still offer pension systems to their public school teachers, but with almost all of these systems in financial crisis, it's hard to imagine they will sustain, at least in their present form, through the next generation of educators.

Gain Experience in the Field

Amazingly, 40% of individuals graduating with a teaching degree never even enter a classroom, instead electing to pursue other fields. Of those who do take over a classroom, 40-50% leave the profession within 5 years.[33] Too often, students studying education do not enter an actual K-12 classroom of any kind on a regular basis until student teaching, which traditionally occurs during one's final undergraduate semester. Colleges of education have been trending toward offering more practicum experience throughout the four years to help give students a more steady diet of actual classroom exposure, but there is no reason not to take matters into your own hands.

One of the beautiful things about gaining experience in the education field is that, wherever you live, a school is never more than a stone's throw away and most will offer ways to get involved. Many K-12 buildings offer chances for community members to tutor or mentor students, supervise after-school activities, or observe a classroom setting upon request. Even when you are still in high school yourself, ask your teachers, counselor, or principal if you can get involved working with younger students—the insight you gain will go a long way in helping you determine whether pursuing a degree in education is right for you.

Think about a Double Major

Given the alarming retention statistics in the field of education, it is not a bad idea to seek a double major. Education degrees from most colleges and universities are generally viewed as less rigorous and selective than other areas of study. Coupling your education degree with a second area of interest, especially in the subject area where you want to teach, can improve your marketability and leave many options open should you choose to enter another field or pursue an advanced degree in a different discipline.

Plan the Financial End

First-year teachers nationwide average close to $40,000 per year. Because teaching pay scales are almost always on a schedule that accounts for years of service and degree status, even higher paying districts very rarely start teachers above $50,000, and it is typically a 15+ year climb to reach the max salary. Except for a smattering of districts across the country experimenting with merit pay, longevity is the sole pathway to incremental raises, which can be frustrating for young teachers.

Avoiding debt prior to entering the teaching field is strongly recommended if not absolutely necessary. Unless your parents or a substantial merit aid package are covering the entire bill, we recommend being very cost conscious during the college selection process. Remember, the selectivity of your college will not have a sizable impact on your ability to obtain a teaching job.

If you intend to stay in teaching for the long haul, plan on eventually pursuing a master's degree. Graduate school is not a barrier to entry in the field of
education, but the majority of teachers pursue advanced degrees at some point
in their careers. At present, 55% of public school teachers hold at least a master's degree and if you look only at industry veterans, that number increases
substantially.[34] Many school districts will pay a portion of their employees'
grad school tuition. In all states, teachers are required to obtain additional
credits as part of continuing education programs tied to maintaining a license,
making post-baccalaureate study of some variety mandatory.

For some, teaching is a rewarding experience that is more a calling than a
job. In the right geographic region, in a public school setting, the combination of solid salary and unmatched retirement benefits can make teaching
a more viable living than many commonly believe. Unfortunately, many
leave the profession due to stress, lack of administrative support, and lack of
academic freedom in the classroom. Yet, for those born to be teachers, those
obstacles are minor when weighed against the opportunity to help bring
learning to life, inspire young people, and play a genuine role in shaping
the future.

SO YOU WANT TO BE A FINANCIAL ANALYST . . .

What Exactly Does Being a Financial Analyst Entail?

Most analysts work for brokerage houses, banking or credit institutions, or
insurance brokerages. In general, the daily work of a financial analyst includes
carefully studying global financial trends for the purpose of accurately pre-
dicting future value of stocks, bonds, and companies. This is accomplished,
in part, through reading voluminous amounts of research and news material
as well as through financial modeling and analysis.

Do I Need to Major in Business?

No. Though many financial analysts do study business administration or
finance, the majority pursue other majors during their undergraduate years.
Economics is the most common major among finance professionals while
mathematics, engineering, and political science are also well represented.[35]
Wall Street employers typically regard intelligence, drive, and certain personality traits as more important than college major, in part because the
technical aspects of many finance-related jobs are learned through on-the-job

training, rather than inside a college classroom. Thus, individuals possessing non-typical majors can still prove competitive in the hiring process, and may even have an advantage over candidates coming from more traditional backgrounds.

Rob Dyer, head of recruitment at Deloitte, insists that non-business and non-finance graduates *make very good employees* because they *often have different thought processes*. "If they've studied history, for example, their research skills give them a huge boost. They're self-starters—they're used to going away, studying on their own, and coming back with a view. These are important skills for us," Dyer says.[36] Dyer's sentiments are substantiated by recruiters at other firms, such as Goldman Sachs, where liberal arts graduates constitute the largest group of employees and significantly outnumber those with undergraduate degrees in business or finance.[37]

Do I Need to Attend a Prestigious Undergraduate School?

Regardless of your major, if you are looking to land a job at a top investment bank or hedge fund, attending a selective undergraduate institution is pretty close to a prerequisite. Ultra-competitive institutions with large alumni bases located in the Northeastern United States provide students with a particular edge.

For example, the US schools most represented at high-powered banks like Goldman Sachs, JPMorgan Chase or Morgan Stanley include Ivies UPenn, Columbia, Cornell, Harvard and Princeton as well as NYU, Georgetown, and Boston College. Other strong but not hyper-selective schools such as Baruch College and Rutgers University are also well represented in the industry, in part, because of their sheer proximity to Wall Street.[38]

What Courses Should I Take in High School?

Taking rigorous math courses including AP Statistics is strongly advised. Students should also consider developing a strong command of spreadsheet/data management software like MS Excel. While more advanced software is used in many investment firms and brokerage houses, becoming proficient in the basics will lay the groundwork for future learning.

The social/communication aspect of the financial world can easily be underestimated and yet is of critical importance. Opportunities to pursue high-level English classes as well as public speaking or drama courses will help hone skills essential to life as a financial analyst.

To assess the undergraduate origins of America's banking elite, we used LinkedIn data to assess the most common college affiliations among a company's employees. We also perused company and college career services websites to learn about the institutions from which top banks are most likely to hire. Results are listed in alphabetical order.

Institution	Top Employer	Runner-Up
Amherst College	J.P. Morgan	Goldman Sachs
Baruch College (CUNY)	J.P. Morgan	Citi
Boston College	Merrill Lynch	Morgan Stanley
Colgate University	Morgan Stanley	Merrill Lynch
Columbia University	Morgan Stanley	Citi
Cornell University	Citi	J.P. Morgan
Dartmouth College	Morgan Stanley	Goldman Sachs
Duke University	Morgan Stanley	Goldman Sachs
Georgetown University	Morgan Stanley	Citi
Hamilton College	Morgan Stanley	Merrill Lynch
Harvard University	Goldman Sachs	Morgan Stanley
Massachusetts Institute of Technology	Goldman Sachs	Morgan Stanley
New York University	Citi	Morgan Stanley
Princeton University	Goldman Sachs	Citi
Rutgers University	Merrill Lynch	Citi
University of Chicago	J.P. Morgan	Credit Suisse
University of Pennsylvania	Goldman Sachs	Morgan Stanley
University of Virginia	Morgan Stanley	J.P. Morgan
Villanova University	Morgan Stanley	J.P. Morgan
Washington and Lee University	Merrill Lynch	J.P. Morgan

The companies incorporated into our analysis:

Bank of America • Merrill Lynch • Barclays • Citi • Credit Suisse • Deutsche Bank
Goldman Sachs • J.P. Morgan • Morgan Stanley • UBS • Wells Fargo

Figure 7.7   Top Feeders (Banking)

Be Prepared for Long Hours

Seventy to eighty hour weeks are commonplace, especially for those in their first few years in the field. In addition to your work hours, it benefits young analysts to network with potential clients as well as others in the field during their limited free time. Do the math, and it's easy to see why work/life balance can be a great challenge in this field. Similar to those starting in the legal field, young financial professionals report a higher level of stress and fatigue than peers in less all-consuming lines of work. Symptoms such as depression, anxiety, weight gain, and other health issues are common.[39]

Salary Expectations

Fortunately, your long hours do not go uncompensated. Salary expectations for financial analysts are quite high, especially when considering that base salary doesn't tell the whole picture. In fact, analysts at many private firms can more than double their base salary through performance bonuses.

The average salary for financial analysts nationwide is $76,000 yet this figure is somewhat misleading as it includes relatively *lower*-paid workers in the insurance field, whose average salary is just under $50,000.[40] Some entry-level jobs at top Wall Street hedge funds pay an average salary in excess of $300,000.[41]

Financial analysts can also be promoted to portfolio or fund managerial positions where top performers have the opportunity to bring home annual salary figures with six zeroes.

Job Outlook

Financial analyst positions are expected to grow at 16%, faster than the average occupation, through 2022.[42] However, competition for these job openings is sure to remain fierce. The industry is so cutthroat that many Wall Street banks and private equity firms begin recruiting top-level prospective candidates 18 months before a position even becomes available.

Additional Education

Unlike many other fields, lucrative entry-level employment is a realistic possibility in the financial industry. Still, nearly half of financial analysts (and many other business professionals) move on to pursue MBAs within their first five years of employment, in order to accelerate their career growth and earn even higher pay. Their decision to pursue further education seems justified, as demand for MBA graduates has never been higher, and reaches far beyond the financial sector.

According to a 2015 survey conducted by the Graduate Management Admission Council, nearly nine in ten US companies have plans to hire MBA graduates, who are estimated to make a median starting salary of $100,000, not including sign-on or year-end bonuses.[43] Graduates of elite business schools now command starting salaries in excess of $130,000, on average, and are about as likely to pursue careers in technology and consulting as they are finance. Given the versatility of an MBA and the significant returns to earning such a degree, it's easy see to why so many future and current college students have their sights set on attending a top-tier business school.

MBA Admissions and the Role of Undergraduate Selectivity

In contrast to other professional degree programs, such as those in law or medicine, MBA programs strongly encourage applicants to possess at least a couple of years of work experience, meaning that few students apply immediately after graduating from college. Still, the competitiveness of one's undergraduate institution is considered in the MBA admissions process. Similar to our analyses of medical and law school students, we relied on LinkedIn to identify the alma mater of those currently enrolled at the nation's most prestigious business schools.

Of the 6,700 students included in our sample, nearly 39% graduated from one of 30 colleges defined as *Elite*, while slightly more than 68% graduated from one of 73 colleges defined as *Elite* or *Extremely Selective* (see the Appendix for a list of colleges and their category of selectivity). Our list of top MBA feeders is comprised almost exclusively of institutions in these selectivity categories. Only Trinity College in Hartford, CT (*Moderately Selective*) is defined as less than *Extremely Selective*.

Although the list is dominated by highly selective schools, several (slightly) less-competitive universities were also well represented, including the following:

- Boston University
- Brigham Young University
- George Washington University
- Miami University
- University of Illinois
- University of Maryland

Using student-level data provided by LinkedIn, we were able to identify the colleges and universities sending the highest percentage of graduates to a top-ranked business school. Results are listed in alphabetical order and suggest that the selectivity of one's undergraduate institution is likely to play a role in the MBA admissions process.

Undergraduate Institution

Amherst College

Bowdoin College

Claremont McKenna College

Colby College

Colgate University

Columbia University

Dartmouth College

Duke University

Georgetown University

Harvard University

Middlebury College

Northwestern University

Princeton University

Stanford University

Trinity College

University of Pennsylvania

Washington and Lee University

Wellesley College

Williams College

Yale University

The business schools incorporated into our analysis:
Chicago (Booth) · Columbia · Dartmouth (Tuck) · Duke (Fuqua) · Harvard
MIT (Sloan) · Michigan (Ross) · NYU (Stern) · Northwestern (Kellogg)
Penn (Wharton) · Stanford · UC Berkeley (Haas) · Virginia (Darden) · Yale

Figure 7.8 Top Feeders to Elite MBA Programs

- University of Texas at Austin
- Whitman College

Alternatives to the MBA

Instead of earning an MBA, a significant number of financial analysts pursue professional certifications and licenses through less formal and more affordable educational means. Many entry-level financial analysts spend their evenings and weekends studying to become a Chartered Financial Analyst (CFA), a designation awarded to qualified individuals by a nonprofit organization called the CFA Institute. To earn the charter, you must have four years of work experience in the financial industry, hold a bachelor's degree, and pass level 1, 2, and 3 exams. Each exam takes an estimated 250 hours to prepare for, and pass rates are low with only 20% of those sitting for the level 1 exam continuing on to pass all three.[44] Those who persevere emerge with an impressive credential that can lead to promotions, raises, and increased desirability on the open market.

Analysts interested in entering certain specialty fields will first have to earn licensure in those areas. For example, anyone wishing to buy or sell securities must first demonstrate proficiency on the Series 7 exam administered by the Financial Industry Regulatory Authority. The vast majority of states will also require would-be securities agents to also pass the Series 63, which covers state laws and regulations.

Bottom Line

Entering this field at the top level is greatly aided by attending a highly selective undergraduate school. Your work as a financial analyst will entail long hours in a highly competitive environment. Yet, those with the right personality and work ethic may end up *occupying* Wall Street for many years as part of this fast-paced and lucrative profession.

Related Careers

Of course, students attracted to Wall Street primarily because of the big money and high prestige should not consider finance as their only career option. The business world is filled with non-finance professionals who have forged equally remunerative and often times more rewarding career paths. There are a few other occupations worth exploring, shown in Figure 7.9.

Profession	Median Pay	Top 10%	Entry-Level Degree
Accountant	$65,940	>$115,950	Bachelor's Degree
Actuary	$96,700	>$180,680	Bachelor's Degree
Economist	$95,710	>$170,780	Master's Degree
Logistician	$73,870	>$113,940	Bachelor's Degree
Market Research Analyst	$61,290	>$116,740	Bachelor's Degree

Figure 7.9   Careers Related to Business

SO YOU WANT TO BE A PSYCHOLOGIST . . .

Which *Helping Profession* Is Right for Me?

The term *psychologist* likely conjures up an image of a professionally attired individual scribbling on a notepad as a patient, reposed on a couch, shares traumas from their adolescence. This image is consistent with the work of a clinical or counseling psychologist, just two of a plethora of options in this diverse field.

A host of specialty areas exist in the field of psychology: school psychology, sports psychology, organizational psychology, experimental psychology, forensic psychology, and neuropsychology, just to name a few. There are also many professional jobs in the mental health field that do not carry the *psychologist* label such as rehabilitation counselor, social worker, special educator, or guidance counselor. Entrance into these positions typically requires a master's degree. However, if you want the title of clinical or counseling psychologist, you must plan to continue your higher education journey, as all states now require these professionals to hold a PhD or PsyD degree.

Plan the Financial End

Salaries in the mental health field will increase significantly based on the level of education required to enter a given field. Those with bachelor's degrees in psychology enter the field making less than $35,000 on average. Most will find entry-level employment in the behavioral/mental health field, working in positions such as a drug and alcohol counselor, probation officer, group home coordinator, or social worker. Master's level psychologists can expect to earn nearly double that of their bachelor's-only peers and those who eventually earn a PsyD or PhD will see average earnings above $87,000 and if you become one of the top 10% of earners in the profession, you can see over $110,000.[45]

Even better pay may await those willing or wanting to explore careers outside traditional mental health settings. For example, the BLS recently cited industrial-organizational psychology as among the fastest growing and highest-paying occupations in the United States.[46] Specializing in human behavior in the workplace, industrial-organizational psychologists help businesses and other organizations improve work productivity, evaluate prospective employees, and design policies and systems that optimize work performance and quality of work life. In 2014, top-earning I/O psychologists took home annual salaries of more than $145,000.[47]

Like I/O psychology, school psychology is also among the fastest growing occupations in the country. Working primarily in K-12 settings, school psychologists use their expertise in mental health, learning, and behavior to aid the academic and emotional development of students. Unlike other psychological specialties, school psychology does not require a doctorate for entry, and most practitioners hold either a master's or specialist degree. Despite this, school psychologists earn robust salaries exceeding $70,000 on average, and many have ample time, especially during summer months (when school is not in session), to pursue consulting, private practice, and other income-generating endeavors.[48]

Does Going to a Prestigious Undergraduate School Help?

Since becoming a psychologist is guaranteed to involve education beyond the bachelor's, the real question here becomes this: Can attending an elite undergraduate school give you a leg up if your goal is to one day attend a top graduate program in the field?

Doctoral programs in clinical psychology are extraordinarily competitive. Admissions rates at schools such as Boston University, Yale, and the University of Michigan are under 3%. Even *less-competitive* psych programs have rates hovering between 5% and 10%.[49] Therefore it figures that attending a highly selective undergraduate school could be a tiebreaker between two similarly qualified applicants. To test this hypothesis, we analyzed data provided by the National Science Foundation's annual Survey of Earned Doctorates (SED). SED collects information on *all* (research) doctoral degree recipients in the United States in a given year, including where recipients received their bachelor's degree. Using this information, we were able to identify which colleges produced the highest percentage of graduates who eventually went on to earn a PhD in psychology. They are shown in Figure 7.10.

Most top-producing institutions are highly selective, suggesting that attending a competitive college may indeed give aspiring psychologists an edge on their competition. In addition, *all* of the top producers are small liberal arts colleges—a finding that is indeed interesting, but not necessarily

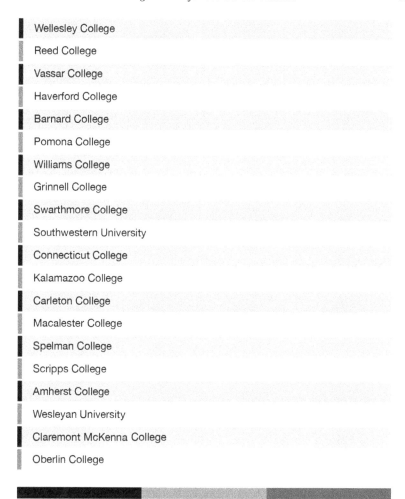

Wellesley College

Reed College

Vassar College

Haverford College

Barnard College

Pomona College

Williams College

Grinnell College

Swarthmore College

Southwestern University

Connecticut College

Kalamazoo College

Carleton College

Macalester College

Spelman College

Scripps College

Amherst College

Wesleyan University

Claremont McKenna College

Oberlin College

Figure 7.10   Colleges Producing the Most PhDs in Psychology

surprising. As discussed in chapter 2, students attending liberal arts colleges are significantly more likely to interact and collaborate with faculty, which often enables them to acquire substantive research experience and strong letters of recommendation—two things that, along with high grades and GRE scores, significantly improve a student's PhD admission prospects.[50]

Do I Have to Major in Psychology?

Psychology has become a wildly popular college major, with the number of bachelor's degrees handed out doubling since the 1990s.[51] Oddly enough, only about a quarter of undergraduates who major in psychology actually go on to enter the field. Instead, many elect to pursue jobs in sales, government, advertising, and a number of other only obliquely related vocations.

For those who are serious about a career in psychology, being a psych major is not necessarily a hardened prerequisite for all graduate programs in the field. While the majority of applicants to master's and doctoral psych programs will possess a BA or BS in psychology or a closely related field, many programs only require the completion of a number of core classes.

Prerequisites vary from school to school. For example, Hofstra's PhD program requires that applicants have achieved a B or better in an undergraduate statistics course and an experimental psychology (lab) course. Pitt's Graduate School of Psychology requires applicants to have completed a minimum of 12 undergraduate credits in psychology, one abnormal psych class, and one advanced mathematics course.

Many programs require applicants to take the GRE Psychology exam as well. It stands to reason that someone who majored in psychology will have an edge since they have received more formal schooling on the subject than non-majors.

PsyD versus PhD

The PsyD, or Doctor of Psychology degree, is a fairly recent creation, having emerged in the 1970s to answer the call for better practical training for future clinicians. PhDs are a better route for those who wish to enter academia or other research-focused areas of the field; however, many who obtain a PhD also enter the field as clinicians.

PhD programs tend to be the more selective of the two, sporting admit rates less than half that of PsyD programs, on average. PhD programs also tend to be more affordable, primarily because most PhD students secure significant financial support in exchange for assisting faculty with research, whereas students admitted into more practice-oriented PsyD programs are usually responsible for paying their own way.

Job Outlook

The job market for psychologists looks decent with positions expected to grow about as fast as average in the coming decade. Those with doctoral degrees or specialty certifications such as school psychology will fare best.

If you plan on pursuing graduate degrees in the mental health field, make sure you select a school with opportunities to participate in research and work closely with faculty. Hands-on experience plus top-notch grades and standardized test scores will make you a quality candidate to continue your studies and eventually land the *helping* job of your dreams.

SO YOU WANT TO BE A PROFESSOR . . .

Fiction versus Reality

Life as a college professor sounds like a delightfully quaint way to make a living. Residing in a rent-free cabin somewhere in New England, clad in your unfashionable yet almost required patch-sleeved sweater, you walk across a picturesque campus each day to deliver an hour or two worth of lecture, engage in intellectual debates with your colleagues, and work on the Great American Novel.

Unfortunately, the realities of working in academia in the twenty-first century are significantly less idyllic. An unfavorable job market, a shift toward part-time faculty, and the corporatization of higher education have made the day-to-day realities challenging and the barriers to entry higher than ever before.

Do I Need to Attend a Prestigious Graduate School?

More than ever before, prestige matters in the field of higher education. A recent study examined 19,000 tenure-track or tenured faculty at over 450 colleges and universities. They focused on three very different disciplines: computer science, history, and business, and reached several overarching conclusions about whether the prestige of your PhD program matters. The findings: Just 25% of the institutions surveyed produced 71–86% of the professors in those fields.[52] Further, half of the history professors hailed from eight schools, half of the business professors from 16 institutions, and half of the computer science professors from 18 prestigious colleges and universities. All of the usual suspects grace these lists: all eight Ivies, Berkeley, University of Chicago, MIT, Northwestern, Johns Hopkins, and a handful of other premier, super-selective institutions.

The takeaway from this research is obvious: Your job prospects in academia are very much tied to the prestige of the school where you earn your PhD.

Do I Need to Attend a Prestigious Undergraduate School?

Knowing that attending an elite PhD program significantly improves your chances of landing a tenure-track academic job, let's examine the next logical question: Do you need to attend an elite undergraduate school to get into an elite PhD program?

One examination of PhD candidates in philosophy found that over 80% had attended top 50 universities or liberal arts colleges,[53] while a more recent study of six top-ranked PhD programs in several disciplines revealed an admissions process that favors students from prestigious undergraduate institutions. Admissions committee members interviewed for the latter study were quoted as saying that they believe elite college attendees were *preadapted* to elite graduate programs, and given their ability to earn admission into a prestigious undergraduate school, *must truly be better.*

Finally, our own examination of National Science Foundation data revealed that prestigious colleges, particularly those of the small, liberal arts variety, also produce a disproportionately high number of PhDs in general. Our findings are made evident in the following *Top Feeders* list, which ranks colleges producing the highest percentage of graduates who eventually go on to earn PhDs in several fields across the humanities, sciences, and social sciences. Surprisingly, selective liberal arts colleges dominate the rankings in every discipline.

The preponderance of liberal arts colleges on this list is due, at least in part, to the fact that liberal arts grads have increased access to faculty and research opportunities, which ultimately gives them a leg up on other PhD applicants (this point was also made in our last section examining psychologists, who also require a PhD to practice). Therefore, it seems fair to suggest that aspiring PhDs should at least consider liberal arts institutions during their college search.

It is also important to note that our advice is not limited to those with elite college admission credentials. Although our *top feeders* list features a high number of very selective liberal arts institutions, several prominently ranked schools do accept students with less than excellent grades and standardized test scores, including Kalamazoo College, Allegheny College, Lawrence University, and others.

Finally, whether attending these schools or the more selective institutions on this list, future PhDs must also account for other equally or more important factors in the PhD admissions process. Aside from college destination, strong grades, excellent GRE scores, research experience, and a publication (or two) can go a long way toward helping you earn admission at a top-notch doctoral program.

A Ranking of Colleges

Rank	All Disciplines	Economics	Math & Science	Political Science	Sociology
1	Reed College	Swarthmore College	Caltech	Swarthmore College	Swarthmore College
2	Swarthmore College	Williams College	Reed College	Pomona College	Wellesley College
3	Carleton College	Reed College	Pomona College	Claremont McKenna	Southwestern University
4	Pomona College	Macalester College	Swarthmore College	Williams College	Pomona College
5	Haverford College	Carleton College	Williams College	Carleton College	Haverford College
6	Caltech	Amherst College	Carleton College	Amherst College	Carleton College
7	Grinnell College	Grinnell College	Whitman College	St. John's College	Reed College
8	Williams College	Wellesley College	St. Olaf College	Reed College	Wesleyan University
9	Amherst College	Pomona College	Haverford College	Oberlin College	Amherst College
10	Oberlin College	Wesleyan University	Rice University	Vassar College	Hampshire College
11	Kalamazoo College	Caltech	Oberlin College	Grinnell College	Pitzer College
12	Wellesley College	Centre College	Minnesota - Morris	Wellesley College	Kalamazoo College
13	Vassar College	Princeton University	Princeton University	Westminster College	Oberlin College
14	Macalester College	Whitman College	Amherst College	Haverford College	Earlham College
15	Allegheny College	Davidson College	Mass Inst. of Tech.	Wesleyan University	Grinnell College
16	Bowdoin College	Knox College	Grinnell College	Lawrence University	Smith College
17	Kenyon University	Haverford University	Knox University	Hanover University	Beloit University
18	Wesleyan University	Ohio Wesleyan University	Bryn Mawr College	Pitzer College	Albion College
19	Whitman College	Mass Inst. of Tech.	Lawrence University	Mount Holyoke College	Williams College
20	Mount Holyoke College	Kalamazoo College	Kalamazoo College	Macalester College	Vassar College

Figure 7.11 PhD Productivity: A Ranking of Colleges

A Ranking of Colleges

Rank	Chemistry	Physics	Biology	History	English
1	Carleton College	Caltech	Reed College	Swarthmore College	Reed College
2	Kalamazoo College	Reed College	Swarthmore College	Reed College	Swarthmore College
3	Reed College	Swarthmore College	Carleton College	Carleton College	St. John's College
4	Caltech	Lawrence University	Haverford College	Grinnell College	Amherst College
5	Wabash College	Carleton College	Grinnell College	Amherst College	Scripps College
6	Allegheny College	Haverford College	Pomona College	Oberlin College	Pomona College
7	College of Wooster	Williams College	Caltech	Kenyon College	Haverford College
8	Franklin & Marshall	Mass Inst. of Tech.	Allegheny College	Vassar College	Oberlin College
9	Grinnell College	CO School of Mines	Kalamazoo College	Pomona College	Vassar College
10	Haverford College	Grinnell College	Oberlin College	Haverford College	Kenyon College
11	Juniata College	Amherst College	Bowdoin College	Bowdoin College	Wellesley College
12	Albion College	Princeton University	Earlham College	Wellesley College	Carleton College
13	Northland University	Wabash University	Ohio Wesleyan University	Wesleyan University	Bowdoin College
14	Knox College	College of Wooster	Williams College	Macalester College	Williams College
15	Pomona College	Gustavus Adolphus	Amherst College	Barnard College	Wesleyan University
16	Centre College	Vassar College	Ursinus College	Williams College	Grinnell College
17	Whitman College	Kenyon College	Mt. Holyoke College	Princeton University	Barnard College
18	Randolph-Macon College	Rice University	College of the Atlantic	Brown University	Bryn Mawr College
19	Hendrix College	Bryn Mawr College	Colby College	Bryn Mawr College	Hampshire College
20	Macalester College	University of Rochester	Whitman College	St. John's College	Rhodes College

Source: *National Science Foundation Survey of Earned Doctorates (SED)*

Figure 7.11   PhD Productivity: A Ranking of Colleges

Earning a PhD Is a Long Commitment

The average PhD takes over eight years to complete. Breaking this down a bit, a doctorate in the physical sciences averages just under seven years, a doctorate in the social sciences just over seven, and a terminal degree in the humanities takes over nine years. As you slog through this intellectual marathon, many of your peers will be out earning money, getting promoted, starting families, and so on. It's important to enter this type of endeavor with the long view in mind and crystal clear about the level of sacrifice required.

Failure to plan and adopt a winning mindset partially explains the attrition rates in PhD programs—50% of those who start a program never finish.[54] Even for those who survive, additional perils await.

The Adjunct Reality

Since 1975, the percent of part-time professors in the United States has increased by 300%.[55] Today, these part-timers known as adjunct professors make up over half of the total faculty members at US colleges. They are paid an average of just $2,700 per class.[56] In an attempt to scratch together a living, many adjuncts take on as many courses as possible each semester, often at multiple universities. Still, the average adjunct's salary comes in right around 20K, which equates to the annual salary of someone making minimum wage. Employing adjunct faculty is an extremely cheap labor source for universities and they have little incentive to hire full-timers with a glut of PhDs available to teach each semester.

If you are going to dedicate eight plus years of your life to obtain a PhD, it's important to understand that your *reward* will be a fierce job market with a limited number of full-time, tenure-track positions. Supply and demand (depending on the field) is not on your side, nor is the hiring trend in higher education.

Adjuncts around the country are beginning to unionize and voice what they perceive as unfair practices on the part of institutions. Whether this leads to substantive change by the time someone in high school right now earns a PhD and enters the job market is yet to be seen.

Salary for Tenure-Track Professors

Tenure-track assistants' and associate professors' average annual salaries fall between 67 and 77K. Full-tenured professors average right around 100K. There is, however, great variability across disciplines. For example, a newly hired computer science professor takes home $83,000 while an equivalent scholar in the field of journalism earns a significantly lower salary of $59,000.[57]

It is important to understand that those hired as tenure-track assistant professors typically have 5–7 years to impress the university with their ability to publish, teach, and aptly fulfill other administrative duties. Generally speaking, most schools, with the exception of some liberal arts schools, place paramount importance on publications over teaching. The higher education cliché of *publish or perish* often guides tenure decisions. The climb toward the top of the hill, becoming a tenured full professor, takes many additional years and much good fortune.

Job Outlook

Postsecondary education jobs are expected to grow 13% through 2024; however, the BLS is careful to note that this includes both full-time and part-time positions.[58] Additionally, these projections vary across disciplines with high job growth expected in fields like health care, nursing, biology, and law and slower growth in areas like agricultural science, library science, and education.

This Must Be a Labor of Love

Unlike other prestige fields with arduous and costly paths to entry, entering academia does not offer a pot of gold at the end of the rainbow. For individuals committed to the idea of teaching and researching at a postsecondary level, proper planning beginning with the selection of an undergraduate institution is necessary. This is a field where elite credentials give candidates a leg up in the pursuit of a tenure-track position. Regardless, your journey to a stable and rewarding career as a professor will likely continue well into your 30s. For those who possess passion and zeal for a given subject, the end result will justify the means. For those picturing that cabin in New England and a relaxing, quiet life, academia is likely not for you.

SO YOU WANT TO BE A JOURNALIST . . .

A Changing Field

In the period following Watergate, roughly 82% of the young people in the world decided to become investigative journalists in the hopes of becoming the next Woodward and Bernstein (perhaps a slight exaggeration). The glamorous appeal of sitting in a cubicle in the newsroom of a major metropolitan paper at 2 am, sporting a short sleeve, white dress shirt and drinking cup after cup of Maxwell House, all while bringing down *the powers that be* was simply too much to resist.

Earning a position at an influential and trusted news source will largely depend on your reporting and writing skills. Yet, all things equal, there are certain colleges that may improve your chances of breaking into the news industry. Using LinkedIn data, we identified the colleges sending the highest percentage of graduates to 15 of the most desirable media outlets. Our list includes a number of highly selective institutions, but also featured are several schools that accept students with less than elite credentials.

Institution	Top Employer	Runner-Up
American University	Washington Post	CNN
Boston University	New York Times	Huffington Post
Brown University	New York Times	Wall Street Journal
Columbia University	New York Times	Huffington Post
Emerson College	BuzzFeed	CBS News
George Washington University	CNN	Fox News
Georgetown University	NPR	Washington Post
Harvard University	Huffington Post	New York Times
New York University	New York Times	ABC News
Northwestern University	Wall Street Journal	Chicago Tribune
Syracuse University	CBS News	CNN
University of California-Berkeley	Huffington Post	Los Angeles Times
University of California-Los Angeles	Huffington Post	Los Angeles Times
University of Maryland	Washington Post	NBC News
University of Michigan	New York Times	Huffington Post
University of Missouri	Wall Street Journal	ABC News
University of North Carolina at Chapel Hill	CNN	New York Times
University of Pennsylvania	Huffington Post	New York Times
University of Southern California	NBC News	Los Angeles Times
Wesleyan University	New York Times	NPR

The media outlets incorporated into our analysis:
ABC News • CBS News • BuzzFeed • CNN • Fox News • Huffington Post
Los Angeles Times • MSNBC • NBC • NPR • PBS • Wall Street Journal •
Washington Post

Figure 7.12   Top Feeders—News and Media

Fast forward forty years, and the career of a journalist is almost unrecognizable from its previous form. Pure print journalism has given way in favor of web-based reporting, independently run blogs, podcasts, tweets, and the technologically oriented like. The media is no longer an exclusive club controlled by a handful of newspaper publishers and the owners of the major broadcasting networks. The gatekeepers that used to have the final say on who got to call themselves a reporter have been overrun by new media advances. While many lament the fall of traditional journalism, the seismic shift of the last two decades has created a field where anyone with an area of expertise and a unique voice can find an audience—a development not without its career advantages.

Journalism versus Broadcast Journalism

The line between these two fields has faded faster than most newspapers circulation counts. Print reporters today are often asked to create video content to accompany articles, seek out media appearances to promote their publication, and snare as many Twitter, Facebook, and Google Plus followers as they possibly can.

To accommodate an ever-changing industry, many institutions, including the University of Georgia, Boston College, and the University of Missouri now offer students a bevy of concentration options under the general umbrella of *journalism*, such as community journalism, entrepreneurial journalism, visual journalism, magazine journalism, health and science journalism, and so on.

Of course, students who want to work exclusively in television news still typically major in broadcast journalism where they learn the ins and outs of the industry, both in front of and behind the camera.

Does Going to a Prestigious Undergraduate School Help?

Journalism is a field built on what you are able to produce. A state college grad who writes beautifully and knows how to tap sources and produce engaging content will never take a backseat to an Ivy Leaguer whose reporting is mediocre.

On the other hand, attending a college with an elite journalism school can help with landing an internship and networking if your aim is to work at a major newspaper, magazine, website, or television market. Schools with notable communications/journalism programs such as Syracuse, UNC, Northwestern, and Columbia can provide grads with huge alumni networking bases and therefore premier internship and entry-level job opportunities. Thus, it should come as no surprise that each of these institutions is featured on our *top feeders* list revealing which schools produce the highest percentage of graduates landing jobs at top news outlets.

Gain Experience in the Field

The beauty of the journalism field is that opportunities to try it out in high school are abundant. Heck, even most middle schools publish a paper and air morning announcements. If you want to be a journalist, start today. There are countless opportunities to begin publishing work outside of your high school. Start a blog, freelance for a small local paper—whatever allows you to write, write, and write some more.

Think about a Double Major

It never hurts to carve out a niche area of expertise in the journalism field. For example, a background in an area like science, computer science, or economics can allow you to write on topics and for publications that many other young journalists simply wouldn't have the ability to tackle. Those with a strong knowledge base in a given area may find better prospects than generalists.

Journalist Salaries

This is a field where salaries are most commonly modest and, in rare instances, where notoriety is achieved, outrageously high. The average salary for someone in the radio, television, or print journalism field is around $37,000.[59] For local news anchors and reporters in small markets around the United States, salaries average as low as the mid-20s. Small market jobs constitute the majority of the positions in this field. However, those who rise to the top of the profession and get plucked up by a top 25 market can expect salaries in the low-six figures. Of course, for those who dare to dream, celebrity journalists are paid like NBA stars. The Matt Lauers and Diane Sawyers of the world take home more than 20 million per year.

Plan the Financial End

Don't plan on hitting that 20 million dollar mark right away. In fact, planning somewhere in the neighborhood of $15 per hour is a safer bet. Then, there is the matter of relocation . . . As a journalist you need to be willing to travel. Very rarely will someone begin their career in broadcast journalism in a major market. If you are a budding sports writer, get ready to cover the Billings Bighorns junior hockey team in Montana before you get a crack at the New York Rangers. From a financial standpoint, two things are important to plan for: the need to travel and the likelihood that you will not make much money early in your career. It goes without saying that taking out massive undergraduate loans could hinder your mobility and therefore stand in the way of essential early career opportunities.

NOTES

1. Jonathan V. Hall and Alan B. Krueger "An Analysis of the Labor Market for Uber's Driver-Partners in the United States," published as Working Paper #587 for the Industrial Relations Section at Princeton University (January 22, 2015).

2. Association of American Medical Colleges, "Table 17: MCAT and GPAs for Applicants and Matriculants to U.S. Medical Schools by Primary Undergraduate Major, 2015–2016," accessed January 25, 2016, https://www.aamc.org/download/321496/data/factstablea17.pdf.

3. Dana Dunleavy et al., "Medical School Admissions: More Than Grades and Test Scores," Association of American Medical Colleges, Analysis in Brief, 11(6), September 2011, accessed February 29, 2016, https://www.aamc.org/download/261106/data.

4. Elite colleges accept fewer than 20% of all applicants AND possess an average composite ACT (25%tile) score of at least 29 or an average combined SAT (25%tile) score (CR + M) of at least 1300. Refer to page () to see which colleges are identified as Most Selective.

5. See, for example: Belasco, A. S., & Trivette, M. J. (2015). Aiming low: Estimating the scope and predictors of postsecondary undermatch. *The Journal of Higher Education, 86*(2), 233–263.

6. Delece Smith-Barrow, "10 Medical Schools Where Students Pay a High Price," *U.S. News & World Report,* May 19, 2015, accessed December 12, 2015, http://www.usnews.com/education/best-graduate-schools/the-short-list-grad school/articles/2015/05/19/10-medical-schools-where-students-pay-a-high-price.

7. Medical Group Management Association, "Primary Care Physicians Outpace Specialists in 2014, according to MGMA Provider Compensation Report," July 23, 2015, accessed December 12, 2015, http://www.mgma.com/about/mgma-pressroom/press-releases/2015/primary-care-physicians-outpace-specialists-in-2014-according-to-mgma-physicians-compensation-repor.

8. Menachem Wecker, "Future Law Students Should Avoid Prelaw Majors, Some Say," *U.S. News & World Report,* October 29, 2012, accessed December 12, 2015, http://www.usnews.com/education/best-graduate-schools/top-law-schools/articles/2012/10/29/future-law-students-should-avoid-prelaw-majors-some-say.

9. Lawyer2B, "Half of Lawyers Wish They'd Chosen a Different Career," March 23, 2015, accessed December 12, 2015, http://l2b.thelawyer.com/solicitor/news/half-of-lawyers-wish-theyd-chosen-a-different-career/3033012.article.

10. C. Stuart Mauney, (n.d.). The lawyers' epidemic: Depression, suicide and substance abuse. Accessed December 31, 2015, http://www.charlestonlaw.edu/charlestonSchoolOfLaw/files/27/274463ca-476c-40cd-9c0a-733676db3cb5.pdf.

11. Most Selective colleges accept fewer than 20% of all applicants AND possess an average composite ACT (25%tile) score of at least 29 or an average combined SAT (25%tile) score (CR + M) of at least 1300. Refer to page () to see which colleges are identified as Most Selective.

12. "Frequently Asked Questions," The University of Michigan Law School, accessed February 29, 2016, http://www.law.umich.edu/prospectivestudents/admissions/pages/faq.aspx.

13. Robert Farrington, "Law School and Student Loan Debt: Be Careful," *Forbes*, December 18, 2014, accessed December 12, 2015, http://www.forbes.com/sites/robertfarrington/2014/12/18/law-school-and-student-loan-debt-be-careful/.

14. Brandi N. Geisinger and D. Raj Raman, "Why They Leave: Understanding Student Attrition from Engineering Majors," *International Journal of Engineering Education* 29 no. 4 (2013): 914–925, accessed December 26, 2015, http://lib.dr.iastate.edu/cgi/viewcontent.cgi?article=1890&context=abe_eng_pubs.

15. Zach Helfand, "Study Reveals Engineering Majors Spend Significantly More Time Studying," *USA Today*, November 23, 2011, accessed December 12, 2015, http://college.usatoday.com/2011/11/23/study-reveals-engineering-majors-spend-significantly-more-time-studying-2/.

16. U.S. Department of Education, Office for Civil Rights, "Data Snapshot: College and Career Readiness," Issue Brief No. 3 (March 2014), March 21, 2014, accessed December 12, 2015, http://ocrdata.ed.gov/Downloads/CRDC-College-and-Career-Readiness-Snapshot.pdf.

17. College Factual, "Highest Paid Engineering Grads," last modified 2013, accessed December 12, 2015, http://www.collegefactual.com/majors/engineering/rankings/highest-paid-grads/p36.html.

18. *U.S. News & World Report*, "Best Engineering Schools," accessed December 12, 2015, http://grad-schools.usnews.rankingsandreviews.com/best-graduate-schools/top-engineering-schools/eng-rankings.

19. PayScale, "2015–2016 PayScale College Salary Report: Best Undergraduate Engineering Schools by Salary Potential," accessed December 12, 2015, http://www.payscale.com/college-salary-report/best-schools-by-type/bachelors/engineering-schools?page=3.

20. John F. Sargent Jr., "The U.S. Science and Engineering Workforce: Recent, Current, and Projected Employment, Wages, and Unemployment," February 19, 2014, accessed December 12, 2015, http://www.fas.org/sgp/crs/misc/R43061.pdf.

21. U.S. Department of Labor, Bureau of Labor Statistics, "Occupational Outlook Handbook, 2014-15 Edition: Civil Engineers," January 8, 2014, accessed December 12, 2015, http://www.bls.gov/ooh/architecture-and-engineering/civil-engineers.htm.

22. U.S. Department of Labor, Bureau of Labor Statistics, "Occupational Outlook Handbook, 2014-15 Edition: Biomedical Engineers," January 8, 2014, accessed

December 12, 2015, http://www.bls.gov/ooh/architecture-and-engineering/biomedical-engineers.htm.

23. U.S. Department of Labor, Bureau of Labor Statistics, "Occupational Outlook Handbook, 2014-15 Edition: Petroleum Engineers," January 8, 2014, accessed December 12, 2015, http://www.bls.gov/ooh/architecture-and-engineering/petroleum-engineers.htm.

24. Joanna Pearlstein, "The Schools Where Apple, Google, and Facebook Get Their Recruits," *WIRED*, May 22, 2014, accessed December 12, 2015, http://www.wired.com/2014/05/alumni-network-2/

25. "Blurbs and Useful Stats," Computer Science Education Week, December 7-15, 2015, accessed 12/31/2015, https://csedweek.org/resource_kit/blurbs

26. College Board, "AP Exam Volume Changes (2004–2014)," accessed December 12, 2015, http://media.collegeboard.com/digitalServices/pdf/research/2014/2014-Exam-Volume-Change.pdf.

27. PayScale, "Software Engineer / Developer / Programmer Salary," accessed December 12, 2015, http://www.payscale.com/research/US/Job=Software_Engineer_%2F_Developer_%2F_Programmer/Salary.

28. U.S. Department of Labor, Bureau of Labor Statistics, "Occupational Outlook Handbook, 2014-15 Edition: Computer Programmers," January 8, 2014, accessed December 12, 2015, http://www.bls.gov/ooh/computer-and-information-technology/computer-programmers.htm.

29. U.S. Department of Labor, Bureau of Labor Statistics, "Occupational Outlook Handbook, 2014–2015 Edition: Software Developers," January 8, 2014, accessed December 12, 2015, http://www.bls.gov/ooh/computer-and-information-technology/software-developers.htm.

30. Center for Education Reform, "K–12 Facts," last modified September 2014, accessed December 12, 2015, https://www.edreform.com/2012/04/k-12-facts/

31. U.S. Department of Labor, Bureau of Labor Statistics, "Occupational Outlook Handbook, 2014-15 Edition: Kindergarten and Elementary School Teachers," January 8, 2014, accessed December 12, 2015, http://www.bls.gov/ooh/education-training-and-library/kindergarten-and-elementary-school-teachers.htm.

32. Steve Billmyer, "NYS Teachers' Salaries by School District: Who Makes the Most Money?" January 29, 2014, accessed December 12, 2015, http://www.syracuse.com/news/index.ssf/2014/01/nys_teachers_salaries_by_school_district_who_makes_the_most_money.html.

33. Liz Riggs, "Why Do Teachers Quit?" *The Atlantic*, October 18, 2013, accessed December 12, 2015, http://www.theatlantic.com/education/archive/2013/10/why-do-teachers-quit/280699/.

34. U.S. Department of Education, National Center for Education Statistics, Institute of Education Sciences, "Total Number of Public School Teachers, Number and Percentage of Public School Teachers with a Master's Degree, and, of Those with a Master's Degree, Number and Percentage of Teachers Whose State, School, or District Helped Pay for Their Master's Degree, by Selected School Characteristics: 2011–2012," Schools and Staffing Survey (SASS), accessed December 12, 2015, https://nces.ed.gov/surveys/sass/tables/Sass1112-478_t1n.asp.

35. Dan Butcher, "Top Majors for Getting an Investment Banking Job on Wall Street," eFinancialCareers, January 8, 2016, accessed February 29, 2016, http://news. efinancialcareers.com/us-en/230786/top-undergraduate-majors-investment-banking-jobs-wall-street/.

36. Sarah Butcher, "Finance Firms Actively Hiring Drama Students, History Majors, Persons with Charisma," eFinancialCareers, October 10, 2013, accessed February 29, 2016, http://news.efinancialcareers.com/cn-en/152746/do-you-really-need-to-study-a-subject-thats-finance-related-to-get-a-job-in-finance/.

37. "Explore Goldman Sachs Careers Quiz," accessed February 29, 2016, http://www.goldmansachs.com/careers/why-goldman-sachs/explore-goldman-sachs-careers-quiz/index.html?Questions=9.

38. LinkedIn, "Best Undergraduate Universities for Finance Professionals," accessed December 12, 2015, https://www.linkedin.com/edu/rankings/us/undergraduate-finance?trk=edu-rankings-ctg-card.

39. Sanjay Sanghoee, "Why Banking and Work-Life Balance Don't Mix," *Fortune*, February 4, 2014, accessed December 12, 2015, http://fortune.com/2014/02/04/why-banking-and-work-life-balance-dont-mix/.

40. U.S. Department of Labor, Bureau of Labor Statistics, "Occupational Outlook Handbook, 2014–2015 Edition: Financial Analysts," January 8, 2014, accessed December 12, 2015, http://www.bls.gov/ooh/business-and-financial/financial-analysts.htm.

41. Katie Holliday, "This Industry Has an Entry Level Salary of $335,000," CNBC, November 1, 2013, accessed December 12, 2015, http://www.cnbc.com/2013/11/01/this-industry-has-an-entry-level-salary-of-335000.html.

42. U.S. Department of Labor, Bureau of Labor Statistics, "Occupational Outlook Handbook, 2014–2015 Edition: Financial Analysts," January 8, 2014, accessed December 12, 2015, http://www.bls.gov/ooh/business-and-financial/financial-analysts.htm.

43. R. Estrada-Worthington, "2015 Corporate Recruiters Survey Report," Graduate Management Admission Council, accessed February 29, 2016, http://www.gmac.com/market-intelligence-and-research/research-library/employment-outlook/2015-corporate-recruiters-survey-report.aspx.

44. Julia La Roche, "14,664 People Just Got Major Cred on Wall Street," *Business Insider*, August 11, 2015, accessed December 12, 2015, http://www.businessinsider.com/cfa-level-3-results-2015-8.

45. D. W. Rajecki and Victor M. H. Borden, "Psychology Degrees: Employment, Wage, and Career Trajectory Consequences," *Perspectives in Psychological Science* 6 (2011): 321–35, doi:10.1177/1745691611412385.

46. Alan Farnham, "20 Fastest Growing Occupations," ABC News, February 5, 2014, accessed February 29, 2016, http://abcnews.go.com/Business/americas-20-fastest-growing-jobs-surprise/story?id=22364716.

47. U.S. Department of Labor, Bureau of Labor Statistics, "Occupational Employment and Wages, May 2014," last modified March 25, 2015, accessed February 29, 2016, http://www.bls.gov/oes/current/oes193032.htm.

48. "Workforce & Salary Information," National Association of School Psychologists, accessed February 29, 2016, https://www.nasponline.org/about-school-psychology/
workforce-and-salary-information.

49. University of North Carolina at Chapel Hill, "Admission Rates by Program between 2006–2011, as Reported on Program Websites," accessed December 12, 2015, http://www.unc.edu/~mjp1970/Admissions%20Rates.pdf.

50. Norcross, J. C., and Sayette, P. M. A. (2014). Insider's Guide to Graduate Programs in Clinical and Counseling Psychology: Revised 2014/2015 Edition. Guilford Publications.

51. Jane S. Halonen, Ph.D., "Are There Too Many Psychology Majors?" February 5, 2011, accessed December 12, 2015, http://www.cogdop.org/page_attachments/0000/0200/FLA_White_Paper_for_cogop_posting.pdf.

52. Aaron Clauset, Samuel Arbesman and Daniel B. Larremore, "Systematic Inequality and Hierarchy in Faculty Hiring Networks," *Science Advances*, February 12, 2015, 1(1), accessed February 29, 2016, http://advances.sciencemag.org/content/1/1/e1400005.full.

53. Scott Jaschik, "Rigor or Snobbery?," *Inside Higher Ed*, November 1, 2011, accessed February 29, 2016, https://www.insidehighered.com/news/2011/11/01/professors-research-raises-questions-about-graduate-admissions.

54. Leonard Cassuto, "Ph.D. Attrition: How Much Is Too Much?," *The Chronicle of Higher Education*, July 1, 2013, accessed February 29, 2016, http://chronicle.com/article/PhD-Attrition-How-Much-Is/140045/.

55. Jordan Weissmann, "The Ever-Shrinking Role of Tenured College Professors (in 1 Chart)," *The Atlantic*, April 10, 2013, accessed February 29, 2016, http://www.theatlantic.com/business/archive/2013/04/the-ever-shrinking-role-of-
tenured-college-professors-in-1-chart/274849/.

56. Laura McKenna, "The College President-to-Adjunct Pay Ratio," *The Atlantic*, September 24, 2015, accessed February 29, 2016, http://www.theatlantic.com/education/archive/2015/09/income-inequality-in-higher-education-the-college-president-to-adjunct-pay-ratio/407029/.

57. Scott Jaschik, "Faculty Pay: Up and Uneven," *Inside Higher Ed*, March 16, 2015, accessed February 29, 2016, https://www.insidehighered.com/news/2015/03/16/survey-finds-increases-faculty-pay-and-significant-gaps-discipline.

58. U.S. Department of Labor, Bureau of Labor Statistics, "Occupational Outlook Handbook, 2014-15 Edition: Postsecondary Teachers," December 17, 2015, accessed February 29, 2016, http://www.bls.gov/ooh/education-training-and-library/postsecondary-teachers.htm.

59. U.S. Department of Labor, Bureau of Labor Statistics, "Occupational Outlook Handbook, 2014-15 Edition: Reporters, Correspondents, and Broadcast News Analysts," January 8, 2014, accessed December 12, 2015, http://www.bls.gov/ooh/media-and-communication/reporters-correspondents-and-broadcast-news-analysts.htm.

Key Takeaways and Conclusions

Now that you've finished reading our research-based, stats-laden, big-picture argument for how parents should approach the college process, we are confident that you have emerged a more informed and empowered higher education consumer. At this very moment, you are fully ready to steer your child through the admissions gauntlet with a steady hand, dauntless and stoic, immune to the multitude of distractions and pitfalls that await on this harrowing journey.

Yet, as the months pass and the unavoidable torrent of admissions-related lunacy pounds your senses, this newfound self-assuredness is likely to erode. You'll hear that lady again in the deli talking about her son's admission to a top 20 school as being a matter of life and death. You'll see a never-ending parade of headlines on reputable news sources about how getting into college has never been more difficult—"Harvard's admission rates down again!" Chatting with other parents from the sidelines of your daughter's JV soccer game, you'll be forced to imbibe the collective fretting, status anxiety, and vicarious aspirations tied to undergraduate prestige.

To combat these unhelpful forces, we advise that you return to this section of *The Enlightened College Applicant*, reread it, and recite it like a mantra. Okay, it's probably too long to recite, but reread it, internalize it, and let it serve as a suit of armor protecting you against misinformation, misdirection, and mania.

1. HIGHER EDUCATION IS A BUYER'S MARKET
AND YOU'RE IN THE DRIVER'S SEAT

Prior to 1984, AT&T had a monopoly on the telecommunications industry. If you wanted to make a call, you had to go through good ol' Ma Bell. Thus, the corporation held all of the power, the customer had absolutely none.

Today, every other advertisement on television is a phone company competing hard for your business, offering free upgrades, buyouts of competitor's contracts—anything to get your business. It's a cutthroat marketplace and you are the beneficiary. The marketplace of higher education is very much the same.

It's critical to remember that the vast majority of quality colleges and universities in the United States are feeling more anxiety than you are about the upcoming admissions season. Outside of a small number of institutions, admissions offices are panicking as we speak over meeting enrollment requirements for next year. With so much competition for even average students, there is a long line of schools looking to woo your son or daughter, even if their GPA and SATs weren't close to perfect.

You don't have to beg T-Mobile, Sprint, AT&T, or Verizon to take your business. The same goes for the overwhelming majority of colleges and universities.

2. THINK ABOUT COLLEGE IN THE CONTEXT OF YOUR LIFE

Our "So You Want to Be a . . ." chapter provided you with a roadmap to some of the most popular career fields. Yet, in a broader sense, we hope this chapter leaves you with one guiding principle: your investment in an undergraduate degree may be the largest (or second largest, behind a mortgage) and most important investment you will ever make in your lifetime—don't make this decision without considering the facts on the ground.

If your child's goal is to work at a top investment bank or enroll at an elite law or medical school, then attending an elite undergraduate institution may pay dividends. If their aim is to work in early childhood education, pursuing a fancy degree may have little upside, especially if you or your kid take on massive debt in order to do so.

The average 17/18-year-old is not ready to select a vocation with 100% certainty but that doesn't mean you can't engage them in a meaningful conversation about how their undergraduate institution *and* undergraduate debt may impact their future. If an *undecided* student elects to attend a wildly expensive college that is beyond their parents' means, it is important for them to understand the future implications. Calculate what their monthly debt payment would be at 22. What salary would they have to earn to make this payment and afford an apartment, car, health care, and so on? These are conversations that are rarely part of the college selection dialogue but, in our opinion, should actually be at the forefront of the discussion.

3. YOUR CHILD'S TALENTS AND MOTIVATION WILL BE THE PRIMARY DETERMINANTS OF THEIR SUCCESS; HOWEVER, THEIR CHOICE OF COLLEGE CAN ALSO MATTER

In laying out the body of research on the subject of prestige and returns to selectivity, we showed a murkier picture than the popular cry of "It doesn't matter where you go" that has gained momentum today. At heart, we are fellow proponents of the belief that talented people do not need a prestigious school attached to their name in order to succeed—simply put: cream rises. Academic studies have shown us that raw talent and winning personality traits often do trump the reputation of the institutional name on a graduate's diploma, *so long as they choose a college that is at least moderately selective.*

Still, it is important to keep in mind that undergraduate prestige can give a person a leg up in certain professional fields. As chapter 7 highlights, there is an undeniable preponderance of elite college graduates at the nation's top business, medical, and law schools. Thus, high-achieving students interested in pursuing any one of these fields are wise to consider the Ivy League, but they should also explore the 60 plus other institutions that are nearly or as prestigious and that may offer a better undergraduate education.

All things equal, choosing Harvard over Henderson State will result in higher earnings and better job prospects; yet choosing Harvard over Hamilton College, an outstanding yet slightly less-selective institution, probably won't. Remember, there is not one but dozens of colleges that can provide the right fit, even for those who aspire to enter the most competitive professions.

4. DON'T OBSESS OVER ADMISSIONS AND FORGET ABOUT THE *BIGGER PICTURE*

Overfocusing on admissions can be a distraction from the more important factors of *fit* and financial sensibility. Many students become obsessed with getting into the most selective college that will accept them, while ignoring other equally reputable schools that would, in the end, make significantly more sense to attend.

Of all the students excitedly scurrying off to college next fall, only a minority will graduate from that school within four years. The majority will transfer, drop out, or slog through six plus inefficient years to earn a degree. Taking the time to find a school that truly meets your child's unique academic, financial, social-emotional, and pre-vocational needs will give them an exponentially better chance to finish their degree and lay the groundwork for later success. In addition to reviewing acceptance rates and average standardized test scores, make sure to also investigate a school's retention rate, graduation rate, and record of job placement. Remember, the admissions process is not an end, but a means to something much greater.

5. LOOK AT FACTORS BEYOND RANKINGS

Brandeis University presently enjoys the distinction of being rated the 34th best national university by *U.S. News*, eleven slots below UCLA at 23rd. Both are wonderful schools, but should this gap in *rank* be considered when choosing which school makes more sense for *your* child? At this point, you've read our book and can likely figure out that the answer is—of course not.

UCLA is almost ten times the size of Brandeis, located on the opposite coast, and known for completely different areas of strength. They can't be compared to one another in any meaningful way and that would be assuming that algorithms employed by *U.S. News* and other ranking systems are actually grounded in research (they are not).

Strength of alumni network, proximity to target employers, and dedication to career services are just a few of the real-world factors that should be placed above where a college ranks in a glossy magazine. Perhaps most importantly, what does actual instruction look like in the classroom? Even among prestige schools, great variance exists with regard to the quality of a classroom experience. Will your child be taught by tenured professors and leaders in their fields or by graduates or even fellow undergraduates (remember our discussion of Harvard vs. Swarthmore)?

6. SKILL ACQUISITION MATTERS

In the 1998 NFL Draft, the San Diego Chargers selected Ryan Leaf, a highly touted Pac-10 quarterback with the second overall pick. That same year, undrafted free agent and University of Northern Iowa graduate, Kurt Warner, was finally signed by an NFL franchise, the St. Louis Rams. Ryan Leaf was immediately handed the starting job with San Diego, a position which he quickly lost due to lack of ability and discipline. Warner, on the other hand, arrived unceremoniously in St. Louis and spent the season as the third-string quarterback. As it turns out, despite his lack of pedigree, Warner was ridiculously good. When he was given a chance the following year, he not only took the Rams to the playoffs, he won the Super Bowl.

All of that football talk is to make the point that the name on your son or daughter's diploma may impact where they start, but their actual skill level will determine where they finish. An individual from a no-name college who writes masterfully, speaks two languages, possesses top-notch people skills, and isn't afraid of a little math is going to have a Warner-like rise. An individual who went to Cornell and scraped by academically while pouring energy into his *jam band* may meet a Ryan Leaf-like fate in the workplace.

7. ENTERING A *LOW-PAYING* MAJOR DOES NOT MEAN YOUR CHILD WON'T MAKE MONEY IN THE LONG RUN

See Warner versus Leaf above or, if you prefer statistics, remember that philosophy majors blow past many assumedly more lucrative areas of study by mid-career. English majors are in demand in the business world for their writing ability and analytical skills. Pressuring your kid to major in engineering or computer science when they lack passion for the subject is a surefire way to precipitate a quarter-life crisis and at least a decade of costly therapy bills.

Additionally, it's important to remember that many of the most desirable, satisfying, and lucrative careers require a graduate degree. As we've referenced, liberal arts majors fare quite well in the workplace and in the graduate school admissions process.

8. FRIVOLOUS DEBT IS THE NUMBER-ONE ENEMY

We chronicled for you the many ways in which excessive debt can impact a young person's personal and professional life well beyond their undergraduate years. If a postsecondary budget is limited (most people), college cost must factor into the equation, as should return on investment. Borrowing thousands of dollars to attend a less-than-elite (or extremely selective) college very rarely makes sense, and will likely result in a young adulthood filled with stress and servitude.

To quote ourselves from chapter 1: "They may want to become a banker; they may want to open a bakery. Either way, it would certainly be nice to have the choice."

9. GOOD PERFORMANCE AND AN EYE TOWARD EARLY COLLEGE CREDIT ARE THE BEST WAYS TO SAVE ON COLLEGE COSTS

While the masses chase the white whale of private scholarships, you and your kid will be exerting all of your energy in areas more within your control and more likely to pay dividends. In reality, there are three main ways to save big on college that are within their control: (1) earn good grades; (2) study like hell for the SAT/ACT; and (3) accrue college credits while still in high school through AP/IB and dual enrollment courses and/or CLEP exams.

In our culture of get-rich-quick schemes, this answer probably lacks sex appeal because it involves hard work, self-improvement, and long-term planning. However, accepting this truth now and tuning out the mirage of private scholarship money will, in the end, be a far more successful strategy.

10. THERE ARE COUNTLESS TRAPS TO AVOID

The admissions maze is fraught with seemingly promising avenues that lead only to dead ends. While everyone's maze is different, there are some generalizable *wrong turns* that should be avoided. There are many private colleges that sport exorbitant tuition prices, offer low return on investment, and leave students with excessive debt. There is the trap of the out-of-state flagship school for which students will pay a sizable premium, likely passing up better values within their home state or at private schools nationwide that have more incentive to generously dispense merit aid awards. There is the all-too-common sales pitch of style over substance: *Look at our brand new multimillion dollar gym! You can study abroad at a Greek resort for a month! Check out our brand new physics lab, ahem, . . .* (trailing off) *that is only open to grad students.*

Students should ignore the frills and deeply investigate the substance of the educational experience. It will be more cost-effective to send your kid to a school with a mediocre but accessible physics lab, buy them a gym membership at LA Fitness, and fork over cash for a summer trip to Greece.

FINAL THOUGHTS

Even the most mature and high-achieving young people are susceptible to the lure of a school's colors (UNC's powder blue often has this effect), dreams of bumper-sticker glory, and the one-upmanship of institutional name-dropping. Parents, of course, are often equally or more drawn in by the trappings of college brand. However, if your child is truly going to maximize the benefits of their higher education, they must first be true to themselves. They should ignore the sensationalism and scare tactics, set aside status-driven tendencies, and situate college in the context of *their* life. Doing so will produce lasting positive effects not only during their next four years, but for the many decades that follow. We hope that we have convinced you to take this step.

Appendix

Elite colleges accept fewer than 20% of all applicants *and* possess an average composite ACT (25%tile) score of at least 29 *or* an average combined SAT (25%tile) score (CR + M) of at least 1300. These include the following:

- Amherst College
- Bowdoin College
- Brown University
- California Institute of Technology
- Claremont McKenna College
- Columbia University
- Cornell University
- Dartmouth University
- Duke University
- Georgetown University
- Harvard University
- Harvey Mudd College
- Johns Hopkins University
- Massachusetts Institute of Technology
- Middlebury College
- Northwestern University
- Pomona College
- Princeton University
- Rice University
- Stanford University
- Swarthmore College
- Tufts University
- United States Air Force Academy

- University of Chicago
- University of Pennsylvania
- Vanderbilt University
- Washington University
- Washington and Lee University
- Williams College
- Yale University

Extremely selective colleges accept fewer than 40% of all applicants *and* possess an average composite ACT (25%tile) score of at least 28 *or* an average combined SAT (25%tile) score (CR + M) of at least 1260. These include the following:

- Barnard College
- Bates College
- Boston College
- Brandeis University
- Bucknell University
- Carleton College
- Carnegie Mellon University
- Colby College
- Colgate University
- College of William and Mary
- College of the Holy Cross
- Connecticut College
- Cooper Union
- Davidson College
- Emory University
- Franklin and Marshall College
- Georgia Institute of Technology
- Grinnell College
- Hamilton College
- Haverford College
- Kenyon College
- Lehigh University
- Macalester College
- New York University
- Northeastern University
- Oberlin College
- Scripps College
- Tulane University

- United States Military Academy
- United States Naval Academy
- University of California, Berkeley
- University of California, Los Angeles
- University of Michigan, Ann Arbor
- University of North Carolina at Chapel Hill
- University of Notre Dame
- University of Richmond
- University of Rochester
- University of Southern California
- University of Virginia
- Vassar College
- Wake Forest University
- Wellesley College
- Wesleyan University

Very selective colleges accept fewer than 60% of all applicants *and* possess an average composite ACT (25%tile) score of at least 26 *or* an average combined SAT (25%tile) score (CR + M) of at least 1190. These include the following:

- American University
- Babson College
- Bard College
- Bentley University
- Boston University
- Brigham Young University
- Bryn Mawr College
- Case Western Reserve University
- Clemson University
- Colorado School of Mines
- Denison University
- Dickinson College
- Emerson College
- Fordham University
- George Washington University
- Gettysburg College
- Hobart and William Smith Colleges
- Lafayette College
- Marist College
- Mount Holyoke College

- Occidental College
- Ohio State University
- Reed College
- Pitzer College
- Rensselaer Polytechnic Institute
- Rhodes College
- SUNY at Binghamton
- SUNY at Geneseo
- Santa Clara University
- Shimer College
- Skidmore College
- Smith College
- Southern Methodist University
- St. Olaf College
- Stevens Institute of Technology
- Stony Brook University
- Union College
- University of Florida
- University of Georgia
- University of Maryland, College Park
- University of Miami
- University of Minnesota, Twin Cities
- University of Pittsburgh
- Villanova University
- Whitman College
- Worcester Polytechnic Institute

Moderately selective colleges accept fewer than 70% of all applicants *and* possess an average composite ACT (25%tile) score of at least 24 *or* an average combined SAT (25%tile) score (CR + M) of at least 1110. These include the following:

- Appalachian State University
- Augustana College, Illinois
- Baylor University
- Beloit College
- Bennington College
- Butler University
- CUNY Baruch
- California Polytechnic State University, San Luis Obispo
- Centre College
- Chapman University

- Clark University
- Clarkson University
- DePauw University
- Drake University
- Earlham College
- Elon University
- Florida International University
- Florida State University
- George Mason University
- Gonzaga University
- Gustavus Adolphus College
- Hampshire College
- Illinois Institute of Technology
- Illinois Wesleyan University
- Kalamazoo University
- Kettering University
- Lewis & Clark College
- Loyola Marymount University
- Loyola University of Maryland
- Marquette University
- Miami University
- Milwaukee School of Engineering
- Muhlenberg College
- New College of Florida
- North Carolina State University
- Penn State University
- Pepperdine University
- Purdue University
- Rochester Institute of Technology
- Rollins College
- Sarah Lawrence College
- Sewanee: University of the South
- St. Lawrence University
- Texas Christian University
- The College of New Jersey
- The College of Wooster
- Trinity College
- Trinity University
- United States Coast Guard Academy
- University of California, San Diego
- University of California, Santa Barbara
- University of Connecticut

- University of Dayton
- University of Delaware
- University of Illinois at Urbana–Champaign
- University of Maryland, Baltimore County
- University of Massachusetts Amherst
- University of North Carolina at Asheville
- University of Portland
- University of San Diego
- University of South Carolina
- University of Texas at Austin
- University of Texas at Dallas
- University of Tulsa
- University of Washington
- University of Wisconsin–Madison
- Ursinus College
- Virginia Tech
- Washington College
- Wheaton College, Illinois
- Wheaton College, Massachusetts
- Wofford College

Bibliography

CHAPTER 1

Allen, Jeff, and Steve Robbins. (2010). "Effects of Interest-Major Congruence, Motivation, and Academic Performance on Timely Degree Attainment." *Journal of Counseling Psychology*. 57. 23–35.

American Student Assistance. "Life Delayed: The Impact of Student Debt on the Daily Lives of Young Americans." 2013. Accessed December 6, 2015. http://www.asa.org/site/assets/files/3793/life_delayed.pdf.

Clark, Patrick. "Debt Is Piling Up Faster for Most Graduate Students—but Not MBAs." *Bloomberg Businessweek*. March 25, 2014. Accessed December 6, 2015. http://www.bloomberg.com/bw/articles/2014-03-25/student-loan-debt-piles-up-for-graduate-students-but-not-mbas.

College Board, The National Commission on Writing for America's Families, Schools, and Colleges. "Writing: A Ticket to Work . . . Or a Ticket Out: A Survey of Business Leaders." September 2004. Accessed December 6, 2015. http://www.collegeboard.com/prod_downloads/writingcom/writing-ticket-to-work.pdf.

Crabtree, Steve. "Worldwide, 13% of Employees Are Engaged at Work." Gallup. October 8, 2013. Accessed December 6, 2015. http://www.gallup.com/poll/165269/worldwide-employees-engaged-work.aspx.

Gallo, Carmine. "The Soft Skill That Could Mean $1 Million Hard Cash for One Manager." *Forbes*. November 7, 2013. Accessed December 2, 2015. http://www.forbes.com/sites/carminegallo/2013/11/07/the-soft-skill-that-could-mean-1-million-hard-cash-for-one-manager/.

Gordon, Virginia. (2007). *The Undecided College Student: An Academic and Career Advising Challenge* (3rd ed.). Springfield, IL: Charles C. Thomas.

Gould, Elise. "2014 Continues a 35-Year Trend of Broad-Based Wage Stagnation." Economic Policy Institute. February 19, 2015. Accessed December 6, 2015. http://www.epi.org/publication/stagnant-wages-in-2014/.

Gould, Elise. "A Decade of Declines in Employer-Sponsored Health Insurance Coverage." Economic Policy Institute. February 23, 2012. Accessed December 6, 2015. http://www.epi.org/publication/bp337-employer-sponsored-health-insurance/.

The Institute for College Access & Success. "Project on Student Debt: State by State Data." Accessed December 6, 2015. http://ticas.org/posd/map-state-data-2015.

Lorin, Janet. "Medical School at $278,000 Means Even Bernanke Son Has Debt." *Bloomberg Businessweek*. April 11, 2013. Accessed December 6, 2015. http://www. bloomberg.com/news/articles/2013-04-11/medical-school-at-278-000-means-even-bernanke-son-carries-debt.

Lowe, Corinne. "70 Percent of Students Change Major After Enrollment, Study Finds." *The Daily Princetonian*. September 18, 2014. Accessed December 6, 2015. http://dailyprincetonian.com/news/2014/09/70-percent-of-students-change-major-after-enrollment-study-finds/.

Lusin, Natalia. "The MLA Survey of Postsecondary Entrance and Degree Requirements for Languages Other Than English, 2009–2010." Modern Language Association of America. March 2012. Accessed December 6, 2015. http://www.mla.org/pdf/requirements_survey_200910.pdf.

Lynch, Mamie, Jennifer Engle, and Jose L. Cruz. "Lifting the Fog on Inequitable Financial Aid Policies." The Education Trust. November 2011. Accessed December 6, 2015. http://edtrust.org/wp-content/uploads/2013/10/Lifting-the-Fog-FINAL.pdf.

National Association of Colleges and Employers. "Starting Salaries." Accessed December 6, 2015. https://www.naceweb.org/salary-resources/starting-salaries. aspx.

Pew Research Center. "Is College Worth It?" May 15, 2011. Accessed December 6, 2015. http://www.pewsocialtrends.org/2011/05/15/is-college-worth-it/.

Rajecki, D. W., and Victor M. H. Borden. (2011). "Psychology Degrees: Employment, Wage, and Career Trajectory Consequences." *Perspectives in Psychological Science*. 6. 321–335.

Saiz, Albert, and Elena Zoido. 2002. "The Returns to Speaking a Second Language." Working Papers 02-16. Federal Reserve Bank of Philadelphia.

Shapiro, Doug, Afet Dundar, Mary Ziskin, Xin Yuan, and Autumn Harrell. (2013, December). "Completing College: A National View of Student Attainment Rates-Fall 2007 Cohort (Signature Report No. 6)." Herndon, VA: National Student Clearinghouse Research Center. Accessed December 6, 2015. http://nscresearchcenter. org/signaturereport6/.

Simon, Cecilia Capuzzi. "Major Decisions." *New York Times*. November 2, 2012. Accessed December 6, 2015. http://www.nytimes.com/2012/11/04/education/edlife/choosing-one-college-major-out-of-hundreds.html?_r=0.

U.S. Department of Labor, Bureau of Labor Statistics. "Employee Tenure in 2014." September 18, 2014. Accessed December 6, 2015. http://www.bls.gov/news. release/archives/tenure_09182014.htm.

U.S. Department of Labor, Bureau of Labor Statistics. "News Release: Number of Jobs Held, Labor Market Activity, and Earnings Growth among the Youngest Baby Boomers: Results from a Longitudinal Survey." March 31, 2015. Accessed June 17, 2015, http://www.bls.gov/news.release/pdf/nlsoy.pdf.

Vedder, Richard. "Why Did 17 Million Students Go to College?" *The Chronicle of Higher Education*. October 20, 2010. Accessed December 6, 2015. http://chronicle.com/blogs/innovations/why-did-17-million-students-go-to-college/27634.

Yale Law School, "Entering Class Profile," accessed November 10, 2015, https://www.law.yale.edu/admissions/profiles-statistics/entering-class-profile.

Yodle. "Survey: SMB Owners are 'Happy' Despite Concerns about Healthcare, Retirement & Customer Acquisition." August 22, 2013. Accessed December 6, 2015. http://www.yodle.com/company/press-releases/yodle-smb-sentiment-survey.

CHAPTER 2

Babay, Emily. "Penn, Villanova Top LinkedIn Rankings Based on Grads' Career Paths." *Philly.com*. October 2, 2014. Accessed December 6, 2015. http://www.philly.com/philly/news/Penn_Villanova_top_LinkedIn_rankings.html.

Brewer, Dominic J., Eric R. Eide, and Ronald G. Ehrenberg. "Does It Pay to Attend an Elite Private College? Cross Cohort Evidence on the Effects of College Type on Earnings." *Journal of Human Resources* 34, no. 1 (Winter 1999): 104–123.

Dale, Stacy, and Alan Krueger. "Estimating the Return to College Selectivity over the Career Using Administrative Earnings Data" (NBER Working Paper 17159, June 2011).

Evans, Teri. "Penn State Tops Recruiter Rankings." *The Wall Street Journal*. September 13, 2010. Accessed December 6, 2015. http://www.wsj.com/articles/SB10001424052748704358904575477643369663352.

Franek, Robert, and Princeton Review (Firm). *The Best 376 Colleges*. New York: Random House, 2011.

Glassdoor. "How to Stay Positive with Your Job Search." July 15, 2014. Accessed December 6, 2015. http://www.foxbusiness.com/personal-finance/2014/07/15/how-to-stay-positive-with-your-job-search/.

Harvard University. "Harvard at a Glance: About the Faculty." Accessed July 8, 2015. http://www.harvard.edu/about-harvard/harvard-glance/about-faculty.

Ho, Margaret W., and Joshua P. Rogers. "Harvard Students Less Satisfied Than Peers with Undergraduate Experience, Survey Finds." *The Harvard Crimson*. March 31, 2005. Accessed December 6, 2015. http://www.thecrimson.com/article/2005/3/31/harvard-students-less-satisfied-than-peers/.

Hoekstra, Mark. "The Effect of Attending the Flagship State University on Earnings: A Discontinuity-Based Approach." *The Review of Economics and Statistics* 91, no. 4 (2009): 717–24. doi:10.1162/rest.91.4.717.

Humphreys, Debra, and Patrick Kelly. "How Liberal Arts and Sciences Majors Fare in Employment: A Report on Earnings and Long-Term Career Paths," Washington, DC: Association of American Colleges and Universities, 2014.

LinkedIn University Finder. Accessed February 1, 2016. https://www.linkedin.com/edu/university-finder?trk=edu-rankings-to-uf.

Long, Mark. "College Quality and Early Adult Outcomes." *Economics of Education Review* 27, no. 5 (2008): 588–602. doi:10.1016/j.econedurev.2007.04.004.

O'Shaughnessy, Lynn. "12 Colleges with Great Professors." CBS MoneyWatch. November 19, 2013. Accessed December 26, 2015. http://www.cbsnews.com/news/12-colleges-with-great-college-professors/.

O'Shaughnessy, Lynn. "The Colleges Where PhD's Get Their Start." The College Solution. January 26, 2012. Accessed December 6, 2015. http://www.thecollegesolution.com/the-colleges-where-phds-get-their-start/.

Oremus, Will. "Where Do Googlers Go to College? A Look at Tech Companies' Top Feeder Schools." *Slate*. May 23, 2014. Accessed December 6, 2015. http://www.slate.com/blogs/future_tense/2014/05/23/tech_company_feeder_schools_stanford_to_google_washington_to_microsoft_sjsu.html.

Penn State Alumni Association. "Alumni Association Overview." Accessed December 6, 2015. http://alumni.psu.edu/about_us/overview.

PER Jobs. "VAP at Pomona College (CA)." February 22, 2012. Accessed December 6, 2015. http://perjobs.blogspot.com/2012_02_01_archive.html.

Princeton University Department of Politics. "Senior Thesis." last modified July 27, 2015. Accessed December 6, 2015. https://www.princeton.edu/politics/undergraduate/independent-work/senior-thesis/.

Qian, Michael. "College Aims to Focus Undergraduate Research." *The Dartmouth*. October 19, 2014. Accessed December 6, 2015. http://thedartmouth.com/2014/10/19/college-aims-to-focus-undergraduate-research/.

Ray, Julie, and Stephanie Kafka. "Life in College Matters for Life After College." Gallup. May 6, 2014. Accessed December 6, 2015. http://www.gallup.com/poll/168848/life-college-matters-life-college.aspx.

Rimer, Sara. "Harvard Task Force Calls for New Focus on Teaching and Not Just Research." *New York Times*. May 10, 2007. Accessed December 6, 2015. http://www.nytimes.com/2007/05/10/education/10harvard.html?pagewanted=1&sq=harvard%20task%20force%20calls%20for%20new%20focus%20on%20teaching%20and%20not%20just%20research&st=nyt&scp=1.

Swarthmore College. "Swarthmore College Class Size Summary." Accessed on December 6, 2015. http://www.swarthmore.edu/Documents/administration/ir/ClassSize.pdf.

Tsang, Kenneth C. "From College Graduate to Chief Executive: A Closer Look at Education and the Fortune 1000 CEOs." *NACE Journal* 75, no. 1 (September 2014): 12–18.

U.S. Department of Education, Institute of Education Sciences, National Center for Education Statistics.

U.S. News & World Report. "Harvard University." Accessed December 6, 2015. http://colleges.usnews.rankingsandreviews.com/best-colleges/harvard-university-2155.

U.S. News & World Report. "Northern Arizona University." Accessed December 6, 2015. http://colleges.usnews.rankingsandreviews.com/best-colleges/northern-arizona-university-1082.

UniJobs. "Preceptor in the Life Sciences." Accessed December 6, 2015. http://www.unijobs.us/harvard-university-jobs/G2PF/preceptor-in-the-life-sciences.

University of Hawaii at Manoa Shidler College of Business. "$100 Million: A Visionary Gift." Accessed December 6, 2015. http://shidler.hawaii.edu/visionary/gift.

Zhang, Brian C. "CS Leads Concentration Growth in SEAS." *The Harvard Crimson.* February 13, 2013. Accessed December 6, 2015. http://www.thecrimson.com/article/2013/2/13/cs-seas-more-concentrators.

CHAPTER 3/4/5

Annicchiarico, Francesca, and Samuel Y. Weinstock. "Freshman Survey Part I: Meet Harvard's Class of 2017." *The Harvard Crimson.* September 3, 2013. Accessed December 26, 2015. http://www.thecrimson.com/article/2013/9/3/freshmen-employment-demographics-geography/?page=2.

Ashburn, Elyse. "At Elite Colleges, Legacy Status May Count More Than Was Previously Thought." *The Chronicle of Higher Education.* January 5, 2011. Accessed December 26, 2015. http://chronicle.com/article/Legacys-Advantage-May-Be/125812/?sid=at&utm_source=at&utm_medium=en.

Belasco, Andrew S. "Creating College Opportunity: School Counselors and Their Influence on Postsecondary Enrollment." *Research in Higher Education.* November 2013. 54(7). 781–804.

Belasco, Andrew S., Kelly O. Rosinger, and James C. Hearn. "The Test-Optional Movement at America's Selective Liberal Arts Colleges: A Boon for Equity or Something Else?" Educational Evaluation and Policy Analysis. (2015). 37(2). 206–23.

Bernhard, Meg. "The Making of a Harvard Feeder School." *The Harvard Crimson.* December 13, 2013. Accessed January 1, 2016. http://www.thecrimson.com/article/2013/12/13/making-harvard-feeder-schools/.

Budryk, Zack. "Should AP be Plan A?" *Inside Higher Ed.* April 23, 2013. Accessed January 1, 2016. https://www.insidehighered.com/news/2013/04/23/new-study-challenges-popular-perceptions-ap.

Center for Community Alternatives. "Education Suspended: The Use of High School Disciplinary Records in College Admissions." May 2015. Accessed January 3, 2015. http://www.communityalternatives.org/pdf/publications/EducationSuspended.pdf.

Chan, Agnes. "Waitlist Admissions See Huge Jump for Class of 2019." *The Brown Daily Herald.* September 10, 2015. Accessed December 26, 2015. http://www.browndailyherald.com/2015/09/10/waitlist-admissions-see-huge-jump-for-class-of-2019/.

Chokshi, Niraj. "Map: The States College Kids Can't Wait to Leave." *The Washington Post.* June 5, 2014. Accessed December 26, 2015. https://www.washingtonpost.com/blogs/govbeat/wp/2014/06/05/map-the-states-college-kids-cant-wait-to-leave/.

Clinedinst, Melissa. "2014 State of College Admission." National Association for College Admission Counseling. Accessed December 26, 2015. http://www.nxtbook.com/ygsreprints/NACAC/2014SoCA_nxtbk/#/28.

College Board. "2013 College-Bound Seniors Total Group Profile Report." Accessed December 26, 2015. http://media.collegeboard.com/digitalServices/pdf/research/2013/TotalGroup-2013.pdf.

College Board. "Institutions Using SAT Subject Tests." Accessed December 26, 2015. https://professionals.collegeboard.com/testing/sat-subject/about/institutions#inst_using_SAT.

Del Giudice, Marguerite. "Grit Trumps Talent and IQ: A Story Every Parent (and Educator) Should Read." *National Geographic*. October 14, 2014. Accessed February 29, 2016. http://news.nationalgeographic.com/news/2014/10/141015-angela-duckworth-success-grit-psychology-self-control-science-nginnovators/.

Espenshade, Thomas J., and Chang Y. Chung. "The Opportunity Cost of Admission Preferences at Elite Universities." *Social Science Quarterly* 86, no. 2 (June 2005): 293–305. doi:10.1111/j.0038-4941.2005.00303.

Espenshade, Thomas J., Lauren E. Hale, and Chang Y. Chung. (2005). "The Frog Pond Revisited: High School Academic Context, Class Rank, and Elite College Admission." *Sociology of Education*. 78(4). 269–293.

Fain, Paul. "Nearing the Bottom." *Inside Higher Ed*. May 15, 2014. Accessed December 26, 2015. https://www.insidehighered.com/news/2014/05/15/new-data-show-slowing-national-enrollment-decline.

Gutting, Gary. "The Myth of the 'Student-Athlete'" *New York Times*. March 15, 2012. Accessed December 26, 2015. http://opinionator.blogs.nytimes.com/2012/03/15/the-myth-of-the-student-athlete/.

Hardy, Susan. "Study Finds That More AP Classes May Not Be Better." *The University Gazette*. The University of North Carolina at Chapel Hill. January 8, 2013. Accessed December 26, 2015. http://gazette.unc.edu/2013/01/08/study-finds-that-more-ap-classes-may-not-be-better/.

Izlar, Mary Camille. "Harvard Summer Program Recommendations Come at Hefty Cost." *Bloomberg Businessweek*. July 17, 2013. Accessed December 26, 2015. http://www.bloomberg.com/news/articles/2013-07-17/harvard-summer-program-recommendations-come-at-hefty-cost.

Jager-Hyman, Joie. "Receiving Testing Accommodations for Learning Disabilities." *The Huffington Post*. February 7, 2014. Last modified April 9, 2014. Accessed December 26, 2015. http://www.huffingtonpost.com/joie-jagerhyman/receiving-testing-accommo_b_4740601.html.

Jaschik, Scott. "Duke Asks the Question." *Inside Higher Ed*. September 2, 2014. Accessed December 26, 2015. https://www.insidehighered.com/news/2014/09/02/duke-u-adds-voluntary-admissions-question-sexual-orientation-and-gender-identity.

Jaschik, Scott. "How Much Admission Misreporting?" *Inside Higher Ed*. January 28, 2013. Accessed December 26, 2015. https://www.insidehighered.com/news/2013/01/28/bucknells-admission-raises-questions-about-how-many-colleges-are-reporting-false.

Kaplan Test Prep. "Kaplan Test Prep Survey: More College Admissions Officers Checking Applicants' Digital Trails, but Most Students Unconcerned." October 31, 2013. Accessed December 26, 2015. http://press.kaptest.com/press-releases/kaplan-test-prep-survey-more-college-admissions-officers-checking-applicants-digital-trails-but-most-students-unconcerned.

Kawano, Kourtney. "Athletics and Socioeconomic Status: NCAA and Ivy League Rules Complicate Recruitment." *The Dartmouth*. May 15, 2015. Accessed December 26, 2015. http://thedartmouth.com/2015/05/15/athletics-and-socioeconomic-status-ncaa-and-ivy-league-rules-complicate-recruitment/.

Kent, Jennie, and Jeff Levy. "Early Decision vs. Regular Decision Acceptance Rates." September 2015. Accessed December 26, 2015. https://www.iecaonline.com/PDF/IECA_Library_ED-vs-RD-Acceptances.pdf.

Massachusetts Institute of Technology. "Admissions Statistics." Accessed February 29, 2016. http://mitadmissions.org/apply/process/stats.

Mulhere, Kaitlin. "Lots More College Admissions Officers Are Checking Your Instagram and Facebook." *Money*. November 9, 2013. Accessed January 31, 2016. http://time.com/money/4179392/college-applications-social-media/.

National Association for College Admission Counseling. "Effective Counseling in Schools Increases College Access, Research to Practice Brief." 2006. Accessed December 26, 2015. http://www.nacacnet.org/research/research-data/Research%20Member%20Only/McDonough.pdf.

National Association for College Admission Counseling. "Factors in the Admission Decision." Accessed December 26, 2015. http://www.nacacnet.org/studentinfo/articles/Pages/Factors-in-the-Admission-Decision.aspx.

National Student Clearinghouse Research Center. "Report: High School Benchmarks 2014." October 13, 2014. Accessed December 26, 2015. https://nscresearchcenter.org/hsbenchmarks2014/#Results1.

Nisen, Max. "Legacies Still Get a Staggeringly Unfair College Admissions Advantage." *Business Insider*. June 5, 2013. Accessed December 26, 2015. http://www.businessinsider.com/legacy-kids-have-an-admissions-advantage-2013-6.

O'Shaughnessy, Lynn. "The Other Side of 'Test Optional.'" *New York Times*. July 20, 2009. Accessed December 26, 2015. http://www.nytimes.com/2009/07/26/education/edlife/26guidance-t.html.

Otani, Akane. "At Top Schools, a Spot on the Wait List May as Well Be a Rejection." *Bloomberg Businessweek*. April 28, 2015. Accessed December 26, 2015. http://www.bloomberg.com/news/articles/2015-04-28/at-top-schools-a-spot-on-the-wait-list-may-as-well-be-a-rejection.

Rosen, Jill. "Johns Hopkins Welcomes First Members of Its Class of 2019." *The Hub*. December 12, 2014. Accessed December 26, 2015. http://hub.jhu.edu/2014/12/12/early-decision-class-of-2019.

Rufus, Anneli. "Your Odds of Getting into College." *The Daily Beast*. September 1, 2010. Accessed December 26, 2015. http://www.thedailybeast.com/articles/2010/09/01/college-admissions-15-ways-to-predict-where-youll-get-in.html.

Ruiz, Rebecca R. "Disclose Disciplinary Infractions, Admissions Officials Say." *New York Times*. October 27, 2011. Accessed December 26, 2015. http://thechoice.blogs.nytimes.com/2011/10/27/infractions/.

Smith-Barrow, Delece. "10 Universities With the Largest Endowments." *U.S. News & World Report*. October 6, 2015. Accessed December 26, 2015. http://www.usnews.com/education/best-colleges/the-short-list-college/articles/2015/10/06/10-universities-with-the-largest-endowments.

Strauss, Valerie. "AP Courses: How Many Do Colleges Want?" *The Washington Post*. January 29, 2010. Accessed December 26, 2015. http://voices.washingtonpost.com/answer-sheet/college-admissions/ap-courses-how-many-do-college.html.

U.S. Department of Education. "The Toolbox Revisited: Paths to Degree Completion from High School through College." Last modified March 2, 2006. Accessed December 26, 2015. http://www2.ed.gov/rschstat/research/pubs/toolboxrevisit/index.html?exp.

Victor, Jon. "Early Apps Increase at Peer Schools." *Yale Daily News.* December 11, 2015. Accessed December 26, 2015. http://yaledailynews.com/blog/2015/12/11/early-apps-increase-at-peer-schools/.

CHAPTER 6

Anderson, Nick. "Colleges Often Give Discounts to the Rich. But Here's One That Gave Up on 'Merit Aid.'" *The Washington Post.* December 29, 2014. Accessed December 21, 2015. https://www.washingtonpost.com/local/education/colleges-often-give-discounts-to-the-rich-but-heres-one-that-gave-up-on-merit-aid/2014/12/29/a15a0f22-6f3c-11e4-893f-86bd390a3340_story.html.

College Board. "Average Published Undergraduate Charges by Sector, 2015–2016." Trends in Higher Education. Accessed December 6, 2015. http://trends.collegeboard.org/college-pricing/figures-tables/average-published-undergraduate-charges-sector-2015-16.

College Board. "CLEP: Getting College Credit." Accessed December 6, 2015. https://clep.collegeboard.org/overview/collegecredit.

College Board. "Retaking the SAT." Accessed September 17, 2015. https://professionals.collegeboard.com/testing/sat-reasoning/scores/retake.

College Board. "Total Undergraduate Student Aid by Source and Type, 2014–15." Trends in Higher Education. Accessed December 6, 2015. http://trends.collegeboard.org/student-aid/figures-tables/total-undergraduate-student-aid-source-and-type-2014-15.

College Board. "Trends in Student Aid 2014. " Accessed December 6, 2015. https://secure-media.collegeboard.org/digitalServices/misc/trends/2014-trends-student-aid-report-final.pdf.

The Daily. "University Tuition Fees, 2015/2016." September 9, 2015. Accessed February 29, 2016. http://www.statcan.gc.ca/daily-quotidien/150909/dq150909b-eng.pdf.

International Baccalaureate. "The IB by Country." Accessed December 28, 2015. http://www.ibo.org/country/US/.

Jaschik, Scott. "More Pressure Than Ever: The 2014 Survey of College and University Admissions Directors." *Inside Higher Ed.* September 18, 2014. Accessed December 6, 2015. https://www.insidehighered.com/news/survey/more-pressure-ever-2014-survey-college-and-university-admissions-directors.

Jaschik, Scott. "Pressure from All Sides: The 2015 Survey of Admissions Directors." *Inside Higher Ed.* October 1, 2015. Accessed December 6, 2015. https://www.insidehighered.com/news/survey/pressure-all-sides-2015-survey-admissions-directors.

Jindal, Shivika. "Most Expensive City in the World–Oslo, Norway." February 13, 2014. Accessed December 6, 2015. http://richglare.com/expensive-city-world-oslo-norway/.

Kantrowitz, Mark. "Reasons Why Students Do Not File the FAFSA." January 18, 2011. Accessed November 11, 2015. http://www.finaid.org/educators/20110118n ofafsareasons.pdf.

Matthews, David. "International and Postgrad Fee Survey, 2014." Times Higher Education. August 21, 2014. Accessed February 29, 2016. https://www.timeshigher-ucation.com/features/international-and-postgrad-fee-survey-2014/2015207.article.

Rivard, Ry. "Summer Scramble." *Inside Higher Ed*. May 21, 2014. Accessed December 28, 2015. https://www.insidehighered.com/news/2014/05/21/colleges-miss-enrollment-targets-step-their-summer-recruitment.

Trinity University. "Academic Merit Scholarships for First-Year Students." Accessed February 29, 2016. https://new.trinity.edu/admissions-aid/financial-aid/academic-merit-scholarships-first-year-students.

U.S. Department of Education. Institute of Education Sciences, National Center for Education Statistics.

World Bank. "GDP Ranking." Last modified December 16, 2015. Accessed December 27, 2015. http://data.worldbank.org/data-catalog/GDP-ranking-table.

CHAPTER 7

Association of American Medical Colleges. "Table 18: MCAT and GPAs for Applicants and Matriculants to U.S. Medical Schools by Primary Undergraduate Major, 2014." Accessed December 13, 2015. https://www.aamc.org/download/321496/data/factstable18.pdf.

Belasco, Andrew S., and Michael J. Trivette. (2015). "Aiming Low: Estimating the Scope and Predictors of Postsecondary Undermatch." *The Journal of Higher Education*. 86(2). 233–63.

Billmyer, Steve. "NYS Teachers' Salaries by School District: Who Makes the Most Money?" January 29, 2014. Accessed December 12, 2015. http://www.syra-cuse.com/news/index.ssf/2014/01/nys_teachers_salaries_by_school_district_who_makes_the_most_money.html.

"Blurbs and Useful Stats." Computer Science Education Week. December 7–15, 2015. Accessed December 31, 2015. https://csedweek.org/resource_kit/blurbs.

Butcher, Dan. "Top Majors for Getting an Investment Banking Job on Wall Street." eFinancialCareers. January 8, 2016. Accessed February 29, 2016. http://news.efinancialcareers.com/us-en/230786/top-undergraduate-majors-investment-banking-jobs-wall-street/.

Butcher, Sarah. "Finance Firms Actively Hiring Drama Students, History Majors, Persons with Charisma." eFinancialCareers. October 10, 2013. Accessed February 29, 2016. http://news.efinancialcareers.com/cn-en/152746/do-you-really-need-to-study-a-subject-thats-finance-related-to-get-a-job-in-finance/.

Cassuto, Leonard. "Ph.D. Attrition: How Much Is Too Much?" *The Chronicle of Higher Education*. July 1, 2013. Accessed February 29, 2016. http://chronicle.com/article/PhD-Attrition-How-Much-Is/140045/.

Center for Education Reform. "K–12 Facts." Last modified September 2014. Accessed December 12, 2015. https://www.edreform.com/2012/04/k-12-facts/

Clauset, Aaron, Samuel Arbesman and Daniel B. Larremore. "Systematic Inequality and Hierarchy in Faculty Hiring Networks." Science Advances. February 12, 2015. 1(1). Accessed February 29, 2016. http://advances.sciencemag.org/content/1/1/e1400005.full.

College Board. "AP Exam Volume Changes (2004–2014)." Accessed December 12, 2015. http://media.collegeboard.com/digitalServices/pdf/research/2014/2014-Exam-Volume-Change.pdf.

College Factual. "Highest Paid Engineering Grads." Last modified 2013. Accessed December 12, 2015. http://www.collegefactual.com/majors/engineering/rankings/highest-paid-grads/p36.html.

Dunleavy, Dana, Henry Sondheimer, Laura Castillo-Page, and Ruth Beer Bletzinger. "Medical School Admissions: More than Grades and Test Scores." Association of American Medical Colleges. Analysis in Brief. 11(6). September 2011. Accessed February 29, 2016. https://www.aamc.org/download/261106/data.

Estrada-Worthington, R. "2015 Corporate Recruiters Survey Report." Graduate Management Admission Council. Accessed February 29, 2016. http://www.gmac.com/market-intelligence-and-research/research-library/employment-outlook/2015-corporate-recruiters-survey-report.aspx.

Farnham, Alan. "20 Fastest Growing Occupations." ABC News. February 5, 2014. Accessed February 29, 2016. http://abcnews.go.com/Business/americas-20-fastest-growing-jobs-surprise/story?id=22364716.

Farrington, Robert. "Law School and Student Loan Debt: Be Careful." *Forbes*. December 18, 2014. Accessed December 12, 2015. http://www.forbes.com/sites/robertfarrington/2014/12/18/law-school-and-student-loan-debt-be-careful/.

Geisinger, Brandi N., and D. Raj Raman. "Why They Leave: Understanding Student Attrition from Engineering Majors." *International Journal of Engineering Education* 29 no. 4 (2013): 914–25. Accessed December 26, 2015. http://lib.dr.iastate.edu/cgi/viewcontent.cgi?article=1890&context=abe_eng_pubs.

Goldman Sachs. "Explore Goldman Sachs Careers Quiz." Accessed February 29, 2016. http://www.goldmansachs.com/careers/why-goldman-sachs/explore-goldman-sachs-careers-quiz/index.html?Questions=9.

Hall, Jonathan V., and Alan B. Krueger. "An Analysis of the Labor Market for Uber's Driver-Partners in the United States." Published as Working Paper #587 for the Industrial Relations Section at Princeton University (January 22, 2015).

Halonen, Ph.D., Jane S. "Are There Too Many Psychology Majors?" February 5, 2011. Accessed December 12, 2015. http://www.cogdop.org/page_attachments/0000/0200/FLA_White_Paper_for_cogop_posting.pdf.

Helfand, Zach. "Study Reveals Engineering Majors Spend Significantly More Time Studying." *USA Today*. November 23, 2011. Accessed December 12, 2015. http://college.usatoday.com/2011/11/23/study-reveals-engineering-majors-spend-significantly-more-time-studying-2/.

Holliday, Katie. "This Industry Has an Entry Level Salary of $335,000." CNBC. November 1, 2013. Accessed December 12, 2015. http://www.cnbc.com/2013/11/01/this-industry-has-an-entry-level-salary-of-335000.html.

Jaschik, Scott. "Faculty Pay: Up and Uneven." *Inside Higher Ed*. March 16, 2015. Accessed February 29, 2016. https://www.insidehighered.com/news/2015/03/16/survey-finds-increases-faculty-pay-and-significant-gaps-discipline.

Jaschik, Scott. "Rigor or Snobbery?" *Inside Higher Ed.* November 1, 2011. Accessed February 29, 2016. https://www.insidehighered.com/news/2011/11/01/professors-research-raises-questions-about-graduate-admissions.

La Roche, Julia. "14,664 People Just Got Major Cred on Wall Street." *Business Insider.* August 11, 2015. Accessed December 12, 2015. http://www.businessinsider.com/cfa-level-3-results-2015-8.

Lawyer2B. "Half of Lawyers Wish They'd Chosen a Different Career." March 23, 2015. Accessed December 12, 2015. http://l2b.thelawyer.com/solicitor/news/half-of-lawyers-wish-theyd-chosen-a-different-career/3033012.article.

LinkedIn. "Best Undergraduate Universities for Finance Professionals." Accessed December 12, 2015. https://www.linkedin.com/edu/rankings/us/undergraduate-finance?trk=edu-rankings-ctg-card.

Medical Group Management Association. "Primary Care Physicians Outpace Specialists in 2014, according to MGMA Provider Compensation Report." July 23, 2015. Accessed December 12, 2015. http://www.mgma.com/about/mgma-press-room/press-releases/2015/primary-care-physicians-outpace-specialists-in-2014-according-to-mgma-physicians-compensation-repor.

Mauney, C. Stuart. (n.d.). "The Lawyers' Epidemic: Depression, Suicide and Substance Abuse." Accessed December 31, 2015. http://www.charlestonlaw.edu/charlestonSchoolOfLaw/files/27/274463ca-476c-40cd-9c0a-733676db3cb5.pdf.

McKenna, Laura. "The College President-to-Adjunct Pay Ratio." *The Atlantic.* September 24, 2015. Accessed February 29, 2016. http://www.theatlantic.com/education/archive/2015/09/income-inequality-in-higher-education-the-college-president-to-adjunct-pay-ratio/407029/.

National Association of School Psychologists. "Workforce & Salary Information." Accessed February 29, 2016. https://www.nasponline.org/about-school-psychology/workforce-and-salary-information.

Norcross, John C., and Sayette, Michael A. (2014). *Insider's Guide to Graduate Programs in Clinical and Counseling Psychology: Revised 2014/2015 Edition.* Guilford Publications.

PayScale. "2015–2016 PayScale College Salary Report: Best Undergraduate Engineering Schools by Salary Potential." Accessed December 12, 2015. http://www.payscale.com/college-salary-report/best-schools-by-type/bachelors/engineering-schools?page=3.

PayScale. "Software Engineer / Developer / Programmer Salary." Accessed December 12, 2015. http://www.payscale.com/research/US/Job=Software_Engineer_%2F_Developer_%2F_Programmer/Salary.

Pearlstein, Joanna. "The Schools Where Apple, Google, and Facebook Get Their Recruits." *WIRED.* May 22, 2014. Accessed December 12, 2015. http://www.wired.com/2014/05/alumni-network-2/

Rajecki, D. W., and Victor M. H. Borden. "Psychology Degrees: Employment, Wage, and Career Trajectory Consequences." *Perspectives in Psychological Science* 6 (2011): 321–35. doi:10.1177/1745691611412385.

Riggs, Liz. "Why Do Teachers Quit?" *The Atlantic.* October 18, 2013. Accessed December 12, 2015. http://www.theatlantic.com/education/archive/2013/10/why-do-teachers-quit/280699/.

Sanghoee, Sanjay. "Why Banking and Work-Life Balance Don't Mix." *Fortune.* February 4, 2014. Accessed December 12, 2015. http://fortune.com/2014/02/04/why-banking-and-work-life-balance-dont-mix/.

Sargent, John F., Jr. "The U.S. Science and Engineering Workforce: Recent, Current, and Projected Employment, Wages, and Unemployment." February 19, 2014. Accessed December 12, 2015. http://www.fas.org/sgp/crs/misc/R43061.pdf.

Smith-Barrow, Delece. "10 Medical Schools Where Students Pay a High Price." *U.S. News & World Report.* May 19, 2015. Accessed December 12, 2015. http://www.usnews.com/education/best-graduate-schools/the-short-list-grad-school/articles/2015/05/19/10-medical-schools-where-students-pay-a-high-price.

The University of Michigan Law School. "Frequently Asked Questions." Accessed February 29, 2016. http://www.law.umich.edu/prospectivestudents/admissions/pages/faq.aspx.

U.S. Census Bureau. "Men in Nursing Occupations." Accessed December 12, 2015. https://www.census.gov/newsroom/releases/pdf/cb13-32_men_in_nursing_occupations.pdf.

U.S. Department of Education, Office for Civil Rights. "Data Snapshot: College and Career Readiness." Issue Brief No. 3 (March 2014). March 21, 2014. Accessed December 12, 2015. http://ocrdata.ed.gov/Downloads/CRDC-College-and-Career-Readiness-Snapshot.pdf.

U.S. Department of Education, National Center for Education Statistics, Institute of Education Sciences. "Total Number of Public School Teachers, Number and Percentage of Public School Teachers with a Master's Degree, and, of Those with a Master's Degree, Number and Percentage of Teachers Whose State, School, or District Helped Pay for Their Master's Degree, by Selected School Characteristics: 2011–2012." Schools and Staffing Survey (SASS). Accessed December 12, 2015. https://nces.ed.gov/surveys/sass/tables/Sass1112-478_t1n.asp.

U.S. Department of Labor, Bureau of Labor Statistics. "Occupational Employment and Wages: Nurse Anesthetists." May 2014. Last modified March 25, 2015. Accessed December 12, 2015. http://www.bls.gov/oes/current/oes291151.htm.

U.S. Department of Labor, Bureau of Labor Statistics, "Occupational Outlook Handbook, 2014–2015 Edition: Accountants and Auditors." January 8, 2014. Accessed December 12, 2015. http://www.bls.gov/ooh/business-and-financial/accountants-and-auditors.htm.

U.S. Department of Labor, Bureau of Labor Statistics. "Occupational Outlook Handbook, 2014–2015 Edition: Biomedical Engineers." January 8, 2014. Accessed December 12, 2015. http://www.bls.gov/ooh/architecture-and-engineering/biomedical-engineers.htm.

U.S. Department of Labor. Bureau of Labor Statistics, "Occupational Outlook Handbook, 2014–2015 Edition: Civil Engineers." January 8, 2014. Accessed December 12, 2015. http://www.bls.gov/ooh/architecture-and-engineering/civil-engineers.htm.

U.S. Department of Labor, Bureau of Labor Statistics. "Occupational Outlook Handbook, 2014–2015 Edition: Computer Programmers." January 8, 2014. Accessed December 12, 2015. http://www.bls.gov/ooh/computer-and-information-technology/computer-programmers.htm.

U.S. Department of Labor, Bureau of Labor Statistics. "Occupational Outlook Handbook, 2014–2015 Edition: Financial Analysts." January 8, 2014. Accessed December 12, 2015. http://www.bls.gov/ooh/business-and-financial/financial-analysts.htm.

U.S. Department of Labor, Bureau of Labor Statistics. "Occupational Outlook Handbook, 2014–2015 Edition: Kindergarten and Elementary School Teachers." January 8, 2014. Accessed December 12, 2015. http://www.bls.gov/ooh/education-training-and-library/kindergarten-and-elementary-school-teachers.htm.

U.S. Department of Labor, Bureau of Labor Statistics. "Occupational Outlook Handbook, 2014–2015 Edition: Occupational Therapists." January 8, 2014. Accessed December 12, 2015. http://www.bls.gov/ooh/healthcare/occupational-therapists.htm.

U.S. Department of Labor, Bureau of Labor Statistics. "Occupational Outlook Handbook, 2014–2015 Edition: Petroleum Engineers." January 8, 2014. Accessed December 12, 2015. http://www.bls.gov/ooh/architecture-and-engineering/petroleum-engineers.htm.

U.S. Department of Labor, Bureau of Labor Statistics. "Occupational Outlook Handbook, 2014–2015 Edition: Physician Assistants." January 8, 2014. Accessed December 12, 2015. http://www.bls.gov/ooh/healthcare/physician-assistants.htm.

U.S. Department of Labor, Bureau of Labor Statistics. "Occupational Outlook Handbook, 2014–2015 Edition: Reporters, Correspondents, and Broadcast News Analysts." January 8, 2014. Accessed December 12, 2015. http://www.bls.gov/ooh/media-and-communication/reporters-correspondents-and-broadcast-news-analysts.htm.

U.S. Department of Labor, Bureau of Labor Statistics. "Occupational Outlook Handbook, 2014–2015 Edition: Software Developers." January 8, 2014. Accessed December 12, 2015. http://www.bls.gov/ooh/computer-and-information-technology/software-developers.htm.

U.S. News & World Report. "Best Engineering Schools." Accessed December 12, 2015. http://grad-schools.usnews.rankingsandreviews.com/best-graduate-schools/top-engineering-schools/eng-rankings.

University of North Carolina at Chapel Hill. "Admission Rates by Program between 2006–2011, as Reported on Program Websites." Accessed December 12, 2015. http://www.unc.edu/~mjp1970/Admissions%20Rates.pdf.

Wecker, Menachem. "Future Law Students Should Avoid Prelaw Majors, Some Say." *U.S. News & World Report.* October 29, 2012. Accessed December 12, 2015. http://www.usnews.com/education/best-graduate-schools/top-law-schools/articles/2012/10/29/future-law-students-should-avoid-prelaw-majors-some-say.

Weissmann, Jordan. "The Ever-Shrinking Role of Tenured College Professors (in 1 Chart)." *The Atlantic.* April 10, 2013. Accessed February 29, 2016. http://www.theatlantic.com/business/archive/2013/04/the-ever-shrinking-role-of-tenured-college-professors-in-1-chart/274849/.

Index

About the Authors

Andrew Belasco

A licensed counselor and independent educational consultant, Andrew's experience in the field of college admissions and transitions spans nearly 15 years. After receiving a BA from Georgetown University and an MEd from Harvard University's Graduate School of Education, Andrew earned a PhD from the University of Georgia's Institute of Higher Education, where his research focused on college access and institutional admission policies.

A recent fellow of the Association for Institutional Research, Andrew's work has been funded by the National Science Foundation, American Educational Research Association, National Center for Education Statistics, and University of Michigan's Inter-university Consortium for Political and Social Research. He has published in education's top academic journals, including *Education Evaluation & Policy Analysis*, *Research in Higher Education*, and the *Journal of Higher Education*, among others, and his research and commentary have been featured in the *New York Times*, the *Washington Post, Forbes, CBS MoneyWatch, U.S. News & World Report, Inside Higher Education*, the *Chronicle of Higher Education, National Public Radio*, and more than a dozen other media outlets. Andrew is a member of the National Association for College Admission Counseling (NACAC) and the Higher Education Consultants Association.

Prior to launching College Transitions, Andrew worked as a school counselor at Abington Senior High School in suburban Philadelphia, as a college admissions consultant and blogger for Kaplan Test Prep, and as a research consultant at the federal level for the Congressional Advisory Committee on Student Financial Assistance.

Dave Bergman

Dave has over a decade of professional experience in the field of education, which includes work as a teacher and administrator at the award-winning Abington Senior High School in suburban Philadelphia, an adjunct professor at Temple University, certified independent educational consultant, and author of a widely read weekly blog on college admissions.

Named a President's Scholar while earning his BA in History from Temple University, Dave continued his education at Temple, earning Master's and Doctoral degrees in Education. While a doctoral student, Dave completed his dissertation on the relationship between adolescent motivation and educational outcomes and published scholarship on how to successfully reach high school students with Teachers College Press and The National Council of Teachers of English. He holds a certificate in college counseling from the University of California, San Diego, and is a member of NACAC.

As a cofounder of College Transitions—an admissions consulting firm— Dave works as an independent educational consultant and essay coach and writes a weekly blog on the world of college admissions for collegetransitions.com that reaches tens of thousands of readers. His work has also been regularly published by Phillyburbs, Carolina Parent, *The Charlotte Observer*, and TeenLife.

CPSIA information can be obtained
at www.ICGtesting.com
Printed in the USA
LVHW040538290620
659220LV00001B/208